Acclaim for *Ayn Rand Explained*

"Ayn Rand is in the news now more than ever—but the media consistently misunderstands her. Read Ayn Rand Explained *for a thorough and clear introduction to her ideas!"*

> —JIMMY WALES, founder of Wikipedia

"Ayn Rand Explained *takes us on an exciting exploration of Rand's provocative worldview and expertly traces its huge contemporary impact on politics, economics, art, and culture. Marsha Familaro Enright provides much new information and probing, in-depth analysis. A surprising, intriguing take on a controversial writer."*

> —CHRIS MATTHEW SCIABARRA, author of *Ayn Rand: The Russian Radical*

"I immensely enjoyed reading Ayn Rand Explained. *Packed with fascinating information, much of it new, the book is a real page turner—and a reminder of why Rand's novels are continuously making their way onto best-seller lists."*

> —VERONIQUE DE RUGY, Senior Research Fellow, the Mercatus Center at George Mason University

Ayn Rand Explained

IDEAS EXPLAINED™

Daoism Explained, Hans-Georg Moeller
Frege Explained, Joan Weiner
Luhmann Explained, Hans-Georg Moeller
Heidegger Explained, Graham Harman
Atheism Explained, David Ramsay Steele
Sartre Explained, David Detmer
Ockham Explained, Rondo Keele
Rawls Explained, Paul Voice
Phenomenology Explained, David Detmer
Ayn Rand Explained, Ronald E. Merrill,
Marsha Familaro Enright

IN PREPARATION

Deleuze and Guattari Explained, Rohit Dalvi

Ayn Rand Explained

From Tyranny to Tea Party

RONALD E. MERRILL

Revised and Updated by Marsha Familaro Enright

OPEN COURT
Chicago and La Salle, Illinois

Volume 10 in the Ideas Explained™ Series

To order books from Open Court, call toll-free 1-800-815-2280, or visit our website at www.opencourtbooks.com.

Open Court Publishing Company is a division of Carus Publishing Company.

This book is a revised and updated edition of the work published in 1991 as *The Ideas of Ayn Rand* by Ronald E. Merrill.

First printing 2013

Printed and bound in the United States of America.

Library of Congress Cataloging-in-Publication Data

Merrill, Ronald E.
    Ayn Rand explained : from tyranny to tea party / Ronald E. Merrill ; revised and updated by Marsha Familaro Enright.
    p. cm. — (Ideas explained ; v. 10)
    Rev. ed. of: The ideas of Ayn Rand.
    Includes bibliographical references (p.   ) and index.
    ISBN 978-0-8126-9798-8 (trade paper : alk. paper)
    1. Rand, Ayn—Philosophy. 2. Objectivism (Philosophy) I. Enright, Marsha Familaro, 1951- II. Merrill, Ronald E. Ideas of Ayn Rand. III. Title.
    B945.R233M47 2013
    191—dc23
                                2012035490

Contents

Preface

When the late Ron Merrill published *The Ideas of Ayn Rand* in 1991, some readers thought he was over-optimistic about the growing influence of Rand's ideas. Instead, the subsequent explosion of interest in Rand, both in the popularity of her fiction and in adherence to her ethical and political message, has exceeded, in so short a period, anything that Merrill might have imagined.

Merrill's successful book, a sympathetic attempt to understand Ayn Rand, itself contributed to this explosion, reaching thousands of people eager for information about her. He presented a detailed, sensitive, and independent look at Ayn Rand's life, work, and thought. In revising and updating Merrill's work, I have again found it to be not only informative but intelligent and original, with much incisive analysis. I learned any number of new ideas from working on this book, although I was already familiar with most of its factual content.

Every part of the book has been scrutinized. Some parts are essentially unchanged, with only slight recasting, while other parts have been extensively reworked or replaced. I do not agree with every opinion of Merrill's and, in some places where this is true, I have given both Merrill's views and my own counter-theories. Even though the lion's share of this new book is still Merrill's contribution, to avoid confusion, Merrill is referred to in the third person, and all uses of the first person singular (except when quoted) refer to me.

Reader, please beware that there are many plot spoilers for Ayn Rand's novels in the pages that follow. Even so, I, like Ron Merrill, encourage you to read her works and decide for yourself on the value of one of the most powerfully influential individuals of the twentieth century.

My thanks go to Diana Smith Butler and Gen LaGreca for their invaluable feedback on the manuscript, to Joel Franck, Molly Hays, Bob Patterson, Duncan Scott, and Ed Snider for their help with exact facts and details, Kira Newman for her hilarious "Objectivist Meme," my editor, David Ramsay Steele for his excellent work, and my encouraging, delightful and always helpful husband, John Enright.

In my account not only of noteworthy people influenced by Ayn Rand, but of noteworthy works about her ideas, I'm sure I've overlooked somebody important. Please forgive me, whoever you are (I'll probably learn of you later).

Marsha Familaro Enright

1

The Controversial Ayn Rand

Ayn Rand died in 1982. Her ideas are marching on.

Rand was a writer of fiction who used the immense popularity of her novels to promote her unique philosophy of life, known as Objectivism. She first became famous with the huge success of her blockbuster, *The Fountainhead*, published in 1943. Fourteen years later she followed this up with *Atlas Shrugged*, even longer, even more popular, and even more clearly carrying a social and political message.

She wrote no more fiction after *Atlas Shrugged*, instead producing popular essays about ethics, society, and politics. Book collections of these essays have also enjoyed large and continuing sales. The success of all these books has pulled up the sales of her earlier fiction, *We the Living* and *Anthem*, and her play, *The Night of January 16th*.

Rand's two great novels, *The Fountainhead* and *Atlas Shrugged*, joined that small class of books which are permanently on the shelves in any typical bookstore. Half a century and more after their initial publication, they continue to enjoy enormous sales. Currently, *Atlas Shrugged* is selling about two thousand copies a week in the United States—more than *Dune* or *The Fellowship of the Ring*, somewhat less than *The Catcher in the Rye*, but that comparison is misleading, as most people who buy *The Catcher in the Rye* buy it because they have to: it's to be read for a class. *Atlas Shrugged* is rarely read for classes, except for a high school essay contest, as it is an affront to the ideological system embraced by most people in the teaching profession.

In 1991, a Book of the Month Club survey found *Atlas Shrugged* to be the second most popular book—next to the Bible.

Some would say it's a secular Bible. Sales of *Atlas Shrugged* soared to new heights following the financial crisis of 2008, with six hundred thousand copies sold in 2009 alone.

Millions of people have been enthralled by Rand's novels and hundreds of thousands have embraced her ideas. This powerful influence certainly does not derive from the approbation of the established intelligentsia. About the best that critics have been willing to say of *Atlas Shrugged* is that it is a ridiculous melodrama interrupted by tedious philosophical speeches. Though a few seasoned scholars have come to identify with Objectivism, broadly speaking, the intellectual establishment is at best unmoved and at worst appalled and outraged by Ayn Rand. Typically, adherents of Objectivism are people who read the novels, often in their teens, experience them as life-changing, and are so intrigued that they go on to read some of Rand's non-fiction works.

> I was fifteen—a common age for converts to the ideas of Ayn Rand. Browsing in the library, I encountered a book called *Atlas Shrugged*. "A man who said he would stop the motor of the world—and did." What was it? Science fiction? Sounded intriguing, anyway, so I checked it out.
>
> I opened it that evening and within a few pages I was hooked. The plot, the characters, above all the ideas—never had I encountered anything so exciting. It was not a book that I couldn't put down. On the contrary, I had to put it down every now and then because I would become so excited that I couldn't keep my eyes on the page. In the early morning hours I finally finished the book. I knew by then that my life had been changed permanently. (Merrill 1991, p. 1)

That account by the late Ronald Merrill is entirely typical of the experience of many thousands of people, most of them young. The process of attracting and recruiting new adherents through the appeal of *Atlas Shrugged* has been going on since 1957 and is still going on today—more powerfully today than in 1957. The army of Rand admirers—some cynics would say Rand worshippers—keeps growing all the time, because of the impact of *Atlas Shrugged*.

Other wildly popular books with a message come and go. Who remembers *The Secret* or *Your Erroneous Zones*? But *Atlas Shrugged* is like the Energizer Bunny. It just keeps on pounding away, always winning over new people to Rand's politically incorrect message.

Back in 1991, Ron Merrill was writing:

> Her ideas are appearing, though anonymously, in a growing portion
> of public discourse. On many fronts in modern intellectual life the
> subterranean influence of Objectivism . . . can be detected. The resur-
> gence of conservatism during the 1980s was to a significant extent
> powered by the quiet theft of Objectivist ideas. George Gilder's con-
> cept of the "altruistic entrepreneur" is a distorted form of Rand's
> insight that the entrepreneur is not and cannot be fully repaid in
> money for what he gives to society. Charles Murray's studies of the
> negative effects of welfare programs validate Rand's concept of the
> corrupting effect of the unearned. Meanwhile, on the other side of
> the political spectrum, liberals bemoan their loss of the intellectual ini-
> tiative; they do not seem to realize, and if they do they certainly never
> admit, that it was Rand's attacks that demolished their positions.

The rising influence Merrill detected in 1991 has now broken
out into a rushing river, bursting its banks and flowing into myriad streams and rivulets of American and world culture. Those of
us who have carefully noted signs of Rand's influence now see her
name popping up all over the media: in magazines and newspapers,
on billboards, shopping bags, blogs and websites, radio and TV
shows.

Formidable Influence

Notable commentators and celebrities regale the public about the
prescience of Rand's ideas. These include radio and TV personalities such as Stephen Moore, John Stossel, Dennis Miller, Rush
Limbaugh, Sean Hannity, Glenn Beck, Andrew Napolitano, Neil
Bortz, Penn Jillette, and Skeptic Society founder Michael Shermer.

Not surprisingly, given her positive portrayal of business,
numerous business people laud her influence on them, and detail
the value of her ideas to their careers and lives. These include busi-
ness-defenders John Allison, former CEO and Chair of BB&T
Bank, and T.J. Rodgers, CEO of Cypress Semi-Conductors; Ed
Snider, Chairman of Comcast-Spectacor which owns the
Philadelphia Flyers; Mark Cuban, businessman-owner of the Dallas
Mavericks; John Aglialoro, CEO of Cybex and independent pro-
ducer of the *Atlas Shrugged* movies, John Mackey, founder and
CEO of Whole Foods; and Donald Luskin, Chief Investment

Officer for Trend Macrolytics LLC, who has written *I Am John Galt: Today's Heroic Innovators Building the World and the Villainous Parasites Destroying It*. Not to overlook the infamous former businessman and Federal Reserve chairman, one-time member of Rand's inner circle, Alan Greenspan.

After Steve Jobs passed away, original Apple partner and engineer Steve Wozniak revealed in an interview with Bloomberg that Jobs:

> must've read some books that really were his guide in life, you know, and I think . . . Well, *Atlas Shrugged* might've been one of them that he mentioned back then. But they were his guides in life as to how you make a difference in the world. And it starts with a company. You build products and you gotta make your profit, and that allows you to invest the profit and then make better products that make more profit. I would say, how good a company is, it's fair to measure it by its profitability.[1]

Jobs was seen at the Shoreline Theater in Mountain View, California, on opening night of the movie *Atlas Shrugged Part I*, on April 15th, 2011.[2] Perhaps it's the reason Jobs gave little to charity, instead spending his time and brain power on "helping to make people's dreams come true" with Apple's ingeniously flexible products. Perhaps even the reason Apple sells "I" products?

Wikipedia founder Jimmy Wales is an outspoken fan of Rand. The methodology of Wikipedia, which requires entries to be well-documented and written from a "Neutral Point of View," encourages contributors to be as objective as possible. Looked upon methodologically, Wikipedia is an enterprise based on facts, reason, and peaceful voluntary cooperation that results in the fulfillment of mutual self-interest—key tenets of Rand's Objectivist philosophy.

Political Impact

David Nolan, founder of the Libertarian Party has said that "without Ayn Rand, the Libertarian Party wouldn't exist."[3] In 2008

---

[1] <www.bloomberg.com/video/74391682/#ooid=8xMWJyMjoT9XMTeW4oIZemoYVXln4cfz>.
[2] <www.facebook.com/mises.institute/posts/151755378244190>.
[3] Barbara Branden 1986, p. 414.

Libertarian Party presidential candidate Gary Johnson gave his fiancée a copy of *Atlas Shrugged* and told her: "If you want to understand me, read this."[4] Texas senator and presidential contender Ron Paul and his son, Kentucky senator Rand Paul are long-time advocates of many of Rand's ideas, as is Florida US Representative Allen West. Dick Armey and Matt Kibbe of Freedom Works openly endorse *Atlas Shrugged*, and Ronald Reagan's private letters reveal he was also an admirer.[5] One *New York Times* article referred to Rand as the Reagan Administration's "novelist laureate."[6]

Congressman and Vice Presidential candidate Paul Ryan and Supreme Court Justice Clarence Thomas both request that their staff read *Atlas Shrugged*. Ryan hosted a hundredth birthday party for Rand in a Library of Congress room in February 2005.[7] Ryan has commented: "Ayn Rand, more than anybody else, did such a good job of articulating the pitfalls of statism and collectivism—you can't find another thinker or writer who did a better job of describing and laying out the moral case for capitalism than Ayn Rand."[8]

Rand is everywhere in the Tea Party. Signs referring to or quoting her hero, John Galt, abound at the rallies, alongside Gadsden "Don't Tread on Me" flags, which capture her philosophy's ethical and political stance. The Tea Party participants' strong ethic of work and self-responsibility, in vivid contrast with leftist demonstrators, leads them to leave parks and public spaces cleaner after their rallies than the way they found them—an ethic that resonates with the characters portrayed in Rand's books. A Bloomberg Op-Ed argued that Rand voiced the Tea Party's views decades before the Tea Party was launched and before CNBC commentator Rick Santelli (an *Atlas Shrugged* fan) ranted on the floor of the Chicago Board of Trade, giving a boost to the Tea Party protests.[9] Polls

---

[4] <www.politico.com/blogs/click/0911/How_Gary_Johnson_wooed_his_fianc.html>.

[5] Ibid.

[6] Burns, p. 279.

[7] <www.atlassociety.org/ele/blog/2012/04/30/paul-ryan-and-ayn-rands-ideas-hot-seat-again>.

[8] Ibid.

[9] <www.bloomberg.com/news/2012-02-27/ayn-rand-beats-out-rick-santelli-as-first-teapartyer-gary-weiss.html>.

reveal that more than a quarter of all Americans identify themselves with the Tea Party movement.

More and more frequently, we observe that political and economic events are compared to dire circumstances in Rand's stories. In April 2011 Kentucky Senator Rand Paul likened the federal incandescent light-bulb ban to Rand's novella *Anthem*, a tale of totalitarian repression in which electric light has long been abolished by the regime.[10]

Portraits and Memoirs

Today there are two organizations specifically dedicated to advancing her philosophy, the Ayn Rand Institute and The Atlas Society. But it's hard to count the number of notable free-market pundits and effective think-tanks influenced by Rand's work, among them the Cato Institute, the Reason Foundation, Atlas Economic Research Foundation, the Heartland Institute, and the Institute for Justice. The State Policy Network encompasses many of these organizations. Universidad Francisco Marroquin in Guatemala has a statue of Atlas on their campus and Junior Achievement of South America was inspired by it.

In 2007, two student fans of Rand at the University of Pennsylvania, seeking political compadres, founded the first Students for Liberty club. One hundred attended its initial international conference in 2008. In February of 2012, over 1,000 students attended, representatives of Students for Liberty clubs all around the nation and world.

Since 1991, several movies have examined her life and work. In 1997, a close associate of the Ayn Rand Institute Michael Paxton filmed the documentary *Ayn Rand: A Sense of Life*, which weaves a tale from still photos and interviews in a remarkably engaging fashion. The film limits its portrayal of her complex personality by glossing over her affair with designated "intellectual heir" Nathaniel Branden. Nor does it probe her life as an artist or philosopher.

In 1999, Barbara Branden's 1986 biography-memoir, *The Passion of Ayn Rand*, was made into a sex-laden movie, focusing on Rand's extra-marital affair with Nathaniel Branden. Helen

---

[10] <www.politico.com/news/stories/0411/53030.html>.

Mirren, Eric Stoltz, Julie Delpy, and Peter Fonda starred. The entire cast performed well, but Mirren was remarkable as Ayn. Unexpectedly, this film conveyed enough of her ideas to interest some viewers in her books.

A documentary telling Rand's tale from her own writing and speeches came out in 2011, *Ayn Rand in Her Own Words*, which has previously unseen archival material. And in the fall of 2011 the documentary *Ayn Rand's Prophecy* delved into her resurgent popularity.

However, the most notable film treatment of Ayn Rand came in the spring of 2011. After forty years of wrangling and setbacks, *Atlas Shrugged* was finally filmed. Until then, like *The Catcher in the Rye*, it hadn't been made into a movie. *Part 1* opened around the country on April 15th, US tax day. The movie competently conveys the essence of Rand's story, despite the fact that it was filmed quickly. Philosopher David Kelley of The Atlas Society, an Objectivist think-tank, was a central figure in ensuring that the script remained consonant with Objectivist philosophy. A number of the performances sharply captured the characters and the cinematography was gorgeous. Although buffs of the novel, as well as film aficionados, disagree on its merits and have many criticisms, it won the Ronald Reagan Presidential Foundation Great Communicator award on Reagan's hundredth birthday in 2011.[11]

Cybex International head John Aglialoro had labored in Hollywood for eighteen years to get the movie produced. When his option was set to run out, Aglialoro took the bull by the horns and produced it himself, reportedly spending $20 million. Lauded by the fans, it was savaged by the movie critics—typical with an Ayn Rand story. With a small marketing budget aimed almost exclusively at fans online, it had a huge attendance in the first weeks, but never made it onto the mainstream movie theater circuit. Despite that, interest from outside investors got behind Aglialoro, and *Atlas Shrugged Part 2: Either-Or* opened on October 12th, 2012 (Christopher Columbus's birthday).

In 1995, New York University scholar Chris Matthew Sciabarra published the first intellectual biography, *Ayn Rand: The Russian Radical*. This book explored her educational background and the ideological influences of her youth, with an eye to their influence

---

[11] <www.prweb.com/releases/AtlasShruggedMovie/ReaganAward/prweb 8407158.htm>.

on her ideas. 2009 saw not one, but two new, independent biographies of Rand, *Goddess of the Market: Ayn Rand and the American Right* from Jennifer Burns and *Ayn Rand and the World She Made* from Anne Heller. Burns (p. 4) captures Rand's cultural power when she says that Rand is "the ultimate gateway drug to life on the right."

The number of blogs, websites, and Facebook groups interested in Ayn Rand and her ideas is growing by leaps and bounds. Ayn Rand in India, Objectivism International, Objectivist Living, Objectivism Online, the Atlasphere dating website, Objectivism.net, and Support the *Atlas Shrugged* Movie are a sample. Her ideas appeal especially to the brainy and accomplished, so it's no surprise that vast numbers of computer technologists and scientists are fond of her. Objectivists are so visible on the web, they now rate a humorous "meme" chart.

A Muse for Popular Art

Rand has impacted many creative minds, and it's only practicable to mention a few examples. One remarkable case is Gene

© Kira Newman

Roddenberry, the creator of the ever-popular and long-lived *Star Trek* franchise. He said: "I read *The Fountainhead* four or five times, *Atlas Shrugged*, but also some of her nonfiction—her book on art [*The Romantic Manifesto*] . . ."[12]

Roddenberry channeled Rand's heroes with the *Enterprise*'s signature goal "To boldly go where no one has gone before." Rand's influence leaks from every pore of the show, first through its emphasis on the use of reason and science and the control of emotions during crisis. But it is also evident in Roddenberry's heroic examples of independent judgment. Captain James T. Kirk often bucks the system, following his own judgment instead. He demonstrates this penchant from the beginning of his career with his handling of the "Kobayashi Maru" battle scenario, a no-win, character-testing situation for Starfleet officers, which requires them to either break a treaty, triggering a war, or leave the *Kobayashi Maru* ship and crew to their deaths. Kirk refuses to accept the no-win situation, circumvents the rules, and changes the scenario so that the ship can be rescued. Throughout the series, Kirk often follows his own standards by leaving the Federation's "Prime Directive" in shreds. This rule requires Starfleet officers not to intervene in alien societies with Starfleet technology or contrary values, whether lives are at stake or not. Kirk never allows the Prime Directive to trump the lives of those under his responsibility.

Individualism triumphed in the show in other ways, too, such as the treatment *Enterprise* crew members accorded any being they encountered. Almost always, they based their judgments and actions towards another on that being's own merits, not its race or group. And the alien Borg hive-being's incorporation of individuals into their collective was the ultimate horror.

James Clavell's mammoth novels, *Shogun, Tai-Pan,* and *Noble House* carved out an influential place in modern culture. These highly plotted, complex and sweeping stories delved deeply into Japanese, Chinese, and Hong Kong culture. Unusual for this day and age, Clavell portrayed ruggedly independent-minded heroes and heroines who are business people, and business as an exciting, creative, positive endeavor.

---

[12] Gary McGath, review of *Star Trek Lives!* <www.mcgath.com/stlives .html>.

These features always made me wonder about Clavell's influences. Then, in a 2005 online auction of items from Rand's personal library, I discovered a copy of *Noble House* inscribed by Clavell as follows:

This is for <u>Ayn Rand</u>
—one of the real, true talents on this earth for which many, many
      thanks
James C
New York
2 Sept 81

Mystery solved!

Giant of science fiction Robert Heinlein, author of *Starship Troopers* and *The Moon Is a Harsh Mistress* stated:

I would say that my position is not too far from that of Ayn Rand's; that I would like to see government reduced to no more than internal police and courts, external armed forces—with the other matters handled otherwise. I'm sick of the way the government sticks its nose into everything, now. (Schulman 1990)

It's hard to tell whether Heinlein was influenced artistically by Rand or simply expressed the fundamental American individualist values which she championed. Known for his individualist heroes, bucking controlling governments across the universe, it's likely that she clarified and sharpened his understanding of his own ideas, expressed in comments such as:

The human race divides politically into those who want people to be controlled and those who have no such desire. The former are idealists acting from highest motives for the greatest good of the greatest number. The latter are surly curmudgeons, suspicious and lacking in altruism. But they are more comfortable neighbors than the other sort.

Creator Ken Levine has revealed that the very popular dystopian videogame *Bioshock* is explicitly based on Rand's ideas. Levine says "I like making videogames where the player has to figure out his own path."[13] Likewise, self-described "recovering

---

[13] <www.wired.com/gaming/gamingreviews/magazine/15-09/pl_games>.

Muslim" and anti-jihadist cartoonist Bosch Fawstin owes her a debt.

One of the world's most consistently popular rock groups, Rush, is known for its intellectual lyrics, written by drummer Neil Peart and drawing heavily on Rand. Rush's album *2112* is based on Rand's novella *Anthem*. No other band as popular and innovative as Rush has failed to be inducted into the Rock'n'roll Hall of Fame, and the denial of this honor to Rush is often attributed to the connection with Ayn Rand. Rock critics, stung by Rush's "intellectual" lyrics, have generally been contemptuous of Rush, often verging on the apoplectic, while other rock musicians usually rate the band very highly.[14]

The New *Atlas Shrugged* Wave

Many attributed the huge increase in sales of *Atlas Shrugged* since 2008 to the fact that the novel always sells well during times of crisis. But David Boaz of Cato had a different theory, which he substantiated with research data: that economist and writer Stephen Moore's *Wall Street Journal* article of January 9th, 2009, "*Atlas Shrugged*: From Fiction to Fact in 52 Years" fuelled the sudden jump in readership. This article went viral immediately through influential blogs such as Glenn Reynolds's Instapundit. By Monday January 12th, sales were afire.

In March 2009 *The Economist* wrote about the climbing sales. Commentators such as Michelle Malkin, the Freakonomics blog, and the Opinionator of the *New York Times* added fuel to the fire. Malkin talked about "Going Galt," like Rand's hero John Galt and the other producers who go on strike in *Atlas Shrugged*. Malkin surmised this because of the pull back from investment and work in response to increased taxes and regulation.[15] In 2012 *Atlas Shrugged* was listed in the "Books that Shaped America" Exhibition as part of the 2012 National Library of Congress Book Festival.

On the flip side, disdain and fear of Rand run rampant as ever. *Atlas Shrugged* was vilified in its day—and remains so by many, many commentators. In 1957, ex-Communist Whittaker Chambers's

---

[14] Berti and Bowman 2011, especially Chapters 2 and 19.
[15] <www.cato-at-liberty.org/what-caused-atlas-shrugged-sales-to-soar>.

book review in William Buckley's *National Review* triggered the decades-long smear that she was a fascist, with Chambers's famous claim: "From almost any page of *Atlas Shrugged*, a voice can be heard, from painful necessity, commanding: 'To the gas chambers—go!'"[16] leading the list of distorting criticisms. Gore Vidal called it "nearly perfect in its immorality."[17] And a 2012 *Guardian* article 'How Ayn Rand Became the New Right's Version of Marx' calls her ideas psychopathic and claims that she thinks poor people should die.[18]

Reviews of the *Atlas Shrugged* movie were similarly hostile. During a FreedomWorks showing, Aglialoro, the producer, expressed dismay at its critical reception, prompting me to congratulate him for telling the story so well that it received the same caliber of criticism as the book.

Rand's publisher, Bennett Cerf, summed it up well: "Ayn believed that the critics were out to get her, and they really did tear her books apart. . . . I said 'most people don't agree with your ideas, and it's your ideas they're attacking.'"[19]

So why do so many people love or hate her books and her ideas? And who was this woman?

"In the Name of the Best within Us"

The key to understanding Rand's enduring appeal and popularity is the panorama of life she paints in her novels, *Anthem, We the Living, The Fountainhead*, and *Atlas Shrugged*.

Here's how some leading business people explain it in a 2007 *New York Times* article, "Ayn Rand's Literature of Capitalism":

John P. Stack is chief executive of Springfield Remanufacturing Company, a retooler of tractor engines in Springfield, Mo.: "There is something in your inner self that Rand draws out," Mr. Stack said. "You want to be a hero, you want to be right, but by the same token you have to question yourself, though you must not listen to interference thrown at you by the distracters." During the 1982 recession

---

[16] <www.orthodoxytoday.org/articles2/ChambersAynRand.php>.

[17] Quoted in *Ayn Rand's Literature of Capitalism*.

[18] Monbiot 2012,
<www.guardian.co.uk/commentisfree/2012/mar/05/new-right-ayn-rand-marx>.

[19] Cerf, p. 252.

when the company lost its main customer, International Harvester, his lawyers told Stack not to pursue a policy of radical transparency with his employees. He defied them. He said *Atlas* helped him. He turned his dream into the successful company it is today.

Darla Moore, a benefactor of the University of South Carolina, spoke of her debt to Rand in 1998, when the business school at the university was named in Ms. Moore's honor. "As a woman and a Southerner," she said, "I thrived on Rand's message that only quality work counted, not who you are."

James M. Kilts, who led turnarounds at Gillette, Nabisco, and Kraft, said he encountered *Atlas* at "a time in college life when everybody was a nihilist, anti-establishment, and a collectivist." He found her writing reassuring because it made success seem rational. "Rand believed that there is right and wrong," he said, "that excellence should be your goal."[20]

And in the fall of 2011, Athleticwear Lululemon's founder celebrated Rand with John Galt shopping bags: "Dennis J. Wilson, the company's founder and chairman, first read *Atlas Shrugged* when he was eighteen years old. Only later, looking back, did he realize the impact the book's ideology had on his quest to elevate the world from mediocrity to greatness (it is not coincidental that this is Lululemon's company vision)," the blog post stated, adding: "Our bags are visual reminders for ourselves to live a life we love and conquer the epidemic of mediocrity. We all have a John Galt inside of us, cheering us on. How are we going to live lives we love?"[21] John Galt is the lead hero in *Atlas Shrugged*.

Now her message is reaching across the Atlantic to long-resistant Europe. Kai John, a young Munich executive, first read *Atlas Shrugged* when he was at Oxford. "It opened my eyes," John says. "It basically put into words all the feelings that I have but couldn't express." Now that Europe's economy is in the toilet and all are looking to Germany for a bailout, John thinks "The time is here to make Germans aware that collectivism has its limits." He's invested a considerable sum of money and time in producing a new German translation of *Atlas Shrugged*.[22]

---

[20] Rubin, <www.nytimes.com/2007/09/15/business/15atlas.html?_r=1>.

[21] <www.nytimes.com/2011/11/28/business/media/combines-ayn-rand-and-yoga.htm>.

[22] <http://moe.businessweek.com/articles/2012-08-02/what-would-ayn-rand-do-about-the-euro-crisis>.

These individuals reveal the secrets to Rand's enduring appeal: her books illustrate lives of achievement, excellence, integrity, and heroism *through productive work*. She appeals to anyone who wants to find a way to live a glorious life. She demonstrates that there is no dichotomy between the spiritual and the material, and these can be integrated in love and work. She justifies the individual's allegiance to his own judgment in the face of opposition from family, friends, and foes. She demonstrates the exceptional goodness of independent, productive individuals and she cheerleads their journey.

As Anne Heller, author of the biography *Ayn Rand and the World She Made* says, "She . . . excelled at making abstractions understandable and complicated notions simple" (p. 132). Not only did she excel at it, she taught others how to do likewise, enabling them to analyze and clearly understand those ideas crucial to their dearest values, whether they are building a company that manufactures springs, enabling anyone with an Internet connection to access the world's knowledge for free, or founding a Montessori school. She helps to cut the Gordian knot—or paradox—of ideas in our culture, which, on the one hand, exhorts us to take care of others, and on the other, encourages us to nurture our own needs and find what's best for ourselves.

She demonstrates that the fundamental principle of good social relations is to treat others as equal trading partners—in spiritual as well as material goods. That in a good relationship there should be no victim—that relationships should be "win-win." That no one should be a sacrificial animal to the needs of others, although anyone should be free to help others.

To those who claim that the highest moral good is to act for the welfare of others (the philosophical meaning of "altruism,") she asks:

> Why is the happiness of another person important and good but not your own? Why are you always the outsider and sacrificial animal? Does it make any sense that your happiness is the highest moral goal of others, but not yourself?

These questions and her answers to them liberate readers from altruistic slavery, from the belief that to be good they must be more concerned with others' needs than their own.

And her ideas reach across boundaries of religion, geography, and generations because they depend on the deepest principles of human nature. Although Rand was a declared atheist, people of many different religions flock to her ideas because she presents a clear moral vision that resonates with the fundamental, universal values of human life and human nature, born of the Founding Fathers' Enlightenment philosophy.

This vision of life, highly esteemed and followed in the nineteenth century, is lyrically summarized in cowboy poet Badger Clark's poem, "The Westerner":

> My fathers sleep on the sunrise plains,
>   And each one sleeps alone.
> Their trails may dim to the grass and rains,
>   For I choose to make my own.
> I lay proud claim to their blood and name,
>   But I lean on no dead kin;
> My name is mine, for the praise or scorn,
> And the world began when I was born
>   And the world is mine to win.

As early as 1944, Rand explained this essence of Americanism: "Man, each single, solitary, individual man, has a sacred value [we] respect," in a piece she did for *Reader's Digest*.

> The right to the pursuit of happiness means man's right to live for himself, to choose what constitutes his own, private, personal happiness and to work for its achievement. Each individual is the sole and final judge in this choice. A man's happiness cannot be prescribed to him by another man or by any number of other men.
>
> These rights are the unconditional, personal, private, individual possession of every man, granted to him by the fact of his birth and requiring no other sanction. Such was the conception of the founders of our country, who placed individual rights above any and all collective claims. Society can only be a traffic policeman in the intercourse of men with one another. ('The Only Path to Tomorrow', pp. 88–90)

When challenged to summarize her philosophy "standing on one leg" at a Random House sales meeting for *Atlas Shrugged* in 1962, she said:

> *Metaphysics:* Objective reality—reality is what it is, no matter your wish or whim. "Nature, to be commanded, must be obeyed."

Epistemology: Reason—the non-contradictory identification of the facts. "You can't have your cake and eat it too."

Ethics: Self-interest—the pursuit of happiness. "Man is an end in himself."

Politics: Laissez-faire capitalism—Government's purpose is to protect the right to life, liberty, and property. "Give me liberty or give me death."

She reiterated the above in a *Los Angeles Times* column she wrote in 1962, reprinted in *The Objectivist Newsletter.*[23]

Against Relativism and Subjectivism

Rand was a model of thinking down to the roots of ideas, to the most basic facts and arguments on which they depend. This practice unmasks ideas that would chain the mind. She often revealed the ways in which ideologies claiming that reason can't know reality *rely* on reason and reality to make their claims.

In her philosophical analysis, Rand emphasized the importance of objectivity, in contrast to the ideologies of relativism and subjectivity rampant in the twentieth century. Relativism, the idea that any set of ideas or values is of equal worth to any other, and subjectivism, the idea that there is no fact-based justification for any set of ideas or values, render reason impotent to know truth and act effectively to protect life.

The idea that "everything's relative" to culture, background, time and place, can fool even a freedom-loving person into unwittingly thinking that "relative" means "individual." For example, what each person likes to eat can be relative to his or her ethnic or family background. If X likes to eat noodles and Y likes to eat steak, that's the person's individual or what economists call "subjective" preference (preferred by the individual from among an array of possibilities). No problem—because, objectively, it's a choice between one kind of life-sustaining value and another: different foods.

But many twentieth- and twenty-first-century ideologists have applied these ideas of relativism and subjectivism far beyond the case of simple choices between life-sustaining values. They apply them to everything, so that all values are considered subjective—without a solid, reality-grounded case for some over others.

---

[23] <www.aynrand.org/site/PageServer?pagename=objectivism_intro>.

The result? Ideas, values, and behavior which we would reasonably think were wrong because they lead to the destruction of life are considered as acceptable as any others. For example, being required to do what your husband or family demand or killed if you 'dishonor' them, is to be respected and allowed. The result is that "honor killings" have been ignored in Britain and other European countries (see Theodore Dalrymple's *Life at the Bottom*).

Rand argues: If there is no truth, if all is relative, then anything is possible. If there is no unified system of logic, tied carefully to the facts, any set of ideas can be "justified." This is one of the ways philosophy enabled the murderous rampage of twentieth-century collectivism, through Communism, Nazism, and other forms of totalitarianism.

Hence, amidst much intellectual ridicule, she made it her project to ground a universal theory of objective knowledge. Her most notable book in this regard is *Introduction to Objectivist Epistemology*.

The Virtue of Selfishness

In the realm of ethics, critics excoriate her philosophy for its admonishment to practice the "virtue of selfishness." Titling her volume on ethics *The Virtue of Selfishness* was a stroke of marketing genius, since so many readers are drawn to its apparent paradox. Yet, critics deeply misunderstand her view. In fact, the meaning of "selfishness" in her work is closely allied to Aristotle's "Great-Souled" man: someone living a life with long-range vision, flourishingly pursuing excellence and achievement—a noble soul. Her literary characters illustrate her meaning: they act with integrity, nobility, and self-control in the service of their long-term goals. They treat others as equals—traders giving value for value, never master or slave.

Rand's vision of life as a heroic journey is at odds with the depressed, cynical, powerless, and terrifying view of existence painted by many modern writers. We have this latter view thanks to a long legacy of ideas, stretching back to the seventeenth century, attacking the human capacity to know reality and to reason efficaciously, disparaging the value of human life itself, and urging a renunciation of self for the sake of others.

These ideas have left millions vulnerable to collectivist leaders who seduce them with the dictatorship of the proletariat, or of the

Volk, or the glory of Allah, or the Emperor, in Europe, Asia, the Middle East, Latin America—they're even creeping into American culture. Her incisive arguments and inspirational stories, urging challenging work and the pursuit of achievement and personal happiness, are a great antidote to this collectivist siren song, and to the angst triggered by the drum-beating doom-and-gloomers throughout our culture.

Her vision of nobility through creative, productive work, born of the individual and his or her independent judgment, strongly resonates with American sensibilities. She shows the reader that success is not based on unknowable, ineffable factors but rests in the individual's hands. She tells us: "With the best use of your reason, you can figure out how to achieve your dreams."

Moreover, she not only shows her readers that they can live life on their own terms, but gives them the moral justification for doing so. The power of moral justification is the power to move the world, as we've seen with many religious movements as well as collectivist atheist regimes in the twentieth century. Humans want money, influence, and power, yes—but they also want the certainty that they are in the *right*. This is how Lenin and Hitler gained their power. As we'll see later, the lack of a moral justification has been a continuing problem for capitalism—and one of the reasons for the power of Rand's philosophy is her moral argument *for* capitalism.

She sums it up in *Atlas Shrugged*:

> "Do not lose your knowledge that man's proper estate is an upright posture, an intransigent mind, and a step that travels limitless roads. . . . Do not let your fire go out, spark by irreplaceable spark. In the hopeless swamp of the not quite, the not yet, and the not at all, do not let the hero in your soul perish and leave only frustration for the life you deserved, but never have been able to reach. . . . The world you desire can be won, it exists, it is real, it is possible, it is yours." (p. 993)

2

Who Was Ayn Rand?

The intensity and drive that fueled Ayn Rand's life were stoked by her passionate love of independent, creative Man, and a hatred for all forms of collectivism that would enslave him—or *her*.

Why the dire dread of collectivism, Communism in particular? Well, she witnessed its devastation first-hand.

Born in 1905 as Alyssa (Alice) Rosenbaum, she was the daughter of a bourgeois Jewish family in St. Petersburg. Like many highly intelligent children, she found school boring, had difficulty making friends, and was more interested in the ideas and people she discovered by her reading than those in her own family. At the age of nine she resolved to become a writer. Overall, her childhood was comfortable and her parents did not obstruct her intellectual development.

This peaceful existence was short-lived. Alice was nine years old, enjoying her first ecstatic taste of the West on a vacation in Switzerland, when the lights of Europe began to go out. The Rosenbaums fled back to Russia to endure the uncertainties and privations of World War I, followed by the Russian Revolution, the Bolshevik *coup,* the Red Terror, and a lengthy civil war. Then came the inexorable crushing of all free thought as Russia was enslaved by the Communists. The Rosenbaums' family business was expropriated, and the family, after gradually eating up all their savings, lived in grinding poverty.

During this hellish period in which the teenage girl lived with the fear of starvation, of disease, and of Siberia, she worked on the development of her literary abilities. She outlined plays and novels (though she did not actually write them). She read widely, admiring Edmond Rostand and Friedrich Schiller and above all Victor Hugo, while disliking Russian authors, George Sand, and Shakespeare. She also became acquainted with the philosophy of Aristotle—and the ideas of Friedrich Nietzsche.

In 1925 at the age of twenty, about a year after graduating from the University of Petrograd, where she majored in history, Rand succeeded in leaving the USSR and came to the United States. This fortunate escape was not without its disadvantages. Rand was cut off from her Russian heritage and had to master a new language—a serious handicap for the aspiring writer. She was also a stranger in a strange land, deprived of whatever comfort she had once had from friends and immediate family. Her position as a new immigrant was precarious both legally and economically. It was not for several years that she was securely placed as an American citizen. Nevertheless, she approached her new life with energy, hope, and conviction.

Rand in Hollywood

After a few months living with relatives in Chicago, she moved to Hollywood with the goal of becoming a screen writer. She went to the DeMille Studio, where she was given the polite brush-off. Then, by chance, she came upon Cecil B. DeMille himself, her favorite director, sitting at the wheel of a parked open roadster. She had admired him in Russia, while escaping the drudgery and fear of daily life through his movies. DeMille asked the little girl with the thick Russian accent and intense black eyes why she was staring at him. This conversation led to her being given a pass to visit the set of *King of Kings*, then a job as an extra for the crowd scenes in that movie, and eventually to a very junior screenwriting job.

Rand's encounter with DeMille and apprenticeship as a screenwriter served her well and had a strong influence on her style. And ever afterwards, DeMille called her "Caviar." Also, on the *King of Kings* set, she met another extra, her life-long husband and companion, Frank O'Connor.

The 1930s were not an easy time for Rand. Perhaps the only bright spot was her happy marriage to Frank, an unsuccessful actor. During that decade she produced the novel *We the Living* and the novella *Anthem*, as well as unpublished material now partially available posthumously. Neither *We the Living* nor *Anthem* was a success at the time. She sold a screenplay, *Red Pawn*, to RKO Pictures. She also wrote three plays, *Ideal*, *Think Twice*, and *The Night of January 16th* (originally *Penthouse Legend*). This last had a modest commercial success, though unavoidable compromises with the producer made it artistically frustrating. But Rand could not earn a living from her writing, and had to continue working at other jobs. This was the Great Depression, and she and her husband often wondered where they'd get the rent money.

To make matters worse, Communism was the intellectual fashion during the notorious 'Red Decade' of the 1930s. The Left was riding high; the traditional Right was helpless, impotent, and reduced to frustrated reaction. The intellectual and social environment was savagely hostile to Rand's ideas, and the situation became increasingly worse throughout most of her lifetime. Having escaped the giant tomb of Soviet Russia, she now feared her beloved United States was following in its footsteps.

Her second novel, *The Fountainhead*, published in 1943, was rejected by many publishers. But when it finally saw print it became a best-seller and gave Rand, for the first time, some degree of financial security. It also gave her significant intellectual stature, placing her among the tiny group of thinkers who were laying the foundation for a renewal of the Right—people such as Isabel Paterson, Ludwig von Mises, and Friedrich von Hayek. Rand's ideas began to attract attention—and disciples, including Nathan Blumenthal and Barbara Weidman (later Nathaniel and Barbara Branden) in the early 1950s.

Meanwhile she was working on her *magnum opus*, *Atlas Shrugged* while Communist thinkers and writers infiltrated the film industry, subtly propagandizing collectivism as a modern heaven. In 1947, her desire to educate the American public on Communism's ills—and threat to American freedom—led her to testify before the House Un-American Activities Committee about Communist infiltration into the movie industry, despite serious misgivings about the Committee's violations of civil liberties. She was mocked by Congressman John McDowell for her criticism of the movie, *Song of Russia*, because it showed Russians smiling.

> It is almost impossible to convey to a free people what it is like to live in a totalitarian dictatorship. I can tell you a lot of details. I can never

completely convince you, because you are free. It is in a way good that you can't even conceive of what it is like. Certainly they have friends and mothers-in-law. They try to live a human life, but you understand it is totally inhuman. Try to imagine what it is like if you are in constant terror from morning till night you are waiting for the doorbell to ring, where you are afraid of anything and everybody, living in a country where human life is nothing, less than nothing, and you know it. You don't know who or when is going to do what to you because you may have friends who spy on you, where there is no law and any rights of any kind. (Binswanger 1987, p. 10)

Ayn Rand once said that she wrote *Atlas Shrugged* so that it wouldn't happen. She'd had enough of that.

The 1950s were the heyday of modern liberalism. Though outright Communism or socialism were not in favor except among the intelligentsia, American culture was firmly in the grip of the 'moderate' Left. Left liberalism dominated the world of ideas—a conservative professor, a conservative journal, a novel presenting a conservative viewpoint—all these were rarities. (In the academic world, a libertarian intellectual was not just a rarity but a freak of nature, like two-headed calves, because they believed in economic *and* personal freedom, in contrast to both the Left and the Right.) Under the Eisenhower administration, a certain amount of public lip service was paid to conservative political values, but for a serious writer to be anything but left-wing was almost a contradiction in terms. Rand had not even the comfort of belonging to the tiny band of brothers clustered around William F. Buckley who formed the embryo of modem conservatism. She could not be fitted into the mold of traditional, religion-based conservatism.

The *Atlas* Phenomenon

It was the publication of *Atlas Shrugged* in 1957 that marked the real beginning of what might be called the Ayn Rand Phenomenon and the renaissance of classical liberalism. The book presented, not just an economic argument for laissez-faire, but a vision of a life of heroic achievement. It seemed an unlikely best-seller. It was an immense tome of one-thousand-plus pages, laden with lectures on philosophy and politics, half science fiction and half melodrama, challenging violently all the most cherished beliefs of the typical reader. Yet it sold like hotcakes and remained at best-seller levels

for decades, until the financial and economic crisis of 2008 pro-
pelled it to the top of the charts again. It continues to demonstrate
the power of a moral ideal.

Atlas Shrugged had an immense appeal to young people, influ-
encing many who later returned to more traditional creeds, such
as George Gilder. Gradually a hard core of 'Objectivist' college
students formed. They read and re-read Rand's books, argued
ferociously with their enemies and with one another, canvassed
for converts, and spontaneously formed clubs and discussion
groups.

There was clearly a market for Objectivism, a hunger for more
of these ideas, and with Rand's endorsement, Nathaniel and
Barbara Branden began in 1960 to satisfy the need with the creation of the Nathaniel Branden Institute (NBI). Rand and
Branden began publishing *The Objectivist Newsletter* (which
evolved into *The Objectivist* and later into the *Ayn Rand Letter*).
Taped lectures provided by NBI unified the various local groups
of Objectivists and built a national network of contacts. The
Sixties were the nascent Age of Objectivism, as what had been a
scattering of isolated thinkers coalesced into an intellectual
movement.

The liberal establishment within the universities was forced to
deal with ideological challenges from an increasing number of
Objectivist students. The resurgent conservatives found, to their
evident annoyance, that the brightest and most enthusiastic young
people on the Right were adherents of, or at least much influenced
by, this abhorrent, atheistic philosophy. The real danger to the
Objectivist movement, however, came from within. So long as she
was a single voice crying in the wilderness, Ayn Rand, that quintessential individualist, was spared from any conflict between ideological purity and human relationships. As leader of an intellectual
movement, she began to encounter disagreement from her colleagues, friends, or students, and seemed to perceive it as a threat
to the purity of her system. Students at NBI lectures began to
whisper rumors of 'excommunications'. Major figures in the
movement, such as John Hospers and Edith Efron, were cast out.[1]

---

[1] For accounts of excommunications, see Rothbard 1989; Hospers 1990;
Machan 1989b; Nichols 1972; Walker 1999. Though associates of Rand,
Rothbard and Hospers never considered themselves Objectivists.

In 1969 Rand's most important protégé and closest friend, Nathaniel Branden, was 'excommunicated', along with his wife Barbara, in an extraordinarily bitter conflict. More on that later. Although the full story of the relationship that caused the break did not come out at the time, enough was exposed to irretrievably damage the personal reputations of both Rand and her former protégés. Few followers knew enough facts first-hand to judge for themselves. Despite that, Rand and her loyalists demanded that all take sides. NBI perforce collapsed, and the Objectivist network fissioned into pro-Rand and pro-Branden factions, with a considerable loss of mass as many students, disillusioned with the behavior of their teachers, left the movement altogether.

The majority of Rand's inner circle, ironically dubbed 'the Collective', took her side in the controversy, perhaps a tribute to her personal and intellectual charisma since most of them were relatives of the Brandens. An attempt was made to continue the work of NBI under a new name, and courses were offered throughout the 1970s by Leonard Peikoff, a philosophy professor, and Allan Blumenthal, a psychiatrist and musician. But, too much was missing and it was impossible to continue at the same level. Even *The Objectivist* could not be maintained. Rand, a slow and scrupulously careful writer, was unable to produce articles fast enough to support regular publication. Her remaining assistants could not contribute enough material of a quality to meet her exacting standards.

In the 1970s Rand's output declined to a slow drip of articles in the *Ayn Rand Letter*. She became increasing isolated, gradually breaking ties with several of her remaining adherents. Unfortunately attacked from all quarters, Right and Left, academia, Christian conservative, and Libertarian and mortifyingly disappointed with the behavior of her vaunted example of Objectivist's best, Nathaniel Branden, Ayn Rand became more and more wary of alliances and "representatives" of her ideas.

The death of her husband was a painful blow. Now an old woman and in ill health, in 1975 she ceased writing almost entirely, continuing only her annual talks at Boston's Ford Hall Forum as well as rare appearances on Tom Snyder's and Phil Donohue's talk shows, and one final speech at a James U. Blanchard monetary conference in New Orleans, which was filled with cheers for her rousing defense of capitalism. This last was given a few months before her death on March 6th, 1982.

The Objectivist Movement

In the 1960s there was an Objectivist movement, organized, growing, gaining members continually. Centered around a monthly journal, *The Objectivist,* and a lecture organization, the Nathaniel Branden Institute (NBI), this movement recruited many of the best and brightest, particularly among college students. College professors, vastly left-liberal in those days as they are today, were horrified.

Many do not realize how violent the opposition to Objectivism was in the intellectual atmosphere of the Sixties, as it is today. An anecdote from Ron Merrill's own experience may be enlightening.

He enthusiastically recommended *Atlas Shrugged* to his college English teacher. She bought a copy, but did not finish reading it; she told him it was "boring." He heard no more about it until the next semester, when she told him the following story.

> On a warm spring day her fiancé visited her apartment. Suddenly spotting *Atlas Shrugged* on her shelf, he said, "You don't want to read that," and without further ado he picked it up and pitched it out the open window. She ran to the window and saw that the book had fluttered to the grass near the building's gardener, who was mowing the lawn. He looked at it—saw the title—and went over it repeatedly with the power mower until it was chopped to confetti.

Such were the emotions that were—and are—aroused by the ideas of Ayn Rand. Many others who like Rand could tell similar stories.

There are many reasons people bemoan Ayn Rand's ideas. 'Bad writing' and 'unrealistic plot and characters' are frequently given; we shan't go into the pros and cons of these judgments here, but suffice it to say that they tend to have the character of pronouncements rather than reasoned arguments. The self-same critics often rave about books with barely a story.

Unfortunately, the kind of vehemence illustrated above is common among those nurtured in Academia, that bastion of collectivism—and it's of a different nature. Those who have eschewed material success and congratulated themselves for the virtue and nobility of their self-sacrificial dedication to others find Rand anathema. This kind of person doesn't like her or her message—or her dramatization of the disasters of a collectivist society. The collectivists have rarely admitted that their ideas lead to disaster, leaving the blame to the evil of human nature. They tend to believe that humans are just not good enough to live up to the requirements of self-sacrifice.

Some people are uncomfortable with her challenge to traditional morality, upon which they have built their self-image. Some don't like her claim that they *are* responsible for their own lives; that they have to have purpose and strive to be their best; that they have to be thinking all the time. This is a tall order many people don't want to fill.

Also, Rand's social analysis can be discomfiting. She shows that the extraordinary achievements of a few make our lives better, far in excess of what anyone pays that few; we all owe such people a debt of gratitude, but some people don't like the idea that others are better than they are, nor, that they owe such a debt. Worst are those who feel envy or what's called "ressentiment"—envy with no ambition to do better, just the desire to tear down.

These are some of the motives for the Rand bashing. The explosive growth of the organized Objectivist movement worried the critics. But as the 1960s wore on, it began to slow. Those who were students at the time could see that the movement was beginning to become less a spontaneous phenomenon, more an organized system. There was a trend toward a sort of intellectual centralization; it was made explicit that only Ayn Rand and a few of her close associates were to contribute original ideas to the movement. The rest of her followers were to act merely as 'transmission belts' to carry these ideas to the uninitiated. They were even forbidden to call themselves 'Objectivists'; the only approved term was 'students of Objectivism'—ironic for a philosophy lauding independent judgment.

Was Objectivism a Cult?

At the same time, there were other disquieting signs. An increasing number of 'true believers' appeared among the ranks. Objectivist doctrine seemed in danger of hardening into dogma. Dissenters, including some of the movement's leaders, began to be formally 'excommunicated'.

Different witnesses have different recollections of the degree of cultishness in the Objectivist movement at that time. Several writers have described the Objectivist movement as a snake-pit of cultism, emotional repression, and thought control.[2] However, the lurid picture painted by these authors is not corroborated by others.

Ron Merrill was an active participant in the movement in the Sixties, including stints as leader of Objectivist groups at MIT and the University of Oregon. On numerous occasions he visited New York for NBI functions. Never did he encounter a single one of the cape-wearing, cigarette-holder-wielding cultists, imitating the dramatic Rand herself, who were allegedly so omnipresent in the movement. Certainly he did meet a number of self-appointed guardians of ideological purity. But he, and the vast majority of his friends in the movement, regarded these characters with amused tolerance rather than quaking fear.

Most published descriptions of the Objectivist movement were written by people who detested it. A leading purveyor of the 'Ayn Rand Cult' allegations was Murray Rothbard, whose polemic (Rothbard 1987) describes an Objectivist movement that other witnesses, including Ron Merrill, somehow never saw. Some of Rothbard's assertions are exaggerations (for example, "Rand's whole-hearted endorsement of Goldwater, Nixon, and Ford"). Others are merely astonishing. That the NBI recommended reading list functioned as "an Index of Permitted Books" was a secret well kept from Merrill and the Objectivists he knew; most of them were enthusiastic admirers of Rothbard's own *Man, Economy, and State*. However, after Nathaniel Branden's excommunication, even *owning* his books was grounds for expulsion.

Perhaps Rothbard knew more of the followers who censored and restrained themselves than Merrill did. The cigarette smokers Merrill knew within the movement would certainly have been surprised and pleased if they'd only known that "smoking, according to the cult, was a moral obligation" as Rothbard claims; they were

---

[2] Tuccille 1972 is a humorous early account of the libertarian movement, depicting Objectivism as a cult. Ellis 1968 grew out of Albert Ellis's debate with Nathaniel Branden. Plasil 1985 portrays the Objectivist milieu as prone to cultishness and recounts her abuse at the hands of Objectivist therapist Lonnie Leonard, though ironically, if Plasil had been a true 'Randroid', she would have dropped Leonard when he was excommunicated, and thus been spared her ordeal. Walker 1999 is a detailed and highly critical compilation of cultish aspects of Objectivism.

used to being criticized by the rest of the participants for irrational and self-destructive behavior.

Rothbard recites a series of anecdotes about unnamed people—"young Randians," "a Randian girl," "high-ranking Randians"—to back up his claims of cultist-like behavior. Merrill reports that he met some fairly flaky specimens in the movement, but none as bizarre as Rothbard's reported acquaintances. Merrill thought that, maybe, he just didn't travel in the right circles.

The central point of Rothbard's essay is the claim that the Randian movement was strictly "hierarchical" and "totalitarian." Certainly there were—and are—those within it who would have liked to make it so. But Merrill cites an anecdote of his own. At NBI, Nathaniel Branden and others taught many lecture classes on Rand's philosophy. Merrill recalls:

> In the mid-Sixties, a friend of mine took some questions to Nathaniel Branden personally. This direct approach was criticized by another student of Objectivism, who said he should have gone through channels. ("First take it to Harry Binswanger. If he thinks it's worthwhile, he'll allow you to see Allan Gotthelf, and if he . . .") Branden, on being informed of this, called that attitude "intellectual feudalism"—which of course it was. *That* is how the "Randian cultists" were regarded within the movement. (p. 4)

Since Rothbard's time, others have claimed Objectivism a cult. Jeff Walker's *The Ayn Rand Cult* is one such examination. Sociologist Benjamin Zablocki defines a cult as an ideological organization held together by charismatic relationships and the demand of total commitment. Objectivism had an organization headed by charismatic leaders which offered a rich, integrated, encompassing framework of thought and a demanding social organization. In this respect, it was similar to other movements which developed cult-like followings, such as Freudianism, Marxism, or orthodox Montessorianism.

But the operative modifier is "cult-*like*." To the extent followers hang on every word, action, attitude, interest, and practice of Objectivist leaders, they are acting in a cult-like manner. To the extent Objectivist leaders demand "total commitment" not just to the philosophy, but the organization and its leaders, they are cultish. Unfortunately, there have been attitudes and practices of some Objectivist leaders and followers which encourage this type of behavior. Fortunately, it's not the whole story.

Nathaniel Branden seems to have forgotten incidents like the one recounted above; indeed, his own memoirs have given a great boost to the legend of the Ayn Rand Cult. The Objectivist movement that Merrill saw from his self-described "worm's-eye view" was very different—and, apparently, much healthier—than the inner circle around Rand. That hotbeds of cultism existed Merrill did not deny, though he never happened to encounter them. That the movement itself was a cult simply is not true. Merrill cannot but suspect that when Branden found it difficult to remember a student of Objectivism who was not a "fanatical repressor," his recollection was colored by his bitter memories seen through a lens of his own making.

The Great Schism of Objectivism

Unknown to most in the Objectivist movement, as it expanded rapidly in the 1960s, there was a worm eating at the heart of it. Some years earlier, Rand had been carrying on an affair with her young protégé and "intellectual heir," Nathaniel Branden. According to the account of Nathaniel's ex-wife, Barbara, the reluctant consent of their respective spouses had been extracted by Rand's extraordinary skill in personal argument—and by their admiration of and gratitude to Rand. I found this an odd explanation: the spouses consented by arm-twisting—personal pressure— *and* from gratitude? One doesn't normally feel very grateful when one is being pressured into doing something.

Rand and Nathaniel's sexual activity, begun in 1955, was suspended in 1959 as Rand went through a terrible depression after the publication of *Atlas Shrugged* and its savaging by liberal and conservative critics alike. Rand and Branden's close personal and professional relationship continued.

Around 1963, Rand began to approach Branden about sleeping together again, and wondered if he still had an interest, while acknowledging that her advanced age might prove a barrier. Branden claimed to Rand that he had too many psychological problems to do so. Rand spent about three years trying to help him with his 'problems', when she finally discovered that Branden had secretly taken up with a younger woman about whom he was too afraid to tell Rand.

Many speculate that Rand denounced them vengefully because she was a 'woman scorned'. Certainly her desire for personal loyalty would have heightened her feelings, but, in contrast, her private diaries show her realistically thinking that she may have been just too old to appeal to Branden at that time (Valliant 2005).

Even if she felt sexually rejected, isn't there plenty of evidence that more was involved? Rand had spent decades carefully delineating her ideas and forthrightly defending them. She had laid on the line her entire career to hew to her own vision. She had fought battles with theater directors, movie producers, and book publishers to have her ideas presented her way, and no less endured thousands of words of ignorant criticism from all corners.

According to her diaries, she was outraged by the years Nathaniel had spent lying to her, not simply lying but building a complicated house of cards to maintain his position. She realized that for an even longer time he had been pretending to be someone he wasn't. Publicly, she said: "I was shocked to discover that he was consistently failing to apply to his own personal life and conduct, not only the fundamental philosophical principles of Objectivism, but also the psychological principles he himself had enunciated and written and lectured about" (Rand 1968b). The person whom she had unequivocally allowed to represent her ideas was a liar and a hypocrite.

Clearly and understandably, she was mortified that she had been so deeply mistaken, and had praised and idolized Nathaniel, allowing him to represent her and her ideas for so long. This was the man to whom she had dedicated her masterpiece, *Atlas Shrugged*; to whom she had given herself body and soul. To find out her hero was a pretender must have been devastating; to realize she had not identified this years-long deception, shaking, especially considering her otherwise unusual ability to see past pretense.

Rand broke off all personal and professional relations with both Nathaniel and Barbara Branden (who had for a while been complicit in hiding Nathaniel's dishonesty, but who eventually was the person to reveal the truth to Rand). She repudiated them both as representatives of her or her ideas. In response, the Brandens revealed part of what had been going on, personally intimating that it was all the reaction of 'a woman scorned'. A longer account of their side was published in Barbara's biography of Rand, *The Passion of Ayn Rand*, in 1986 and, later, in Nathaniel's memoir, *Judgment Day*.

Barbara Branden's account has been challenged in several respects. On one detail, she seems to have overestimated the secrecy of the affair between Rand and Nathaniel. Rand and the Brandens were the object of concentrated attention from hundreds of New York 'students of Objectivism' who were interested in everything from their musical tastes to what they wore. Under the circumstances, it's not surprising that rumors of a Rand-Branden intimate relationship were circulating long before the 1968 break.

Shrinking of the Movement

The result, back in 1968 when Rand publicly broke with the Brandens, was the radical down-sizing of the organized movement. The Nathaniel Branden Institute was disbanded. Branden himself moved across the country and went into full-time practice as a psychotherapist. Gradually his psychological theories trended toward the California standard 'get in touch with your feelings' approach, and he became much less involved with, and occasionally critical of, Objectivism. His first book, *The Psychology of Self-Esteem*, published shortly after the break with Rand, was a big success and helped to give shape to the new self-esteem movement. It is profoundly philosophical in its first half, laying out the groundwork for a philosophical psychology. The second half puts forth his theory of self-esteem as a fundamental force in human psychology.

The books he published later were well-written and of great psychological help to many people. However, they are not deeply intellectual or scientifically original works; they are excellent popular psychology. Mostly, they repeat and refine his initial theories of self and self-esteem. His "sentence completion" technique, was a new addition to the arsenal of psychotherapy. The few additions to his theory regarding, for example, the importance of understanding emotions and "honoring the self" were very close to well-established ideas of humanistic psychology practiced by the likes of Carl Rogers and Fritz Perls; Branden fruitfully cast these attitudes into an Objectivist framework.

Many of the movement's true believers left and moved on to real cults. Some of the rank and file clustered around the remaining official Objectivists in New York. Others joined the nascent libertarian political movement which was beginning to stir, especially in California. Many simply abandoned all confidence in the leaders and concentrated silently on living as Objectivists.

The movement drastically shrunk. Loyalists, Leonard Peikoff, a philosophy professor, and Allan Blumenthal, a psychiatrist-musician, continued with lecture courses, in-person and on tape through much of the 1970s. Yet, like an ideological neutron bomb, the Great Schism destroyed the idols but left the ideas intact. While Objectivism faded from the public eye, new waves of young people continued to read *Atlas Shrugged* and find that these ideas made sense. They accepted Objectivism if not in whole then in part, and as the years went by they graduated from college and began to take their places as potential intellectual leaders. Rand's ideas were carried with them.

Leonard Peikoff became legal heir to her estate when Rand passed away in 1982. Shortly thereafter, Ed Snider, owner of the Philadelphia Flyers and a friend and supporter of Rand for many years, suggested to Peikoff that he start an institute in Rand's honor. To make this happen, Snider organized a meeting of wealthy supporters at the Helmsley Palace in New York City. In 1983, Snider and Peikoff re-started the organized movement with the founding of the Ayn Rand Institute (ARI). But, after a Prague Spring, the movement was once-again plunged into conflict in the late 1980s with yet another schism, this time between Peikoff and philosophy professor David Kelley.

Some think Peikoff denounced Kelley because, as a board member of the publication *On Principle*, Kelley did not object to a review of Barbara Branden's *The Passion of Ayn Rand*, which was the first account to detail the Rand-Branden affair. Peikoff did not believe the affair had transpired, and condemned anyone who said anything favorable about Barbara Branden's book. Officially, Kelley was reproached for speaking to libertarians at the Laissez-Faire Supper Club. Peikoff, like Rand before him, contemptuously denounced all those who called themselves libertarians. Then-ARI chairman Peter Schwartz developed the anti-Kelley criticism into a full-blown anti-libertarian doctrine in his pamphlet "Libertarianism: The Perversion of Liberty."

Libertarians were denounced as evil for refusing to require a moral justification, specifically Objectivism, for their political doctrine based on the "non-coercion" principle—that no one should initiate force against another. Most libertarians are united in this principle as their fundamental political belief. Ironically, the purpose of Kelley's speech at the Laissez-Faire Supper Club had been to convince libertarians they needed to accept Objectivism as the philosophical underpinning for their political views.

Kelley was subsequently thrown out of ARI, and philosophy professor George Walsh left on principle as a result (Walsh was one of the first already-established professors who recognized the value and power of Rand's philosophy). Around 1988–89, computer consultant Bob Patterson conceived of a competing organization, and he and fellow consultant Mary Ann ('Molly') Hays convinced and helped Kelley and Walsh to create the Institute for Objectivist Studies, now The Atlas Society. The Atlas Society takes the position that: "the philosophy is a body of knowledge open to expansion and revision, through rational inquiry and open discussion and debate," which position they call "Open Objectivism."[3]

This became one of many disputes with personal undertones which were justified by supposed philosophical breaches. ARI refused to have any truck with libertarian organizations, and followed a policy of denouncing libertarians and anyone who interacted with them in a friendly manner. This trickled down into the orthodox Randian world, enforced by denunciations, excommunications, and banishments everywhere. However, under businessman Yaron Brook, who became Executive Director in 2000, the Institute has fruitfully collaborated with many libertarian and conservative organizations. Long-time ARI supporter John Allison is now head of the libertarian Cato Institute. Oddly, though reversing a decades-long policy of condemnation of libertarians and Objectivists who remained friendly to libertarians, these recent collaborations have transpired with no special justification from ARI.

Under Brook, ARI has grown enormously and he has spearheaded its expanded presence in all forms of media. Brook himself, a highly articulate, passionate, and knowledgeable representative of Rand's ideas, acts as a commentator on numerous TV shows, blogs with Don Watkins in *Forbes,* and is a contributing editor to

---

[3] <www.atlassociety.org>.

The Objective Standard, a quarterly journal "written from an Objectivist perspective."[4] ARI's essay contests for high school and college students and the Objectivist Academic Center have helped spread Rand's ideas among the young.

While a smaller organization, The Atlas Society (TAS) has remained a haven for independent Objectivist thinkers. Respectful discussion and rational debate are hallmarks of its events and products. Its Business Rights Center, headed by Roger Donway, advocates for businessmen such as Greg Reyes, who have been unjustly persecuted by ambitious government prosecutors using non-objective laws. TAS worked closely with Aglioloro on the *Atlas Shrugged* movies. And Kelley's work in philosophy, whether in epistemology or ethics, has pushed the boundaries of Objectivism.

From Individualism to the Morality of Capitalism

In the larger ideological world Rand remained swept under the rug for decades. The renaissance in conservative thought owes much to the vitality of ideas imported from Rand's work, yet she remains anathema to many in the traditional Right, especially because of her atheism, advocacy of rational self-interest, and pro-abortion stance. The libertarian movement has deep roots in Objectivism and much, if not most, of its initial strength and growth was provided by her books.

For decades, libertarians championed capitalism as "free markets" to distinguish the kind of capitalism they advocated from highly regulated businesses using political pull. But the ultimate Achilles' heel of capitalism is the fact that it fosters self-interest. Traditionally, the pursuit of self-interest has been considered at the least, amoral, at the most, the root of immorality. Yet, as Adam Smith long ago observed, "By pursuing his own interest," a person "frequently promotes that of the society more effectually than when he really intends to promote it." Therefore, capitalism must be morally grounded and self-interest must carefully be defined and properly justified if it is to triumph as an honored instrument of human society.

---

4 <www.theobjectivestandard.com>.

Capitalism grew up and became ever more productive as individual rights were recognized and protected, from the late Middle Ages onward. When men are free to follow their own thinking, keep its results, and trade with others, commerce blossoms and wealth expands. But, since these rights are ultimately the rights of the individual to pursue his or her own interests, they fly in the face of the millennia-long collectivist ethical belief that the highest moral purpose is to live for others and to put others' interests ahead of one's own. This is why Objectivists argue that libertarian political doctrine needs Objectivism as an ethical basis.

Instead, many libertarians have tried to use a utilitarian justification for capitalism, that capitalism brings the greatest wealth to the greatest number. But this justification is at root a collectivist one. In it, what matters is the group, the numbers of people capitalism serves. If this is accepted as a moral justification for capitalism then, logically, capitalism and the freedom to trade peacefully with whom and how you want, can be limited and controlled for any 'higher purpose' which serves the group.

Without justifying the individual's right to live for his own sake, no amount of economic superiority, of ability to produce the goods for the most people, will morally validate capitalism because of its root in self-interest. Any time self-interest is seen as being at odds with the "needs" of "society," it can be forcibly curtailed. In this ethical view, self-interest will always be seen as unfair because it doesn't serve "other people." Today we very often see this collectivist criticism in the complaint that capitalism doesn't distribute wealth evenly—the way the Left thinks is "fair."

Rand's analysis shows that the individual human being is the primary ethical unit. The cogent facts are these: Humans live by the use of their reason applied to material in the world; they need various forms of property to live. Each individual's life depends on the operation of his or her reason. A person can learn from others and collaborate on thinking about things with others, but, in the end, each person's reason operates individually. Further, a person cannot be forced to think—only motivated to think by fear or reward—because no amount of force will cause a thought to happen. Therefore, humans must be left free to make up their own minds and choose their own course of action, if they are to live and live well.

Each person is an end in himself, not the means to the end someone else chooses; to be the means to an end someone else chooses is to be a slave. Thomas Jefferson's "pursuit of happiness" is each person's highest purpose. A society in which men are free to live as they see fit, as long as they are not forcing others, is the optimal, the just, the good society. The natural consequence of this freedom is capitalism. In the last analysis, what is good for the individual is good universally—for all humans. In other words, what is good for *each* is good for *all*.

Both the Ayn Rand Institute and the Atlas Society writers have long championed Rand's ethic of self-interest. Since the 2008 financial crisis and its consequent anti-capitalist rhetoric, libertarian and conservative intellectuals alike seemed to have realized the necessity of providing a moral justification for capitalism. Many pro-capitalist intellectuals are producing a rich array of commentaries, articles, blog posts and books addressing the moral issues. And, after decades of arguing for "the free market," libertarians are finally defending "capitalism."

Arthur Brooks's *The Battle* and the muti-author *Morality of Capitalism*, a combined effort of the Atlas Economic Research Foundation and Students for Liberty, are two recent examples. In *The Battle*, Brooks argues that America's culture values "earned success based on enterprise, work, and merit." In *The Morality of Capitalism*, authors ranging from Mario Vargas Llosa to Deirdre McCloskey make a variety of arguments for capitalism's moral superiority to other systems.

Still, both conservatives and libertarians are so aware of Rand's potency and importance that some have stepped up their attacks on her. The conservatives attack her atheism and moral approval of abortion; both conservatives and libertarians attack her for her advocacy of the virtue of 'selfishness'. Yet, Ayn Rand and the power of her ideas are triumphing.

3

Ayn Rand in Person

It was inevitable, considering the dramatic events of Ayn Rand's life, that attention would focus as much on her character as on her thinking. For one thing, people want to know: can someone actually live like one of her heroes? For another, the titillating details of her personal—especially sexual—behavior have caught the interest of the public.

Ron Merrill reported that he could not testify much as to Ayn Rand's personality. He met her several times, briefly, at public appearances. But he, like almost everyone else who met her, found it an unforgettable experience. "She *radiates* intelligence," he told a friend. Merrill reported that, on a stage, seen from the audience, this short, dumpy, ugly old woman with a dense Russian accent was intellectually exciting though personally unimpressive. But when you approached her closely, "an inverse-square law took hold, and her mind shone out at you through her incredible eyes with an intensity that seemed almost physically sizzling." Merrill could easily understand that bright young people would give anything to orbit around this stellar intellect, even though it might burn away their own personalities.

I met Ayn Rand only after "The Break" with the Brandens, when she was in her seventies. However, I did have a number of close encounters with her while attending lecture series by Leonard Peikoff and Alan Blumenthal, during the years 1974 to 1979. I was in my mid-twenties and attending graduate school. Rand regularly accompanied Peikoff and Blumenthal to their lectures and answered questions afterwards. I noticed that most attendees dressed like conservatives in 1960s-style suits and ties, dresses and skirts, that they looked severely uncomfortable, and that some seemed to play at posing with arrogant confidence. But few approached her either in the intermissions or after the lectures.

In my experience, many attendees (as many followers today) seemed able to think only within a narrow Objectivist context and set of concepts, and they didn't seem to come up with their own examples to illustrate Objectivist principles. I didn't find many people at these lectures actively trying to integrate Objectivism with new information and ideas. Wide-ranging, independent thought seemed to be at a minimum, and self-censored.

During breaks and after lectures, I took advantage of her presence to regularly pepper her with questions, whether it was about free will or where she got some delightful plastic jewelry she was wearing. We even talked about cats and she looked at pictures of mine.

During a break between series, I found an adorable pin of a cat arching its back and brought it to her office as a birthday present. Her secretary was going to refuse it with "Miss Rand doesn't accept gifts," until I said "It only cost me $3." The next fall, I saw Rand wearing the pin. When I approached her and said "Oh, I gave you that pin," she replied in her heavily accented English, "It is ze *essence* of cat!"

Another time, I asked her who should be cast for a movie of *Atlas Shrugged*. We talked about actors dead and alive. I suggested Errol Flynn for Francisco (Flynn was a childhood hero of mine from *The Sea Hawk* and *Robin Hood*, fighting for the rights of the oppressed). She said "Oh no dahhling!" and instead offered an English actor, John Justin, as her ideal for this part. During the middle of this conversation, she enthusiastically commented, "Now *ziss* is the kind of conversation I like!"

Other delightful comments I heard her make were, for example, when I asked her to autograph a copy of *The Fountainhead* for my husband, John Enright, and she said "Zat's a nice name, isn't it?" I chuckled: Roger Enright is an important minor character in *The Fountainhead*.

And then there was the time I discovered, upon reading Victor Hugo's first novel, *Hans of Iceland*, that the hero became the first of the Counts of Danneskjöld. Clearly, the name of her *Atlas Shrugged* hero, Ragnar Danneskjöld, was a reference and tribute to Hugo. But when I mentioned this to her, she was quick to make sure I didn't think she was riding on Hugo's coattails: she said "Oh, but there really were Counts of Danneskjöld!" She wouldn't want me to think she was plagiarizing Hugo.

Overall, I found her to be nothing but seriously interested in my questions, always earnest in her answers, and enthralled with conversation about ideas, or her works. If her answer revealed that she hadn't understood my question, I'd let her know and re-formulate what I meant. She patiently listened and then once again tried her best to give a clear answer. She seemed to me deeply authentic—she said what she meant and meant what she said. She never approached me as a superior of any kind, intellectual or social, but always spoke to me mind-to-mind. She was one of the most passionate and authentic people I've ever known.

Mind you, I did experience the famous Ayn Rand temper—the woman *was* a hot-headed Russian, as a Russian friend once commented. Before one lecture, I was waiting to speak to her while she and Alan Blumenthal discussed something. Frank O'Connor, her husband of many decades, was sitting next to her and close to me as I stood in the aisle. I had noticed that Rand was very affectionate with him, often holding hands. It was clear to me that he suffered from aphasia, a neurological disorder which makes it difficult to formulate one's words, a disorder often caused by strokes in old age. Also, I knew he was an artist and not known to be interested in discussing ideas. So I made conversation with him about his painting.

As we talked, Rand repeatedly darted angry looks at me until she finally burst out with a comment something like "Don't bother him, he's not an Objectivist, he's my husband!" Although, of course, chagrined at her reaction, I knew she had no idea what we were talking about. I also realized she was being protective of him. I went back to my seat.

At the next break, she found me across the lecture hall and said "Please dahling, forgive me, I didn't know what you were talking about!" I said "Of course! Thanks." Frank must have straightened her out about our conversation.

What stood out loud and clear to me was that, despite her fame and position, she wasn't above rectifying her mistake, her injustice, towards a young woman. Moreover, she was concerned to do so even though I'm not sure she ever even knew my name.

Neurosurgeon and inventor Joel Franck had a similar experience with Rand. He was a boy of twelve when his brother, Murray, now a retired intellectual property attorney and writer, introduced him to Rand's works. Subsequently, he attended the opening lecture to an NBI series, and had piled his high school books along with tomes of Rand favorites, Austrian economists Ludwig von Mises, Frédéric Bastiat, and Carl Menger, under his seat in the front row.

Sitting on the stage alone, Rand kept looking at him and his books. Then she crooked a finger, motioning for him to approach her. She asked if he was taking the lecture series; but, no, he couldn't afford it. She said "Now you can—I'm giving you a scholarship." Later in the lecture series, she took him to dinner, learned he was interested in the brain and wanted to discover the nature of consciousness.

Dr. Franck attended every lecture he could throughout high school, MIT, Rockefeller University, and Yale Medical School. Sometimes, he wouldn't see her for more than a year, yet she remembered everything about him. When she spoke at the Ford Hall Forum in Boston, no matter the mobs around her, she took five minutes to catch up with her "scholarship student" Joel.

When he had some questions, he was given her telephone number, and free license to call her. He says she exuded nothing but warmth towards him, and was like his Jewish grandmother, always asking about his goals, interests, and achievements, and remembering every detail about them. He thinks that she and her ideas are what made him who he is today, not only a neurosurgeon and inventor, but knowledgeable about a vast array of subjects in the arts, economics, history, and science, of which he would not have learned otherwise. She taught him how to think, how to integrate ideas, and how to learn.

Partisan Accounts

Contrary to my experience or Dr. Franck's, the confessions of Barbara and Nathaniel Branden paint an ugly picture of Ayn Rand's treatment of her followers. According to them, Rand was routinely inconsiderate and often cruel. She stifled intellectual independence and crushed originality, apparently violating the ideal behavior she dramatized in her heroes.

It's hard to judge what actually transpired, since almost all accounts of Rand and her behavior are partisan. Even independently researched books, such as Heller's *Ayn Rand and the World She Made,* are heavily influenced by the Brandens' accounts. The

Brandens, though they admit to being accomplices as well as victims of Rand, still seem not to recognize fully the influence they and the other members of 'the Collective' had on her (this was the ironic name she gave to the group of friends and disciples which Nathaniel collected around her). To the extent that they passively accepted the sort of intellectual bullying of which they accuse her, they corrupted her—as slaves always corrupt their masters. Surrounded as she was by the distorting mirrors of her sycophantic admirers, it's not surprising that Rand lost touch with a common-sense approach.

Later accounts written by loyalists Mary Ann and Charles Sures in *Facets of Ayn Rand*, Leonard Peikoff's accounts, and many of the accounts in *100 Voices: An Oral History of Ayn Rand* present a different picture of the woman than the Brandens'—a picture of a helpful, understanding, nurturing, albeit demanding woman. (The Sures account resonates the most with my own experience.) However these are published by the Ayn Rand Institute, which severely edited other works of Rand's such as *The Art of Fiction Writing*. (This book was based on a class she gave to some students during the 1960s, the tapes of which I heard in the 1980s and I remember many relevant sections of the classes that were left out of this book entirely.)

Looking from the outside of her circle, Rand's public behavior and the complaints of only too many people, including people favorable to her philosophy, add up to an unfortunate picture of her behavior at times. For example, at the Ford Hall Forum, I saw her react strongly, with condemnatory comments, to questioners on abortion and other topics. Sometimes the questioners deserved her reaction for their disingenuous attempts to 'get' her, but sometimes the questioners were seriously confused.

In contrast with the calm way she seemed to handle questioners in early video interviews, in her later years she seemed to get more and more impatient and angry while talking in public. Sometimes I think she was simply sick of hearing the same tired criticisms, and terribly disappointed that no one could come up with a challenge she found intellectually serious.

Rand and Her Hangers-on

Atlas Shrugged publisher Bennett Cerf and editor Hiram Haydn, non-Objectivists who worked with Rand on editing her books, gave intelligent and astute accounts of her. As Anne Heller aptly sums it up: "Bennett Cerf and Hiram Haydn . . . were among the first to notice" that "in professional settings, their 'most interesting' author was a simple, often modest, spellbinding person, even if she was singularly sure of her ideas and impossible to vanquish in an argument. Cerf called Nathaniel Branden and his circle "hangers-on," "brown-nosers," "sycophants," and "stooges."

As an outsider with serious ideological differences, Cerf was never required to agree with Rand's ideas because he wasn't trying to follow Objectivism. It seems that the more fully one advocated her ideas, the harsher was the judgment, which practice continues to this day amongst a significant portion of her followers, causing ever more ridiculous and unproductive schisms. What's particularly shocking is that they occur among people purportedly advocating a philosophy of reason, not a religion or emotionally based doctrine. The idea of "the reasonable" is all but lost. Apparently "rational men," cannot have reasonable disagreements.

Rand's heroes act in the opposite manner, treating other heroes who think and act against them with careful respect. Their attitude is summed up in a scene from *Atlas Shrugged* in which the heroine, Dagny Taggart, is trying to make a decision as to whether to remain with the group of heroes and act with them, or leave their secret enclave and go back to working in the world—which the group considers the equivalent of fighting against them. What do they say to her?

"Yes or no, Miss Taggart?"

"She looked at the faces of the four men in the soft twilight of Mulligan's living room. . . .

"I have one more day," she said steadily. "Will you let me have it? I think I've reached my decision, but I am not fully certain of it and I'll need all the certainty possible to me."

"Of course," said Mulligan. "You have, in fact, until morning of the day after tomorrow. We'll wait."

"We'll wait after that as well," said Hugh Akston, "though in your absence, if that be necessary." . . .

"Consider the reasons which make us certain that we are right," said Hugh Akston, "but not the fact that we are certain. If you are not convinced, ignore our certainty. Don't be tempted to substitute our judgment for your own."

"Don't rely on our knowledge of what's best for your future," said Mulligan. "We do know, but it can't be best until *you* know it."

"Don't consider our interests or desires,' said Francisco. "You have no duty to anyone but yourself." (p. 740)

This is only one, but one of the clearest, examples of the way in which her heroes act in a manner utterly respecting the independent reasoning mind—so unlike the practices of many of her followers. What's worse is that the followers' unreasonable practices add up to the use of social pressure. They attempt to influence other's opinions not by reason and facts, but by threats of condemnation and ostracism.

The Owner of Objectivism?

The rationale for Rand's insistence on the ideological purity of followers usually leads back to Rand's apparent belief that she owned her philosophy in the same way she owned her fiction. She said:

> Since Objectivism is not a loose body of ideas, but a philosophical system originated by me and publicly associated with my name, it is my right and my responsibility to protect its intellectual integrity. (Rand 1968c)

Also in 1968, this statement showed up in *The Objectivist*:

> **Legal Notice signed by Henry Mark Holzer**
>
> The principle involved had once been identified as follows: "An 'Objectivist Society' with which Miss Rand has no connection, and of which she has no knowledge, is misrepresentation and entails a misappropriation of her intellectual property. No admirer of her work can wish to be guilty of this." (Nathaniel Branden, *The Objectivist Newsletter*, April 1965)

At her 1971 Ford Hall Forum appearance, she expanded on her policy:

> There is nothing wrong in using ideas—anybody's ideas—provided you give appropriate credit. You can make any mixture of ideas that you want; the contradiction will be yours. [*Audience snickers.*] But *why do you need the name of someone with whom you do not agree*, in order to spread your misunderstandings, or, worse, your nonsense and falsehood? . . . anything which you do not hear from me or read under my name, *do not accept it* as in any way emanating from or

representing Objectivism. If you want to know what Objectivism is, learn it from me and my publications. Nobody else is authorized to speak for me. And if he doesn't want to speak for himself, then you know what to think of him. . . . When and if a student is ready to contribute to Objectivist theory, the place to do so is in the pages of this magazine—if his theories are consonant with Objectivism; if they are not, he should not designate them as 'Objectivist'.[1]

Rand also said:

Philosophy is the science that studies the fundamental aspects of the nature of existence. The task of philosophy is to provide a comprehensive view of life. (Rand 1975, p. 107)

She seems to have forgotten that no one can own a scientific theory since it is not a creation, but a discovery, an identification, of reality.

No One Owns Objectivism

What does she mean by "science"? Today, this word is usually reserved for the study of nature, apart from the study of humans, although the line blurs with neuropsychology, experimental psychology, experimental anthropology, or economics. But there's an older, broader meaning of science from the Ancient Greeks, which distinguishes science from religion or other paths to forming ideas and beliefs. Physicist Laurence I. Gould defined it as "a rational and systematic study of the natural world with the object of formulating general laws." I think this is close to Rand's application of the word 'science' to philosophy, above. If so, what are the implications for the use of her philosophy?

The Branden-Holzer policy implies that Rand "owned" Objectivism—it was her "intellectual property," and this issue seems to revolve around the idea that the name "Objectivism" is tied to all the specific tenets and beliefs she identified. Of course, she owned the books and the particular way she wrote up her ideas. And any decent person honors her for what she discovered, just as we honor Newton's genius. But she did not own the ideas

---

[1] <www.objectivistliving.com/forums/index.php?showtopic=7801&st=0&p=82479&#entry82479>.

themselves, or their implications and extensions. This is especially important because she acknowledged that her philosophy wasn't finished—that there was much more to discover and explain. She said "the elaboration of a system is a job that no philosopher can finish in his lifetime. There is an awful lot of work yet to be done" (Interview with Garth Ancier of Focus on Youth, 1976, reprinted in Podritske and Schwartz 2009).

Here's the problem: what does she mean by "elaboration" of her "system"? The ARI people seem to take that to mean: applications of the ideas she already enunciated. What, then, of her epistemology, for example, which was only an "introduction"? Who is to develop it into a full epistemology and would that be an 'elaboration'? What about her metaphysics, of which we know only the smallest amount? What about her ethics? She wrote but a slim volume specifically about ethics, supported by some of the writing in her novels. Anyone who thinks about her ideas with any depth and seriousness realizes that there are many further issues and principles to be identified and developed.

Going back to the issue of philosophy as a science, let's consider how we treat scientific theories by looking at Newton and his discoveries. We call his theories of physics 'Newtonian physics', just as we call Rand's theories of philosophy 'Objectivism' (and perhaps the distinction as to what was hers versus others' contributions might have been clearer if we called her ideas 'Randian philosophy'). But many physicists have added discoveries to Newtonian physics—identifications of theories and laws that incorporate and build on Newton's. Maxwell's and Farady's ideas on electro-magnetism, for example; or Boyle's Law. The fact of the matter is: if a scientist or philosopher correctly identifies the facts, that is, arrives at truth, then others properly using the truths will find untold new discoveries as a consequence. So, if Objectivist principles are identifications of universal truths, they are ownershipless and timeless.

And, regarding the "students of Objectivism" Rand mentions in the quote above: if Objectivism is a system of ideas like a science, *who* is to decide when "ideas are consonant with Objectivism" if not each person for himself? If Objectivism is a philosophy based on reason and lauding independent thought, then it cannot require an authority. In practice, in science or any other truth-based system of ideas, we exercise a long process of debate and discovery which results (sometimes) in a set of ideas generally accepted as truth, like the identification of gravity or inertia, because they are the most reasonable and encompassing in fitting the facts.

For a person as dedicated to reason as Rand, how did she miss this obvious problem? Why didn't she see that only reason and reality can be the final authorities for her ideas—as for any?

Horrified by Hypocrisy

Clearly, her horror at Branden's hypocrisy while representing her ideas made her even more sensitized to anyone representing her ideas but her. Also, she was very concerned with maintaining the integrity of her system and avoiding further misunderstandings about her ideas; having been so deeply misunderstood so often would naturally cause a person to be on the lookout about this issue. And perhaps her lifelong passion to save the individualist freedom of the West fuelled her concern that everyone get the ideas just right. She often evinced deep worries about subtle variations on Western ideas that could lead to the destruction of the West's institutions of freedom.

She had seen the way sly collectivists could spin ideas towards their mind-confusing, power-mad purposes. The New Left was especially clever in taking concepts appealing to American sensibilities (rooted in the American Founders' Enlightenment ideas of liberty, equality, and rights) and twisting them to mean something entirely different.

For example, we see the fruits of the New Left's control of Academia today with the widespread confusion over 'equality' and 'fairness'. Does 'equality' mean everyone having exactly the same stuff, does fairness mean that everyone deserves an equal share of all goods and values, regardless of how they were produced? Or does equality mean equality before the law: that all individuals' rights are equal and that each individual should be treated the same by our system of government? Does 'fairness' mean that each person gets what he or she deserves when that person gets what he or she has earned?

Her emphasis on integrity seems related to another idea she had, which became more pronounced with what George Walsh called Peikoff's "coherence theory of truth." This is a kind of Hegelian 'the truth is the whole' belief that to disagree with one part of Objectivism is to reject the entire system. Rand had argued that an incorrect idea, a contradiction to a set of principles, can directly or insidiously undermine the whole. Just as a belief that self-interest is evil or, at the least, amoral, undermines the value of capitalism, so Rand saw anyone potentially going the wrong way if he or she held an idea which Rand thought contradicted her set of principles. This is a kind of "bad ideas drive out good" theory, similar to the economic principle that "bad money drives out good."

What this view doesn't seem to acknowledge is that systems of ideas are not closed-ended, like the airways in an hermetically sealed building. Systems of ideas should be carefully built, thoroughly grounded on facts, and ideologically interlinked with excellent logic. But if they are to fulfill their service to Man's Life, their highest purpose, they must be open-ended, admitting of new facts and arguments. This applies to Objectivism as to any other system of ideas. Even though Rand was a genius, she wasn't omniscient; she hadn't thought of everything, as she recognized. This view fits with Rand's contextual theory of truth.

Internecine warfare over who originated what idea is common even in science, so perhaps Objectivism's problems don't need any special explanation. But, maybe there is another factor which added to the problem. Her philosophy was so dramatically illustrated first in her fiction, the ideas seemed all one piece with the fiction. Since she constantly referred to her characters and scenes to explain her principles, this confusion is almost a certainty. And it also explains some of her vehemence. Rand thought of herself as a paragon of rationality and she was an expert reasoner. However, she was also a highly passionate artist—and artists are unusually sensitive to criticism and proprietary about their artworks. It's a psychological pitfall of the profession, caused by the difficulty of separating one's self from the artwork. Anyone who has children recognizes this phenomenon, the difficulty of looking at one's children objectively; they and what they become are experienced as a deep reflection of self. So also with art and the artist, but the two are even harder to keep separate, as the art has no separate life, or will.

Rand had many motives for her fierce claims to her philosophy. But, the demands that she and only she could pronounce what were and weren't part of the philosophical system of Objectivism were not reasonable. Worse, such demands encourage a cultish atmosphere among those willing to remain part of her group.

From the Political to the Personal and Back

Confusion and cultishness continue to this day in Objectivist circles, between the tiresome, ARI-led denunciations of David Kelley and the kow-towing to Peikoff's condemnations of this person or that. There are various groups of "denouncers" and "enforcers" among Objectivists who are tolerated by ARI. One might think that Yaron Brook could quash this cultish behavior with a statement that would distance the Institute from approving. But nothing is done. Peikoff, of course, holds all the copyrights to Rand's works.

The orthodox followers have never seemed to notice the deep and tragic irony that they are behaving just like Rand's worst characters, creating a community rife with social climbing. Under the guise of "pronouncing judgment," many jostle to prove how righteous—and therefore morally superior—they are. Under the guise of hero worship, they elevate the movement leaders to authorities not to be questioned—at least too closely. In the end, they demand allegiance to person and not principle. They sometimes argue from authority and often use what Rand called the fallacy of the "Argument from Intimidation' in which they threaten moral condemnation to those who disagree.

Lost among the schisms and condemnations are the paragons of independent thought and action as well as the emphasis on her uplifting vision. Where, in these groups, are the people like her heroes, highly original creative producers? Not among the orthodox followers. Instead, they're most apparent in the business people who thrive on her philosophy.

To be fair, those among the orthodox have produced some valuable work, although they are caught between a rock and a hard place: they can't "add" to her philosophy because they adhere to her belief that it was all hers. All they're "allowed" to do is "applications," although the definition and limits of those is far from clear.

Many people have learned much about her philosophy from Leonard Peikoff's *Objectivism: The Philosophy of Ayn Rand*. It is a competent summary of her principles and her best examples, creating a good philosophical introduction. Unfortunately, as is apparent to anyone thoroughly familiar with her writing, it adds almost nothing new to an understanding of her ideas, not even new examples. If one really grasps a set of ideas, one should be able to put them in the context of one's own examples.

In contrast, Peikoff's *The Ominous Parallels* is an original take on the origins and development of Nazism, its effects on German society, and the parallels to American society today. It took Peikoff some ten years to complete this book, under Rand's detailed guidance. Also, in 2010, David Harriman and Leonard Peikoff published a book, *The Logical Leap*, offering an expansion on Rand's theory of induction based on a lecture series by Peikoff. The value of this book is controversial, at the least because of the accuracy of its historical examples, according to Stanford professor of history and philosophy of science, John McCaskey.[2] More recently, Peikoff published *The DIM Hypothesis*.

Other orthodox Objectivist scholars have produced worthwhile explanations of Rand's ideas. Philosophy professor Tara Smith's works such as *Viable Values* and *Ayn Rand's Normative Ethics,* and essays by various writers such as James Lennox, Allan Gotthelf, and Darryl Wright are some examples. *The Objective Standard*, a periodical, has good contributions from Yaron Brook, Alex Epstein, Bradley Thompson and others, expanding on the meaning or Rand's work. Brook and others have contributed to political theory, especially on foreign and military policy. These positions diverge considerably from the common libertarian belief in non-intervention and highly limited military engagement.

Fortunately, independent thinking is accepted and encouraged among the non-orthodox groups of Objectivists. Some examples are: David Kelley's work in epistemology and sociology, *Truth and Toleration* (now *The Contested Legacy of Ayn Rand*), and 'Rand Versus Hayek on Abstraction', and in ethics, *Unrugged Individualism*; Murray I. Franck's 'The State, the Market, and the Morality of Taxation' in politics and law; Kirsti Minsaas's and John Gillis's work in esthetics, 'Mimesis and Expression in Ayn Rand's Theory of Art' and the website ArtGrok.org respectively; Stephen Hicks's work in philosophy, *Explaining Postmodernism*, and Chris Sciabarra's in the history of ideas, *Ayn Rand: The Russian Radical*.

This issue of originality among her followers is pertinent to the

---

[2] <www.amazon.com/review/R33YO57MMEDAJ7/ref=cm_cr_dp_title?ie=UTF8&ASIN=0451230051&nodeID=283155&store=books>.

public's fascination with Rand's life. They want to know: if you believe in her radical set of ideas, if you admire the heroes presented in her books, how would you live your life? They want to see how she lived hers and whether she was able to live up to her ideas and ideals. They want to know if living according to her ideas is possible on earth and they want to see more concrete examples of how to do it.

They have good reason to be skeptical of anyone consistently living up to a set of abstract principles. Given the evidence of history, whether it's the Assembly of the French Revolution or battling over who first discovered the cause of AIDS, human groups find it difficult to respect the rational independence of their members. Instead, humans tend to factions of belief and action, and use social pressure, condemnation, and even force to align members.

Yet, just as it is surprising to read of the vitriol between Thomas Jefferson and John Adams, those close friends and devotees of Enlightenment reason, so it is shocking to learn of the unreasonable ways in which Ayn Rand and her disciples treated admirers who might diverge from exact agreement with her views.

It behooves us to ask what forces exist in human nature, or in these individuals, that overtake men's reason and cause them to be so unreasonable? Unfortunately, human psychology is rife with causes.

Once someone has accepted the framework of a set of beliefs, that person has to work very actively to notice counter-examples, exceptions, elisions, and non-integrated material. One must keep a vigilant eye on reality in order to avoid succumbing to the habit of using the ideas without question.

It's hard work to maintain that vigilance. In the division of labor, it is the domain of intellectuals to delineate all the details of an ideology. Most people spend the lion's share of their time thinking hard about the subject of their professions. Although they should be reflective and educated enough to have thought through their own basic philosophical principles and justifications, most won't have time to continually question the detail.

Moreover, people like certainty. It is cognitively difficult, and can be emotionally shaking, to question a once-accepted whole. A careful examination and control of one's emotional reactions and high skill at introspection—in other words, an entirely elevated development of reasoning habits—is necessary to live with ideological uncertainty. Only if one's self-image, one's self-esteem, is firmly based on an unshakeable loyalty to the facts and the truth, can a person weather the turmoil of questioning deeply held ideas and values (like Rand's character, industrialist Hank Rearden). Usually, such questioning leads to a deep psychological shake-up, or a rejection of the questioning and an attack on those who question. We often see these latter two effects when people question their fundamentalist religion.

When intellectuals are stifled by an interpretation of an ideology which says that it is complete and all-encompassing, or when its followers' reverence for the achievements of the founder is rigidified into an habitual acceptance of the founder's authority, following a philosophy or theory becomes a dogma and schisms are inevitable.

Rand's Personality in Context

To put Rand's personality in the context of her life, she came from one of the worst collectivist totalitarian countries that has ever existed. The Soviet Union crushed the life and individuality out of millions. When she arrived in the US, she thought she had escaped to the haven of individual rights and freedom, only to find out that its culture and its government were being attacked, infiltrated, and undermined by adherents of the very Communism she thought she had escaped. It must have felt like a nightmare in which she couldn't escape the evil psychopath.

Desiring the career of an artist, she realized that she had to define her own point of view, not merely artistically, but philosophically—in order to save the civilization she loved.

Once again, Bennett Cerf, who knew, liked and admired Rand, but was not an advocate of her ideas, gives us some more insight into her context. In *At Random*, Cerf says:

> Ayn is a remarkable woman, but, in my opinion, she was not helped by her sycophants. She's like a movie queen with her retinue, or a prize-fight champion who's followed by a bunch of hangers-on, or a big crooner and his worshippers. They all come to need this adulation. These people tell her she's a genius and agree with everything she says, and she grows more and more opinionated as she goes along. You can't argue with Ayn Rand. She's so clever at it, she makes a fool

out of you. Any time I started arguing with her, she'd trick me into
making some crazy statement and then demolish me.

   At any rate, Ayn and I became good friends. What I loved to do
was trot her out for people who sneered at us for publishing her. She
would invariably charm them. For instance, Clifton Fadiman, who
had snorted at the idea of our publishing Ayn Rand, sat talking with
her until about three in the morning. George Axelrod, author of *The
Seven Year Itch*, toward the end of a long, long evening at Ayn's, dis-
appeared with her into another room and we couldn't get him to go
home. Later he said, "She knows me better after five hours than my
analyst does after five years." (pp. 250–51)

Hiram Haydn, her editor at Bobbs-Merrill and Random House,
paints an accompanying picture in his reminiscences, *Words and
Faces,* which delineates the power and force of her thinking and
personality:

   To gather with her New York adherents, which I did several times, is
   a disquieting experience. . . . She has been idolized and ridiculed,
   called a great thinker, a crackpot, a fascistic counterrevolutionary, a
   fake, but to me the truth is that her mind is all of one piece, a marvelous logical machine before which most computers and cyborgs
   would cower. And at such meetings, the very whining, toadying quality of the camp followers there throw into brilliant relief the wholly
   dedicated, crusading, intrepid nature of the leader. . . .

   What were your premises? [she would ask] And in every argument
   in which she engaged, she emerged victorious no matter with whom,
   or about what. First driving him to defensiveness with that all-impal-
   ing question, then catching every single point that admitted of any
   inconsistency, however marginal, and pressing on with more questions. . . . Many are the people who laughed at my description of her
   dialectical invincibility, only later to try their hands and join me
   among the corpses on the Randian battlefield. (pp. 258–59)

Perhaps this power made many followers cower?

   It's somewhat baffling that so many of those writing about
Rand either believe everything she said about herself without question, or believe almost none of it—yet are willing to believe the
reports of those on the short end of her relationships. Instead of
using Occam's Razor, by which the explanation with the fewest
assumptions is most often best, they immediately leap to conclusions—for example, about Rand's relationship with her father or
her motives for marriage. Using Occam's Razor, shouldn't we at

least begin by taking Rand's statements about her motives at face value to see if they seem to fit the facts?

Ayn and Frank

Except for the orthodox, almost every writer seems to see Rand's marriage to Frank O'Connor as a puzzle because he wasn't a genius inventor or a ground-breaking artist or titan of industry, like her heroes. They tend to assume she must have deluded herself in order to explain why she said she was so deeply in love with him, or that he was her model for Roark or the other heroes. More than a few fall back on his looks for an explanation, presuming she projected a heroic character into him because he looked like her fictional ideal. But is such a delusion possible to maintain for decades? Is that enough to explain a lifetime's relationship?

Few seemed to have known him well except the Brandens, and can their views be impartial? She cast them out and denounced them. One would only expect they would have had a hard time being evenhanded about her. And their relatives and friends—the 'Collective' of Jewish intellectuals who formed her inner circle—would they be objective as to what Frank was like? Not only would their cultural differences and expectations have been vast (he was an Irish-American by background), but also by their own accounts, they were boisterously obsessed with ideas, barely paying attention to the quiet artist in the corner.

Is there another way to view him, his character, and his relationship with Ayn? I haven't seen any commentator consider the idea that, as a sensitive artist, not especially intellectual, and not a genius, but intelligent and sharp about what was happening in the world, he could have had a towering moral character, worthy of *The Fountainhead's* dedication, and of her love and loyalty for fifty years. As she said after he died, "he was so *good*" (Donahue interview, 1979). Apparently, most commentators don't know much about his moral character—but who would, with so little knowledge of him?

Ayn met Frank when they were two artists in their twenties. She was immediately attracted to him by his looks *and* bearing—"my kind of man," as she would say. She picked him out in Hollywood, from among very many attractive actors. When she first saw him "She felt a shock of astonishment—a sense almost of recognition—

and an emotion of such intensity that she could not know if it was pleasure or pain." Months later when she ran into him again, they spent hours talking.

> They discussed movies and writing and acting and what they intended to do in the future; they talked eagerly, without strain and with no sense of being strangers. By the end of the day, she knew that what she had seen in his face, that first morning on the streetcar, she now had found in his character." (Branden and Branden 1962, pp. 174–77)

He must have been quite the conversationalist to hold *her* interest. She never suffered fools—or small talk—gladly. As she repeatedly said, they had a lot in common: their ambitions, sensibilities, and outlooks. She also said he complemented and supported her with his insouciant American sense of life—those who knew him even a little agreed he was quite humorous and witty. And she seemed to be very supportive and encouraging of his artistic pursuits. Their array of nicknames for each other such as "Fluff" and "Cubbyhole" convey something of their close affection. For decades, through very tough times, they worked on their careers, and had difficulty making ends meet. On the day in 1943 before *The Fountainhead* was published, Frank told her "We've made it, this time", conveying the sense that they were a team in their pursuits (pp. 204).

And he must have understood and enjoyed her tremendously—since, with his looks and elegant manner, he likely could have had his pick of Hollywood beauties. The fact that he married her and stayed with her all the time they were poor, when divorce would not have been any kind of social problem for him, speaks volumes.

In the introduction to the twenty-fifth anniversary edition of *The Fountainhead*, she reveals how depressed she was at the state of the world in the late 1930s, with Nazism and Communism running rampant, turning Europe into one gigantic slave state, and no one apparently able to stop it. She was so depressed she almost quit writing the novel; she recounts how Frank talked her out of it.

He talked her out of something? He argued her out of something? Who could do that? Just look at the testimony of Cerf, Haydn, and myriad others to get some perspective on that feat. Clearly, he was a person of discerning judgment, whose counsel she deeply valued.

So why, after this intense intimacy, did Ayn take up with

Nathaniel Branden?

Indeed, the attentions and attraction of a young, handsome man would have had a great deal of flattering excitement for an older woman. But Branden, by many accounts exceptionally brilliant, offered much more. After three decades of intellectual isolation and misapprehension by others, Rand would have been starved for thoughtful, intelligently appreciative, and deeply enthusiastic feedback about her ideas, from an "outsider," someone not of her world, who could give her a sense of objective feedback. She longed to find some accomplished intellectuals who recognized her value. Then, along came the brilliant Nathan Blumenthal (Nathaniel Branden's original name) who had deeply studied every word she'd written and was ready to mirror all she was. And he did just that—to a fault.

By trying to embody, and then acting the role of Randian hero, he offered her an intellectual mirror unavailable elsewhere. By worshipping her artistry and appreciating it in detail, he offered a new reflection of her passion. And, by his own admission, he cultivated this role with vigor. This complex of intense experiences apparently was irresistible.

This relationship did not destroy her marriage to Frank O'Connor. Some writers have argued that he stayed because he had no other financial support. Perhaps, but it's likely he could have gotten a big divorce settlement. Given the close and affectionate way they acted until the end of O'Connor's life, it's just as likely that their loving relationship survived.

4

The Young Nietzschean

Commonly Rand's critics, as well as her supporters, have based their discussion on her philosophical and political essays, with an occasional reference to Galt's speech in *Atlas Shrugged*. Rand was a master polemicist who could, while writing passionate, persuasive prose, keep it tightly reasoned. Yet for most of her life she saw herself as a writer of fiction, and her fiction works were the workshop in which she hammered out her philosophy. In the next three chapters we'll look at the development of Rand's ideas by examining her fiction works in chronological order.

Rand's philosophical roots in the Aristotelian tradition are well known. Not so well understood is her ambivalent attitude toward Friedrich Nietzsche. Rand started her career as a follower of this enigmatic philosopher. By looking at Rand's literary work chronologically, we can trace her intellectual odyssey. Her ethical, political, and esthetic values, woven together in a complex manner, developed by a process of rejection and revision of the Nietzschean vision.

Alone Against the World

Often, we can fully understand the positions Rand takes only by contrasting them with what she rejects. And aside from specific influences, Rand's life-long struggle against a hostile intellectual climate left its mark on her philosophy and her art. A corollary of this determined resistance was the consistent theme, prominent in all her fiction, of integrity and loyalty to values.

Ayn Rand was not merely an intellectual but also an artist. Only her relentless consistency made it possible for her to integrate the varied aspects of her work. It is this total integration which makes her ideas so compelling, which hits the first-time reader with that feeling, 'But of course! How could I have ever thought otherwise?' Unfortunately, it's too easy to take this certainty for granted, and thus fail to examine and understand the architectural ingenuity which underlies it. Neither should we miss the sheer fun that was always a part of Ayn Rand's writing. Her pleasure in the paradoxical, the bizarre, the shocking, enhanced the talent that made her such a superb teacher. Whether satirizing Gertrude Stein or slipping the needle to collectivist science with a casual allusion to "the Seventeen Illustrious Inventors of the Candle," she entertains as she instructs.

Rand was a genius, but a genius bedeviled by her sex and by her birthdate and in violent conflict with her environment. This conflict led to her worst despair and her greatest triumph. In a personal context, a central theme of Rand's life is her struggle with despair. She fought for decades, alone against the world, a battle as horrible as any endured by her fictional heroes.

The constant thread which runs through all of her work is the problem of the moral individual trapped in an evil society. This was Rand's own dilemma in life, a dilemma which she resolved by her artistic and philosophical vision of the individual's power to create his own life, expressed through her writing. Through this vehicle, she overcame all obstacles, to become famous and influential.

Rand was, for the most part, alienated from the society in which she lived. She saw herself, with no small justification, as being a lone figure of reason and morality in a viciously evil culture. All of her major works of fiction deal with the same theme: the able and moral person trapped in an oppressive society. How is he to survive? How can he preserve his psychological health? How can he triumph? To one with this perspective on life, there is constant danger that resolution will degrade into depression, that alienation will evolve into paranoia. Rand recognized this hazard and explored it in her novels.

'Repression', in something approaching the Freudian sense of the word—a denial or cutting-off of emotions from one's consciousness so habitualized that one is hardly aware of the process—was an important part of Objectivist theory through Nathaniel Branden's articles. It was regarded as not just a psychological phenomenon, but at least potentially a moral offense, for denial of emotions can lead to denial of facts. And, for an Objectivist, refusal to face reality is a cardinal sin. Nevertheless, ignorance and denial of emotions and motivations was—and is—prominent in practice among some Objectivists.

As we shall see in discussing her novels, particularly *The Fountainhead* and *Atlas Shrugged,* Rand was well aware of the phenomenon of repression, and of its dangers, and had much counsel to offer on dealing with it. Her complex and subtle understanding of motivation made her a master of psychological insight—illustrated in real life by playwright George Axelrod's testimony (Cerf 1977, p. 251).

The Evolution of Objectivism

Rand claimed that she had held the same beliefs throughout her life, though she gradually expanded and improved her understanding. This is a distortion of the facts.

Rand, at the time she wrote *We the Living,* was highly influenced by Nietzsche. As her thinking developed, she began to abandon the emotionalism of Nietzsche for the rationalism of her own philosophy, Objectivism. At the same time, her sense of life—at least as expressed in her writing—changed from one of existential despair to one of hope and confidence. Ultimately, her understanding and experience of the freedom of American society taught her that good will triumph, if fought for properly. Further, she learned that under the reign of freedom no one needs to be sacrificed to anyone else, not the ordinary to the supermen nor the producers to the consumers.

This can be seen in the progression of her four novels. In *We the Living* the struggle is between good (represented by Kira, Leo, and Andrei) and evil (the Communist State)—and evil wins. *Anthem* deals with the same fight, but this time the good is triumphant. *The Fountainhead* progresses further; now the conflict is between the good (Roark) and the imperfect (Dominique and Wynand). With *Atlas Shrugged* Rand dismisses the power of evil entirely, and the conflict is between good and good (the strikers versus the scabs).

After the completion of her fictional output Rand went through a brief sterile period of severe depression before turning to non-fiction. She elaborated and systematized the philosophy of

Objectivism, adding some major innovations to the ideas she had presented in *Atlas Shrugged* in articles eventually collected into controversial books, including, *For the New Intellectual, The Virtue of Selfishness, Capitalism: The Unknown Ideal, Introduction to Objectivist Epistemology, The Romantic Manifesto*, and *The New Left* (now retitled *Return of the Primitive*).

Other articles were published posthumously in *Philosophy: Who Needs It* and *The Ayn Rand Column. The Early Ayn Rand* encompassed her unpublished fiction. ARI has also published some of her journals, her letters, a book of her marginalia, a book of transcripts of her interviews, a book of her answers to questions posed at interviews and lectures, and books based on highly edited transcripts of courses she gave on fiction and non-fiction writing.

The Randian Style

Ayn Rand was one of the most innovative writers of the twentieth century, and it's worth noting some of the outstanding aspects of her unique style. Rand's writing is characterized by the following qualities:

- **Paradox.** Rand's conscious and explicit commitment to logical consistency is a most obvious trait. One way in which it shows up in her fiction is her predilection for paradox. Repeatedly she challenges the reader with contradictions to be resolved. Sometimes the paradox appears in a major theme of the work; in *Think Twice,* for instance, a rich altruist, the benefactor of many people, turns out to be a vile sadist, and the recipients of his help the victims of torture. Sometimes paradox is a plot device: the scientific genius who works as an unskilled railroad laborer. Sometimes it appears in characterization; recall the scene in which Dagny Taggart admires Rearden's appearance of "ruthless asceticism"—at a moment when he has just been fantasizing a sexual assault on her. Or it may appear in the background—as in *Red Pawn,* where a Soviet prison is located in an old Russian Orthodox monastery with religious murals on the walls.

- **Surprise**. Rand took great delight in surprising and astonishing her readers. In her short story, 'The Simplest Thing in the World', Rand describes what seems to have been her own plotting technique: Think of an obvious, trite bromide of a theme—and give it a totally unexpected twist. Nathaniel Branden has described (in *Who Is Ayn Rand?* and *Judgment Day*) Rand's personal pleasure in the denouement of *Atlas Shrugged,* in which the villains torture the hero—to force him to become dictator of the country. This habit of reversing clichés gives Rand's work much of its freshness and impact.

- **Épater les Bourgeois (shocking the middle classes).** Rand takes an almost childish delight in defying the conventions and shocking the reader. This is true not only in her presentation of philosophical principles ("The Virtue of Selfishness") but in her social attitudes (making a heroine out of a sexually unconventional forger in her play *Penthouse Legend,* for instance) and in her literary style (deliberately mixing melodrama, science fiction, and heavy philosophical discourses in *Atlas Shrugged).* Perhaps the classic example (though it might better be described as *épater l'intelligentsia)* is her essay on fiction-writing technique in which she selects passages to show how Mickey Spillane is superior in style to Thomas Wolfe.

- **Visual imagery.** Rand's experience writing for the movies shows up strongly in her literary style. Take for example Andrei's suicide in *We the Living.* The scene is strikingly visual—the silent room, the burning of Kira's clothing, the loading of the pistol. Then there is the movie-like dissolve from the silence to the band playing in Andrei's funeral procession, with the ironic counterpoint of the marching women's mundane and cynical conversation. The whole sequence could be translated to the screen with scarcely any revision. All of Rand's fiction shows this cinematic obsession with visual imagery.

- **Psychological insight.** Rand has the faculty, rare among even the best writers, of getting into the minds of all her characters. Few novelists have surpassed, or even equaled, Rand's ability to make a character's deepest motivations understandable.

- **Moral focus.** Though Rand is a figure of the twentieth century, her books have very much the flavor of the nineteenth.

This stems from her choice of plot-themes. Any serious fiction is centered on a conflict within the protagonist. What can be the source of this conflict? Roughly speaking—there are of course many exceptions!—one might make the following generalization. In the eighteenth century, novels tended to focus on 'manners' as a source of conflict: the hero wants to do something, but the dictates of custom forbid it. In the nineteenth century, the conflict tends to be moral in nature: the hero wants to do something, but his moral principles forbid it. In the twentieth century, the conflict tends to be psychological: the hero wants to do something, but is incapable because of his neurotic problems. In this analysis, Rand is quite definitely a nineteenth-century writer rather than a twentieth-century writer, in that the focus of her books is on moral issues rather than psychological problems.

- **Philosophical Themes**. It takes some courage to write a novel about philosophy. Again, Rand, in doing this, is more of the nineteenth century than of the twentieth. The illustration of ethical principles by fictional action is today casually dismissed as 'didactic writing' or 'morality play'. Rand's essays on philosophy within the novels, presented as speeches by her characters, are universally denounced by literary critics. Oddly enough these are often the same professors who have no problem with the use of this technique by writers like Tolstoy or Thomas Mann—and who sneer at students who find the sermons in Dante heavy going.

Nietzsche's Influence on Rand

According to *Who Is Ayn Rand?*, the Objectivist movement's official, Rand-approved account published in 1962, Friedrich Nietzsche's influence on Ayn Rand was brief. She flirted with his ideas in college, attracted by Nietzsche's view of the heroic in man and his denunciation of collectivism and altruism. But she soon discovered Nietzsche's explicit repudiation of reason, and "that finished him as an intellectual ally."[1]

---

[1] Rand's early rejection of Nietzsche is reported by Barbara Branden both in *Who Is Ayn Rand?* (p. 132) and in *The Passion of Ayn Rand* (p. 45). In the latter

By Rand's own account she quickly and completely abandoned Nietzsche's philosophy, and developed her own philosophical ideas under the sole influence of Aristotle. Yet, during the first part of her career, Rand's writings are clearly and explicitly Nietzschean—so much so that even her later substantial textual revisions are insufficient to conceal the evidence. It was not until the late 1930s, when she was in her mid-thirties, that Rand finally broke with Nietzsche, and this break is an important theme in *The Fountainhead*.

During this Nietzschean period of her career Rand, as a new immigrant to the United States, developed her writing skills and began the effort to express her ideas in fiction. But this very effort seemed to challenge, and ultimately refute, much of what she believed. With the completion of *We the Living* it became clear that she could not integrate her philosophy with her art; there was something wrong in Nietzsche, something that imposed on her stories either a tragic sense of life, or an optimism that threatened to degenerate into mere frivolity. It was in this crucible that Objectivism was smelted.

The Nietzschean Vision

Many critics of Objectivism have casually assumed that it is merely a variant of Nietzsche's philosophy. Objectivism's defenders have indignantly denied the charge. Few on either side have displayed much familiarity with the actual ideas of that notoriously obscure and difficult thinker, Friedrich Nietzsche. Mostly he is described in vague terms as an advocate of 'selfishness' and inventor of the 'superman' who built the ideological foundation for Nazism.

Nietzsche viewed himself as leading the opposition to one of history's most influential philosophers, Immanuel Kant. Nietzsche accused Kant of attempting to set limits to the validity of reason as a means of rescuing Christian, altruistic morality. He agreed with Kant that reason and altruism were incompatible. Unlike Kant, he was prepared to jettison religion and altruism, so Nietzsche rejected Kant's attack on reason. Rand adopted this view of Kant as her own, and never abandoned it. Like Nietzsche, to the end of

---

work (pp. 114–15) Branden discusses the Nietzschean passages in *We the Living* and suggests that Rand really didn't mean it. However, the only evidence she can adduce is Rand's much *later* writings on the issue of force.

her life she considered Kant her intellectual arch-enemy. It's uncertain what of Kant's works she read herself.

Though Nietzsche regarded himself as, in a sense at least, a defender of reason, he extended the common conception of reason to include the entire capability of the human entity: Not just deductive reasoning, but intuition, imagination, perception, and feeling were to him included in 'reason'. In developing Objectivism Rand rejected Nietzsche's idea that emotion is actually a form of reason. However, she retained the basic idea behind Nietzsche's concept of reason, the idea that human beings are unitary, that mind, soul, and body are inherently inseparable. This viewpoint is at the root of Rand's rejection of the 'mind-body dichotomy'. For her, as for Nietzsche, there is no inherent separation between mind and body. Note how Randian this quotation from Nietzsche sounds:

> I have my word to say to those who despise the body. I am not asking them to learn better or teach better, but merely to say farewell to their body—and so be silent.[2]

Since there is no separation between mind and body, there is none between reason and emotion. While Rand argued that emotions may not be "tools of cognition," in the well-integrated person they do not conflict with reason. Here, for instance, is a passage from Rand's journal, written in 1934:

> It may be considered strange and denying my own supremacy of reason—that I start with a set of ideas—then want to study in order to support them, and not vice-versa, that is, not study and derive my ideas from that. But these ideas, to a great extent, are the result of a subconscious instinct, which is a form of unrealized reason. All instincts are reason, essentially, or *reason is instincts made conscious*. The "unreasonable" instincts are diseased ones. This—for the study of psychology. For the base of the reconciliation of reason and emotions.[3]

---

[2] *Thus Spoke Zarathustra*, 'On Those Who Despise the Body'. All Nietzsche quotations are from *Nietzsche: An Anthology of His Works*, edited by Otto Manthey-Zorn. Compare this passage with Galt's speech, *Atlas Shrugged*, pp. 1026–27.

[3] Emphasis added. See 'From Ayn Rand's Unpublished Writings: Philosophic Journal (1934)', *The Objectivist Forum*.

One corollary to Nietzsche's expanded notion of human reason is the danger of being ruled by one's 'passions'. If emotions are to contribute to reasoning they must be held under strict control. Though Rand developed her own theory of emotion, all her fiction, as we shall see, emphasized heroic emotional control, sometimes almost to the point of repression. However, all of her heroes are so exquisitely self-aware that their self-control doesn't seem to result in repression.

The logical next step for Nietzsche was the utter repudiation of religion and the supernatural, and man's acceptance of human life as an end in itself. The Nietzschean 'superman' accepts the obligation to make the most of himself, to constantly develop and improve his ability, courage, and creative will. Nobody can fully understand Rand's thinking without realizing that this emphasis on personal ability and strength of character, on what one is and is becoming, lies at the root of her morality, as it did for Nietzsche.

Finally, Nietzsche is compelled by his view of reason to proceed 'beyond good and evil'. It is not sufficient to repudiate the authority of priests. No exterior moral authority may be recognized, since 'reason' is not objective for Nietzsche, it is personal. Thus the 'superman' must be a law unto himself—philosophically, and therefore socially.

But what if two people's 'reasoned' views are in conflict? Then the only resolution lies in force. Hence the 'will to power'; the 'superman' establishes the correctness of his views by forcing them upon those who disagree. This leads, obviously, to a social hierarchy, with the superman at the top and the 'masses' at the bottom. The morality of Judeo-Christian altruism is a 'slave morality'; the superman and those who aspire to that title must follow a morality of 'masters', a morality focused on power. This sentiment seems to have caused Rand some queasiness from the start, and she later repudiated it.

Nietzsche's political views were confused at best. He, like Rand, knew what he was against—socialism and statism—far better than he knew what he was for. He was a perceptive opponent of the Marxist vision, though, as events turned out, too optimistic:

[Socialism] desires a degree of political power as high as despotism has ever had. Indeed, it out-rivals all the past in that it aims at the complete annihilation of the individual. . . . it can hope to exist only here and there and only for a short time by means of extreme terrorism. (p. 473)

Let it not be thought, however, that Nietzsche was an advocate of egoism. His concern was with the welfare of the race more than of the individual. This was at the root of his concept of the 'superman'.

Nietzsche, like most intellectuals of his time, was profoundly influenced by the concept of evolution. He believed passionately in the evolution of the human species into a higher order of being—a 'superman' (or 'overman', as his term *Übermensch* is sometimes translated)—a being who would be to man what humans are to apes. Unlike the Social Darwinists, however, Nietzsche saw this evolution as occurring not through 'survival of the fittest' and natural selection, but through 'sublimation'—the effort of the individual human being to make himself into something higher.

Nietzsche was, in fact—not a Social Darwinist, but, shall we say, a Social Lamarckist. Just as Lamarck's giraffe lengthened its neck by striving for leaves on high branches, and transmitted that characteristic to its descendants, so Nietzsche saw human intellectual ability rising by the same process. He therefore exhorts men, most particularly the best, to better themselves and their descendants by striving to accomplish great things, so that the superman may be created by this Lamarckian process. According to Nietzsche, it is the duty of every human being, to the extent of his capacity, to sacrifice himself for the creation of the superman:

> I love those who . . . sacrifice themselves for the earth so that the earth may some day belong to the Overman.
>   I love him who lives in order to know and who seeks knowledge so that the Overman may live. And thus he wills his own passing.
>   I love him who works and invents in order to build a house for the Overman and to prepare for him the earth, the beasts, and the plants; for thus he wills his passing. (p. 4)

Yet for all this, Nietzsche's superior man, who is to pave the way for and evolve into the superman, is not completely an altruist. Nietzsche visualizes human fulfillment, at least for the superior man, as lying in a continual process of self-improvement, self-renewal, and self-challenge. His aphorism "The noble soul has reverence for itself" fitted Rand's thought perfectly; she nearly adopted it as the epigraph for *The Fountainhead*. Rand saw human fulfillment in much the same terms, though she extended it explicitly to all rational men, not just the strongest of the human race.

One of Nietzsche's most oft-stated themes is the necessity for continual challenge of one's intellectual substructure.

> Convictions are greater enemies of truth than lies. (p. 483)

> The presupposition of every man of faith of any shade was that he could not be refuted. If the arguments against it prove to be too strong he could still take resource in belittling reason itself. (p. 630)

> Are we under obligation to be true to our errors even when we realize that by doing so we do harm to our higher selves? . . . No, there is no law, no obligation of this kind; we must be traitors, must be disloyal, again and again must abandon our ideals. (p. 629)

Here we may discern the root of Rand's "Check your premises" dictum, as well as the realization that those who cannot justify their beliefs may reject reason rather than accept the truth.

More subtle but still detectable in its influence on Rand's work is Nietzsche's belief that intellectual and moral growth is inherently painful and indeed cruel. His view is that self-improvement involves not only effort but suffering—a sort of intellectual 'no pain, no gain' principle. This theme is recurrent through Nietzsche's work. To take just one example:

> Consider, that in his search for knowledge even the scholar, by forcing his intellect to know *against* the inclination of his mind, and often also against the wishes of his heart—that is to say No where he would prefer to affirm, love, and worship—is acting as an artist and transformer of cruelty . . . In every desire to know there is a drop of cruelty. (p. 229)

As Manthey-Zorn puts it, "Growth is taken to mean the sublimation of the beast in man. According to the nature of growth it is painful and attended by cruelty" (p. 215). A number of Nietzsche's aphorisms reinforce this point. "Whatever does not kill me makes me stronger." "Spirits and vigor grow through a wound."

Ayn Rand seems to have accepted and retained this idea herself. Rand's heroes are described in her early works as cruel; in her later works as "implacable." In spite of her emphasis on "the benevolent universe premise," she never completely lost the conviction that to grow and improve oneself is painful, that one must not be stopped by the pain, and that to assist others means, in a sense, to be cruel to them. Considered in this light. Henry Cameron's brusque treatment of Howard Roark; Francisco D'Anconia's deception of Dagny; and John Galt's cruelty toward both Dagny and Hank Rearden become more comprehensible.

In addition to these contributions to the content of her thought, Nietzsche also influenced Rand's literary style in several ways. Like Nietzsche, Rand often wrote in an aphoristic style. Like Nietzsche, she could be bitterly, even viciously polemical. The two writers are similar in their pleasure in shocking the reader, one announcing that "God is dead," the other proclaiming "the virtue of selfishness." Yet Ayn Rand, like Friedrich Nietzsche, was irreligious though not irreverent.

In her essay on the philosophical significance of the space program, 'Apollo and Dionysius', Rand invokes a metaphorical dichotomy taken directly from Nietzsche. But, unlike Nietzsche, who portrayed himself as a worshipper of Dionysius, Rand comes down on the side of the Apollonian worldview.

Rand, as a philosopher and as a writer, derived much of her intellectual impulse from Nietzsche. Yet, as we shall see, she was in the end by no means his follower. Indeed, the significance of his influence was most marked in how she created Objectivism by struggling against it.

Literary Influences

No author, not even one as independent as Ayn Rand, can completely avoid the influence of other writers. A number of sources contributed to Rand's literary technique and style.

The earliest inspiration for Rand's work came from the adventure melodramas she devoured as a young girl. Above all she was attracted by the heroes she found in these magazine serials: strong, resourceful, self-confident men who laughed at danger and were never at a loss for a way to deal with it. Her childhood experiments with writing concentrated on similar stories. But when she began serious work as an adult, the melodramatic hero was for the most part suppressed; he did not return as a major factor until *Think Twice* and *Atlas Shrugged*.

Rand was familiar from her schooldays with the major Russian authors. She detested them for their sense of life, though admiring some (especially Dostoyevsky) for their powerful technique. She was more receptive to foreign authors, especially Schiller and Ibsen, and she loved Rostand's *Cyrano de Bergerac*. But the closest approach to her literary ideals was Victor Hugo.

Hugo, the leading Romantic of nineteenth-century literature, showed heroic men fighting for ideas. To portray this sort of struggle became Ayn Rand's own literary ambition. Hugo was her model, and in spite of her conscious effort to avoid imitation, the influence of Hugo is clear, especially in her early works.

Even Hugo was not quite *dramatic* enough for Rand's taste. Her work shows, almost from the beginning, a theatrical approach which appears to owe much to Henrik Ibsen. She must have thrilled indeed to *An Enemy of the People*. "The strongest man in the world is he who stands most alone," says Ibsen. "Every loneliness is a pinnacle," responds Rand.

Rand's predilection for paradox and her pleasure in surprising and shocking the reader probably owed much to the influence of O. Henry and Oscar Wilde. And, as we shall see, several authors may have contributed to specific plot devices or characters in her later novels. But overall, only Rand's earliest work is occasionally derivative; she established her literary independence far more quickly than most writers.

Rand's Early Fiction

Rand began writing in English shortly after her arrival in the United States. Her first efforts functioned primarily as exercises—apparently she made no effort to publish any of them—and they have little philosophical or intellectual content.

The earliest story by Ayn Rand that we have in print is 'The Husband I Bought', written in 1926. This seems to have been the first story Rand actually completed since her childhood efforts (she suspended her writing at age twelve, contenting herself with outlines and scenarios). This story of a failed marriage, while immature, is lavishly Romantic in its heroine's approach towards love. It incorporates a hallmark of Rand: turning a convention on its head. Rather than out of revenge, the wronged wife fakes an affair out of love. Her all-encompassing love for her husband moves her to give her husband an honorable way out of the marriage so that he can be happy in his new relationship.

In view of its stylistic deficiencies Rand probably would not have preserved it had it not had a strong emotional significance to her. Both Barbara Branden and Leonard Peikoff suggest that in this story Rand worked out her emotional reaction to her first love, the Russian "Leo."

Though Peikoff attempts to put 'The Husband I Bought' into the context of Rand's work, the story is incapable of bearing much philosophical burden. Certainly the theme—loyalty to values—is one of the main unifying ideas of Rand's thought. Irene in dreary exile, kneeling before the portrait of her lost love, gives us a faint hint of Francisco d'Anconia's sad cabin in the forest. In the final analysis, the story is the maiden literary effort of a twenty-one-year-old woman.

'Good Copy', written a year or so later, shows a very substantial improvement in technique. It is a humorous, almost slapstick account of a cub reporter's effort to stimulate his career by faking the kidnapping of an heiress. The stunt begins to backfire when the madcap heiress proves entirely too co-operative. The story is pure fun, of a type popular in the 1920s, and competently handled.

'Escort', a short-short written in 1929, is a conscious imitation of O. Henry, not nearly as good as that master's best but perhaps better than his worst.

Also written in 1929 was 'Her Second Career'. This is the first story that is recognizably written by Ayn Rand, showing the signs of Rand's mature fiction. First, there is the distinctive Randian 'gimmick': A Hollywood star is challenged to try starting over again at the bottom, to prove that her success is due to talent rather than luck or pull. Then, there are typical Randian heroes, the writer Winston Ayers and the aspiring actress Hedy Leland. The ironic twists of the plot are characteristic of the mature Rand.

And, an important sign of progress, Rand is now writing about reality. The settings of her earlier stories, though ordinary, are imaginary; Rand had no more direct knowledge of small-town 'society' or the newspaper business than she did of the African veldt. But the Hollywood milieu of 'Her Second Career' is unquestionably grounded in the personal experience of the author. Rand is now writing as an adult for the first time, drawing on experience rather than fantasy. Her description of the trials of aspiring actresses—including the petty indignities of the casting office and the not-so-petty indignities of the casting couch—has a gritty realism that adds impact to the story.

The story carries a limited but significant message. Rand indicts Hollywood for lacking the courage to develop new ideas, new stories, and new faces. She portrays effectively the movie industry herd phenomenon, with studio executives, each attempting to follow all the others, afraid to take the smallest chance on innovation.

Red Pawn

In 1930 Rand began work on her first novel, *We the Living*. A year later she interrupted the project to write a movie scenario, *Red Pawn*. This was her first commercial work to be completed, and her first sale.

Comparing *Red Pawn* to 'Her Second Career' shows that Rand's improvement in technique has not only continued but accelerated. The scenario is clearly a sketch for *We the Living;* theme and plot are identical with those of the novel. A woman (Joan/Kira) becomes the mistress of a dedicated Communist (Kareyev/Andrei) in order to save the life of the man she loves (Michael/Leo). Unexpectedly she comes to admire, and even love, the man she deceives; he in turn learns, from her example, that he must renounce his faith in Communism. But in the end her loyalty is to her first and greater love.

The two stories differ in two important respects. *Red Pawn* takes place in a prison, a limitation that effectively provides dramatic unity for a movie. In *We the Living*, Russia itself is the prison; the novel can handle the wider scope.

More interesting is the contrast between the denouements of the two stories. In *Red Pawn*, Kareyev's renunciation saves Joan and Michael, and they escape to Japan and freedom. In *We the Living*, Andrei's renunciation is futile; Leo and Kira are doomed. Rand may have felt that a 'happy' ending was mandatory for the film treatment.

Red Pawn marks another quantum leap in Rand's skill as a writer. The integration of plot, theme, and symbol is superb; Rand clearly is already a master of the esoteric art of writing for film. The characters of Joan and Kareyev are brilliantly drawn; the only deficiency is Michael. Rand fails to dramatize him as an effective hero, so that Joan's obsessive dedication lacks some credibility. She faced the same problem in *We the Living*.

Penthouse Legend

In 1933 Rand again interrupted her work on *We the Living* to write her first stage play. *Penthouse Legend,* now more commonly known as *The Night of January Sixteenth*. The play has been published in at least three editions: the McKay edition, intended for amateur productions; the Longmans, Green edition; and the authorized edition, put out by World Publishing.

Rand claims in her introduction to the authorized edition that it is essentially unchanged from her original manuscript. One may wonder whether this is wholly true; her similar claim with respect to *We the Living* is demonstrably false, as we shall see. However, there seems to be little in the authorized edition which could not have been written by the Rand of the 1930s, though she may have done a little philosophical airbrushing. Certainly the text is far more authentic Rand than either of the other two editions. There is only one passage missing from the authorized edition which seems authentic. It occurs at the end of the Longmans, Green edition: In both of the play's alternate conclusions, whether the verdict is guilty or not guilty, the judge chews out the jury and strikes their names from the rolls. *That* has Rand's hallmark on it!

Rand goes to great pains in her introduction to the authorized edition to emphasize her rejection of the criminal-as-hero and to downplay the Nietzschean aspects of the work. A tortuous and unconvincing explication of the idea of a "sense-of-life play" is invoked to explain away the play's obvious philosophical thrust. A Nietzschean theme is so central to *Penthouse Legend* that Rand could never have hoped to Bowdlerize it—she would have had to eviscerate the plot.

Penthouse Legend is dominated by a character who never appears on stage: Bjorn Faulkner. He is a classic Nietzschean superman, a colossus of finance who is literally 'beyond good and evil' ("Bjorn never thought of things as right or wrong. To him, it was only: you can or you can't. He always could," p. 102). His only value is power: his "whip over the world" (p. 122) and his ownership of Karen Andre.

Karen Andre is drawn with a sure hand and is a striking character even in the elite group of Rand's heroines. In her combination of competence and sexuality she prefigures Dagny Taggart, and in her insolent defiance of morality she prefigures Dominique Francon. She is, of course, a consummate hero-worshipper. Rand's lifelong theme of loyalty to values forms the basis of the plot: Karen Andre allows herself to be tried for Faulkner's murder to help him escape with his loot—not knowing that he really is dead. Reinforcing the theme is the comparable loyalty of the gangster 'Guts' Regan to Karen.

The play is a powerful and eloquent plea for the Nietzschean world view. Its epigraph might be Milton's, "Better to reign in hell than serve in heav'n." But in the end, the Nietzschean vision must conclude with tragedy. What would be a happy ending for Faulkner? What could be? To rule the world? What would he do with it? He would be revealed as chasing a goal that would be useless if achieved; so he cannot be allowed to achieve it. Even the lesser goal of getting away with his ten million dollars cannot be practical. Is this the triumph of Bjorn Faulkner—to hide in Buenos Aires and play with his mistress and his money? Faulkner cannot succeed *and remain a hero*—so he must fail and die.

Just look at what happens. This 'superman' gives away his master plot by carelessly telling an underling too much. As Faulkner tries to sneak away, he is easily tailed by an amateur sleuth. And, finally, he is out-shot in a gunfight with a wealthy philanthropist. Poor Karen! Her hero not only dies, he dies ignominiously; he is not only murdered, he is humiliated.

On a technical level, the play is a skillfully constructed drama with a beautiful gimmick and extremely strong characters. Its only defect is Rand's peculiar inability to write an effective mystery plot without leaving holes. There are just too many problems with the prosecution's case: If the drunken man wasn't 'Lefty' O'Toole, who was he and what was he doing there? How did Karen Andre manage to throw Faulkner over a parapet? Why was no ballistics evidence presented?

Rand's stated theme in *Penthouse Legend* is envy. Why are the great hated? Why do people gloat over the fall of the successful? Though she may well have started out with this theme in mind, the story apparently took on a mind of its own (as often happens) and the true theme ends up somewhat different: Do we prefer hypocrites who hem in their lives with conventional morality and concern for what other people think—or figures of such vitality and independence that they commit downright fraud, open and unashamed?

The play, as *The Night of January Sixteenth,* had a moderate success on Broadway. Rand, like any writer for the stage, found that actually staging a play is a frustrating process of argument and compromise. In view of her hatred of compromise, and the philosophical chasm between author and director, it is not surprising that she found the entire process extremely unpleasant. Though she later wrote two more plays, neither made it to the stage—partly, perhaps, because she did not want to run the gauntlet again. Exhausted from her struggle over *The Night of January Sixteenth,* and disgusted by the outcome, she resumed work on her first novel.

We the Living

Purely in terms of literary technique, *We the Living* is an extraordinary first novel. That a beginning writer, working in a language not her own, could produce a book so complex, subtle, skillfully structured, and emotionally powerful, and in the process deal with important philosophical and political themes in an original manner, marks her at once as a genius.

We the Living resembles most first novels in having strong elements of autobiography. Kira Argounova, like Ayn Rand, is the daughter of a Russian businessman; like Rand, she is a college student under the Soviet regime; like Rand, she works as a tour guide in a Bolshevik museum for a while. The details of life in the USSR in the 1920s, from the omnipresent melody of "John Gray" to pumping up the Primus stove, are impressed on the reader vividly in a way possible only to an author who has lived through the experience.

On its most superficial level, *We the Living* is a powerful political novel. "Tell them that Russia is a vast prison, and that we are all dying slowly," begged a young man as Rand prepared to leave the USSR. And Rand does so, depicting a totalitarian society with a painful, immediate realism.

On the next level, Rand deals with the theme that haunted her and drove her all her life: How does the heroic person survive in an evil society? In this book, she cannot even begin to develop a solution to this conundrum. Her heroes are destroyed, and only Kira's last smile hints that something better is possible.

On a still deeper level, the book is organized around another of Rand's universal themes: loyalty to values. This is the source, in fact, of the novel's plot. For the book's heroine, Kira Argounova, there is, essentially, a single value: her love for the aristocrat Leo Kovalensky. Her attitude toward this value is very simple, and very characteristic of Rand: price no object.

The Theme

With her typical ingenuity, Rand bases her plot on an ancient, hackneyed device—and gives it a new twist. A woman, to save the life of the man she loves, is forced to become the mistress of another man. As Nathaniel Branden has pointed out, this ancient cliché provides the plot for *Tosca* and many other stories. Rand's twist is that the other man, Andrei Taganov, is not the one who forces the heroine into his bed; indeed, he does not even know her motive but sincerely believes that she loves him. Nor is he despicable; Kira likes him and increasingly admires him.

The plot is shrewdly designed to give Rand the opportunity to build tension and develop a dramatic climax. Like any woman with two lovers, Kira is faced with the ever-more-difficult task of keeping them both in ignorance. The looming threat of discovery underlies the entire story like a pedal point as sub-plots develop on the upper stave.

Like most first novels. *We the Living* shows some derivative traits. The book owes much of its style and structure to techniques Rand had learned from Victor Hugo. In particular, Rand's narrative structure is in many ways parallel to that of *Ninety-Three*. Like Hugo's novel, *We the Living* has a plot based on a complex love-hate relationship between three primary characters, set against a background of revolution. In both books, the theme involves a conflict between the political beliefs and the personal moral values of the protagonists. And both novels climax with a series of intense personal confrontations between the three heroes.

Trio for Heroes

Kira Argounova bears little resemblance to the corresponding character in *Red Pawn*. Joan is a mature, sophisticated woman;

Kira is a naive young woman, eighteen as the novel begins. She is perhaps the least effectual of Rand's heroines, as befits the theme—the impossibility of a human life under totalitarianism. Her one positive accomplishment in the entire book is saving Leo from death by tuberculosis. For the rest, in spite of all her courage and determination, her life is one failure after another.

Kira's loyalty to values is expressed primarily in her love for Leo Kovalensky. Though Rand equips her with a career ambition—to become an engineer—this becomes impossible because of the Soviet state's control of the universities. There's a parallel between Kira's ambition to build bridges out of aluminum, and the Rearden metal bridge in *Atlas Shrugged*. But Kira's interest in engineering is less encompassing than that of Rand's later heroine, Dagny Taggart. When Kira becomes involved in her love affair with Leo she finds her classes boring and cuts them. When a Communist purge expels her from the university and her career plans are ruined, she is by no means crushed. One cannot help but suspect that her interest in engineering is an artificial part of her characterization, tacked on by Rand to make her more 'unconventional'.

It is Kira's love for Leo that is her driving force. Her behavior in this love affair shows Rand at her most typical. Kira meets Leo by allowing herself to be taken for a prostitute. When her family is outraged by the relationship, she cuts ties with them without a moment's hesitation. She is prepared to face death or imprisonment for Leo's sake. She becomes the mistress of a GPU officer to save Leo's life. One could scarcely ask for a stronger embodiment of Rand's theory that the good person will do anything—"price no object"—in defense of his highest value. Many will find this more credible in the case of Kira, whose highest value is a man, than in the case of Dagny, whose highest value is a railroad. But Rand regards the cases as essentially equivalent.

Leo, however, is a hero who does not satisfy. Rand, a daughter of the Russian bourgeoisie, retained an admiration for the aristocracy throughout her life, or at least the aristocratic manner; it is still visible even in *Atlas Shrugged*. Leo Kovalensky, the aristocrat, is her first fully-formed hero. Handsome and cruel, born to carry a whip, he seems a good candidate for the Nietzschean superman. But already Rand is beginning to show just the whisper of a doubt. Leo has arrogance, and even courage; he does not hesitate to insult his tormentors to their faces. One feels that he would face a firing squad well; it would be his finest moment. Yet his courage, like his beauty, is of the delicate sort. Just as his godlike body is that of a consumptive, so his arrogant soul cracks under prolonged pressure.

Like another fictional Nietzschean, Dorian Gray, Leo maintains a handsome exterior while his character gradually corrodes. From an aristocrat he descends to being an ordinary student; from that to a black market operator; from that to a gigolo. Kira fights in vain to save him from corruption.

For, like his fellow superman Bjorn Faulkner, Leo has no real place in the world. Perhaps in the old Russia he might have found his métier applying the knout to his serfs. But once again Rand is compelled by loyalty to her art to the conclusion that the Nietzschean superman does not really belong on this earth. Having portrayed her ideal, she can find no place for him. When Leo is making large profits in the black market, he shows no desire to save the money to escape from Russia. He could do no better anywhere else.

Andrei Taganov, too, shows the earmarks of a character who has escaped his author's hands and taken on a life of his own. In many ways he steals the show. Rand had a brilliant idea in making her villain-hero a Communist—and not just a Communist but a Chekist. But the logic of her plot and theme resulted in the development of a character who, in the end, overshadows her intended hero. Taganov is an authentic hero, a real soldier, a man of strict integrity and true courage. Leo Kovalensky, the son of a White admiral, did not carry arms in the Civil War. He cuts a rather poor figure in comparison to Taganov.

Andrei in the end is much closer to Kira than Leo. He too has a value to pursue: Communism. It is this which draws them together initially; though their values are antithetical, they are alike in having a loyalty to a supreme value. But as the true face of Communism appears, Andrei, like Kira, finds his idol turning to corruption before his eyes. Though he transfers his loyalty to Kira, she is irrevocably Leo's.

A Cinematic Style

As in plot, so also in style does *We the Living* closely follow Hugo. Though Rand made a conscious effort to avoid imitating Hugo, she nonetheless ended up adopting many of his devices, especially in her descriptive passages—her essay on St. Petersburg could easily have come directly from Hugo's pen—and in her carefully positioned flashbacks. She also borrowed from Hugo the use of short, sometimes one-sentence paragraphs to provide impact. Indeed, she continued to use this technique throughout her fiction career, though not so heavily; in her 1958 revision of *We the Living* she substantially reduced the use of this device. Again imitated from Hugo is sharp, significant dialogue very much in the French style.

However, perhaps the most striking aspect of the novel's style is its powerful visual element. Even more than her other works, *We the Living* shows the influence of Rand's experience as a Hollywood screenwriter. Andrei's suicide scene has already been mentioned, but the novel is full of other scenes, which are visually dramatic—not merely 'theatrical' but specifically cinematic. The student meeting with its green and red caps and the *Internationale* competing with the traditional student song was custom-tailored for the silver screen. Kira's pickup of Leo in a red-light district was ready without modification for a Griffith or Welles or Lang. And the book's climax could hardly be bettered for suitability for the cinema.

It is not surprising that Italian director Goffredo Alessandrini was driven to film the story during World War II. Thanks to the efforts of Henry and Erika Holzer,[4] this superb movie is now available on DVD. Unlike the movie of *The Fountainhead*, Rand had nothing to do with the production, but when she was finally able to see it she was very pleased. And her input was critical to the editing of the Italian original into the version we have today. After the Holzers obtained the film in the 1970s, they engaged a young director, Duncan Scott, to edit it. Rand worked with Scott to reduce the original four-hour-plus Italian version to conform more precisely to Rand's original story. According to Scott, much irrelevant material was edited out. Consequently, the film is strikingly faithful to the novel. In the end, they produced the superb version we have today.

Some years ago, Scott interviewed the then ninety-something Massimo Ferrara, General Manager of the studio Scalera Films,

---

[4] Henry Mark Holzer and Erika Holzer, both lawyers, were members of Rand's inner circle. Erika was encouraged to write by Rand and later wrote the novels *Double Crossing* and *Eye for an Eye*.

about the making of the movie. Mussolini's son advocated for the movie, part of the reason it was allowed to be made. The Fascists thought it was an anti-Communist movie; when it became hugely popular, the Nazis discovered its anti-totalitarian message and wanted it destroyed.

Ferrara had a typically Italian genius for misdirection of the bureaucracy (during World War II, of the 45,000 Jews censused by Mussolini, the Italians managed to "lose" 30,000—the Nazis couldn't seem to find them). When Ferrara was told to send the negatives to the authorities, he switched the negatives out of their container and replaced them with others. Then he gave the can of the *We the Living* film to "a little, little man who worked in my studio"—someone with a very insignificant title—and told him to hide it in his house.

Fortunately the authorities were Italians. Ferrara said that that was lucky, because if they had been Germans, they would have checked the film in the can. Instead, it was saved until, decades later, the Holzers found it.

Textual Changes in *We the Living*

We the Living was published in 1936 with almost no marketing. Just at it was beginning to sell, the publisher, Macmillan, destroyed the type, and the book went out of print. After the success *of Atlas Shrugged* the earlier novel was revived, with revisions by Rand, in 1959. Rand, in her introduction to the revised version, asserted that she merely cleaned up grammar and awkward wording: "In brief, all the changes are merely editorial line-changes." This is not entirely true.

One must not exaggerate the importance of Rand's revisions. They are not extensive, and most of them are minor. Some choppy paragraphs are consolidated. One character's style of speech is changed. A rather gory description of Bolshevik atrocities is expunged (p. 455). Some changes are merely puzzling: an allusion to Kira's virginity is removed (p. 141); Leo quotes Spinoza rather than Kant (p. 156).

One short passage is excised in which Leo is described as "not a lover, but a slave owner," and Kira longs to be under his whip (once again, inverting the conventional image of slave and slave owner). Throughout her fiction Rand presents a model of female sexual submission that sometimes seems to border on masochism; perhaps she decided this particular passage went a bit too far.

However, two passages have been modified in a way which clearly shows an intent to expurgate Nietzschean ideas. Both occur (pp. 92–95) in an argument between Kira and Andrei shortly after they have first met. In the first passage, Kira, speaking of Communism, says (starting out with a typical Randian cliché-reversal):

> "I loathe your ideals. I admire your methods. If one believes one's right, one shouldn't wait to convince millions of fools, one might just as well force them. Except that I don't know, however, whether I'd include blood in my methods."
>
> "Why not? Anyone can sacrifice his own life for an idea. How many know the devotion that makes you capable of sacrificing other lives? Horrible, isn't it?"
>
> "Not at all. Admirable. If you're right. But are you right?"

Rand removes this entire passage; in the revised edition. Kira says merely, "I loathe your ideals."

A few paragraphs further on, Kira becomes brutally explicit:

> "Don't you know," he asked, "that we can't sacrifice millions for the sake of the few?"
>
> "You can! You must. When those few are the best. Deny the best its right to the top—and you have no best left. What are your masses but mud to be ground underfoot, fuel to be burned for those who deserve it? What is the people but millions of puny, shrivelled, helpless souls that have no thoughts of their own, no dreams of their own, no will of their own, who eat and sleep and chew helplessly the words others put into their mildewed brains? And for those you would sacrifice the few who know life, who *are* life? I loathe your ideals because I know no worse injustice than justice for all. Because men are not born equal and I don't see why one should want to make them equal. And because I loathe most of them."

Here is the revised version:

> "Don't you know," he asked, "that we can't sacrifice millions for the sake of the few?"
>
> "Can you sacrifice the few? When those few are the best? Deny the best its right to the top—and you have no best left. What are your masses but millions of dull, shrivelled, stagnant souls that have no

thoughts of their own, no dreams of their own, no will of their own, who eat and sleep and chew helplessly the words others put into their brains? And for those you would sacrifice the few who know life, who *are* life? I loathe your ideals because I know no worse injustice than the giving of the undeserved. Because men are not equal in ability and one can't treat them as if they were. And because I loathe most of them."

These passages display Andrei Taganov as a committed and consistent Communist. His goal, as he states elsewhere in the argument, is to raise the masses to his own level. Any means, including massive bloodshed, is justified by this end; but he finds the necessary killing horrible.

Kira counters, in the original passages, with a classical Nietzschean point of view. The masses are worthless; they are to be exploited, or even destroyed, for the sake of the "best." She personally dislikes bloodshed, but she admires those who are not limited by what she seems to regard as her overfastidiousness.

These passages, unlike the revised versions, are perfectly in character for Kira. They are consistent with her thought and speech and behavior throughout the book. The revised passage, on the other hand, is anachronistic and—in terms of Kira's personal style—out of character. Nowhere else in the book does she speak about superior abilities or the giving of the undeserved. Though she might well agree with such sentiments, Kira Argounova simply does not think in those terms. They represent the Rand of the 1950s, not the Rand of the 1930s; it is Dagny Taggart speaking, not Kira Argounova.

What may we conclude? We certainly can't accept Rand's assertion that her revision only "reworded the sentences and clarified their meaning." Her meaning was perfectly clear in the original. Kira Argounova, speaking for Rand, adopts in the most explicit terms possible the ethical position of Friedrich Nietzsche.

But Rand was already showing signs of challenging this position. Kira's reluctance to resort to violence is a portent. And a few sentences later she says that she does not want to fight for or against the people, she wants to be left alone to live. This clearly foreshadows the Objectivist position.

The Failure of Nietzsche

We the Living is the neglected stepchild of Rand's novels. This is partly due, no doubt, to the fact that it is less didactic and carries less philosophical content than her later works. Further, the story is extremely depressing; one might admire the literary technique while feeling little inclination to reread the book for pleasure. However, it may be that *We the Living* receives less than its due because of its embarrassing and disturbing Nietzschean themes, which are still evident even in the revised version. Yet to any serious student of Rand's work, this book is an essential starting point.

With *We the Living* Rand reached complete maturity as a writer. Through her fiction she had begun to grapple seriously with ethical issues. And, as a direct result, she began to develop the ideas which were to grow into Objectivism.

It's easy to criticize Rand for having once held to ethical precepts which are invalid, even evil. It is still easier to criticize her for dissembling about these beliefs in later life. Yet these ideas provided a necessary foundation for the edifice that she was later to erect. Just as Aristotle taught her logic and metaphysics, so Nietzsche provided Rand with the root of her sense of life, the emphasis on achievement, on aspiration, on pursuing supremely important values. It is to her credit that she was able to clear away the debris of his ethical monstrosities and keep what was good as she built Objectivism.

With the completion of *We the Living* Rand entered a period of philosophical transition. Ayn Rand was never a person who changed her mind easily, and the repudiation of her Nietzschean beliefs must have involved a formidable internal struggle. Out of this struggle grew the work which made her famous—*The Fountainhead*.

5

Scourge of the Second-Handers

Rand's career was close to its nadir in 1934. *We the Living* could not find a publisher; *Penthouse Legend* could not find a producer. With her savings running out, her husband unable to find work, her adopted country deep in the Great Depression, Rand might have been excused had she given way to despair.

During this period of stress—and perhaps in some way as a result of her emotional turmoil—Rand took the first decisive steps away from Nietzsche. Unfortunately, it's difficult to follow her progress in this critical transition; we only know that somehow, during the next three years, she renounced the Nietzschean superman and formulated a new kind of hero, Howard Roark.

Some evidence of Rand's thinking during this period is available from two plays: *Ideal* and *Think Twice*.

The Enigma of *Ideal*

In all of Rand's output no work presents so many problems to the analyst as *Ideal*. Almost everything else she wrote is absolutely pellucid; the reader need never be in doubt as to what she is saying and what she means. *Ideal* provides a striking contrast.

The basic story is straightforward enough. Kay Gonda, a much-worshipped movie star, disappears; she is suspected of murder. We see her approach, one by one, a series of people who have written adoring fan letters, and ask for asylum. Each one fails her. A left-wing writer tries to sell her out for the reward money; an artist who has painted her again and again cannot even recognize her in the flesh; a preacher exhorts her to confess. All those who idolized her fail, when challenged, to value their ideal—except for Johnnie Dawes, an unemployed drifter. To clear her of suspicion, he confesses falsely to the murder of which she is accused, then commits suicide. In the final scene, we learn that Kay Gonda was innocent of the 'murder'; she framed herself for the crime, in order to discover the reaction of her fans.

Ideal was initially written as a novella, and later transformed into a two-act play; it was never produced. The story (as Rand herself recognized[1]) would have been better left as a novella; the narrative is simply not well suited to the stage, though Rand achieved a number of well-crafted dramatic touches. But it is not primarily literary problems that the play poses.

The direct interpretation of *Ideal* is straightforward. When put to the test, Gonda's admirers betray their professed ideal. On this level, the story is a condemnation of their almost universal lack of integrity, and the theme is very efficiently handled. As always, Rand retains her theme of loyalty to values.

The problem arises with the motivation of the two principle characters, Gonda and Dawes. Why does she go to such lengths to search for integrity? How could a person like Dawes possess that integrity?

Rand's difficulty in expressing these critical factors in the story indicates the deep-seated questioning of her own values while she was writing it. She was groping for an entirely new view of life at this time. Had *Ideal* been written a couple of years earlier perhaps it would have had a different ending with a disillusioned Kay Gonda staggering into a police station to give herself up and face trial and execution. In a Nietzschean world there is no integrity to be found in the masses, and the superman—or superwoman—whose spiritual fuel runs dry is doomed.

This is Gonda's motive: she creates for her fans an ideal world, an ideal person; but who is to be *her* ideal? She gives them the courage to face life; but who is to give *her* courage? She must know; is she the only person on earth who still pursues an ideal with integrity, who has not given up her childhood dreams? Is integrity possible at all? Like Nietzsche's Zarathustra, she comes

---

[1] Branden 1986, p. 148.

down from her lonely pinnacle to the world of men—only to be disappointed.

Leonard Peikoff points out that Gonda, like Dominique in *The Fountainhead,* and like Rand herself ("in a bad mood"), suffers from an idealistic alienation from the world. In this sense, *Ideal* may be considered a first sketch for *The Fountainhead.* But Peikoff unjustly classes Gonda below Dominique. For, as we shall see, Dominique has almost despaired as *The Fountainhead* begins; convinced that her ideal is unattainable, she acts as a destroyer. Kay Gonda, on the other hand, has not given up. She is desperate but not despairing. And in the end she does find—in a way—the integrity she is seeking.

But this brings us to the character of Johnnie Dawes, a most unlikely Rand hero. Physically he fits the bill: tall, a gaunt face, a hard mouth and steady eyes. But what else is there? A college graduate (with an unspecified major), he fails to hold even the job of a bellhop or a waiter. He shows no purpose in life; he is unable to live in the world as it is, but lacks the resolution to change it. "I'm nothing," is his description of himself.

His one value is his ideal, Kay Gonda. His one redeeming trait is his determination to act to protect his ideal. And to save her he dies, as he tells us, "perfectly happy."

In actual fact, Johnnie's action is unnecessary. Gonda is innocent—indeed, the 'murder' never even happened—and she is in no danger. But when her press agent condemns her for allowing Johnnie to die, she replies, "That, Mick, was the kindest thing I have ever done." For, as she has realized, his death was a kindness; like Leo in *We the Living,* Johnnie Dawes had no future. Rather than turn into a Leo, he died protecting the one thing he loved and idolized.

Yet, in another way, Johnnie's death does save Gonda's life. This ultimate testimony to the possibility of human integrity gives her the conviction to go on living.

As Kay Gonda surveys her fans, Rand compares different responses to the disillusionment of childhood ideals—as a means, perhaps, of confronting the crisis in her own ideals. George Perkins, the first fan, simply gives them up for a life of pure convention. Chuck Fink, the leftist, holds to his ideals even when he learns that they are actually evil, and thus descends into an amoral viciousness. Dwight Langley, the artist, holds to an ideal but considers it impossible of achievement on earth. Claude Hix, the preacher, goes even farther; if an ideal should appear on earth rather than in heaven, it must be sacrificed. The playboy, Esterhazy, finds that he cannot climb out of the quicksand of cynicism which he so casually entered.

But Johnnie Dawes is no hero, either. He has retained a child's dedication to an ideal, but at the price of remaining a child. He has an ideal, he is faithful to her, he knows that he must not merely admire but act. He has a child's piercing emotional insight and empathy. But he has despaired—not of the world, but of himself. He too has betrayed his ideal—by refusing to grow up.

We now see the dramatic unity in the play's conclusion. Kay Gonda is not, after all, revitalized at the end. We see her exhausted, indifferent, almost bitter. She has not found what she wanted; but she has found, in the most direct possible way, that she must live. She is loyal to her ideal; Johnnie Dawes's escape is not for her. She has found the one person in the world with integrity: herself. And that integrity will not let her quit.

Ideal seems to have served Rand as a preliminary study in which she experimented with the theme of treason to values. This germ of an idea blossomed into the extraordinary plot of *The Fountainhead*.

Think Twice

While writing *The Fountainhead,* Rand several times interrupted her work on the novel to complete smaller projects—primarily in the hope of developing some income. *Think Twice,* a two-act play written in 1939, was one of these projects. The play prefigures *Atlas Shrugged* in certain respects—notably in its combination of philosophical and mystery elements, and in its scientist hero. However, it appears to have functioned primarily as a sketch for *The Fountainhead*—in particular, for the character of Ellsworth Toohey. Walter Breckenridge, the villain of *Think Twice,* is clearly a primitive, unfinished version of Toohey, her most complex and fascinating badman.

Breckenridge, like Toohey, is a power-luster acting in the guise of a humanitarian, who controls his victims by 'helping' them. This provides the root of the play's mystery element. On his birthday Breckenridge invites his victims to his new house, and uses the occasion to torment them with a sophisticated but nonetheless vicious sadism. It is hardly surprising that he is murdered before the first act ends.

As a mystery, the play fails; one can easily deduce the murderer, and not in the way Rand suggested either.[2] However, it is an exciting and entertaining drama. It richly merits production, and it is a pity that it never made it to the stage.

As a sketch for the character of Toohey, Breckenridge is only a skeleton. His characterization, in the final analysis, is the play's major weakness. Breckenridge has too little to say for himself, and his final confrontation with his murderer is thereby lacking in the dramatic tension it deserves. It seems likely that Rand learned from this sketch that Toohey must be a more eloquent villain, more self-consciously evil—though, as we will see, this introduced new problems.

On the other hand, as a philosophical drama *Think Twice* is highly effective. In a marvelous piece of integrated symbolism, Rand dates the play on July Third and Fourth, with Independence Day for Breckenridge's slaves announced by fireworks—climaxed by the pistol shot which kills him. Rand brilliantly exercises her talent for making a philosophical theme concrete.

The hero of *Think Twice,* Steve Ingalls, is clearly in the Objectivist rather than the Nietzschean mold—he seems more similar to John Galt than to Howard Roark. However, the play was revised as late as the 1950s, while Rand was writing *Atlas Shrugged;* the published version may not give us an accurate vision of her thinking at the time the play was originally written.

Writing these two plays clearly gave Rand a chance to develop key themes and characters which would appear in *The Fountainhead.* She now felt ready to tackle her masterwork, the novel she'd wanted to write all her life, the story of her ideal, her ultimate hero.

The Fountainhead

Many consider *The Fountainhead*, judged purely as a piece of literature, Rand's best work. Although it lacks the enormous philo-

---

[2] Serge Sookin is deliberately given an alibi by Steve Ingalls. Since only the murderer could have known in advance the time of the murder, Ingalls must be the culprit.

sophical scope and the intricate multi-level organization of plot and theme that we find in *Atlas Shrugged,* the earlier book presents a fascinating and subtle interplay of ethical and psychological themes.

On one level, *The Fountainhead* is a treatment of Rand's professed theme: the ideal man, Howard Roark. She set out initially to portray the ideal man. It's no coincidence that the book begins and ends with the words, "Howard Roark."

But she did not get far into the construction of the novel before encountering two serious problems. First, she simply was not ready to portray the ideal man; her ideas, her ideals, were in a state of flux at that time and she was far from having developed them sufficiently to accomplish her self-assigned task.

Second, from the point of view of literary technique, problems arise in writing a story about an ideal person. To use a central character who is morally perfect makes it difficult to center the story on an internal moral conflict. Adopting a hero who has no psychological problems rules out centering the story on psychological conflict. Thus when we encounter an ideal hero, the story usually involves a basic dilemma of some less fundamental sort, such as a physical challenge.

Rand resolved this problem in *The Fountainhead* by removing Roark from the lead role. In the novel as it exists, Roark is off stage for over half of the book. Instead, Dominique Francon becomes the real protagonist. The plot-theme of the book now becomes something different: 'How would imperfect people react to the ideal man?' This makes it possible to center the plot on a moral conflict within Dominique—and, later in the book, within Gail Wynand.

On this level, *The Fountainhead* is a novel about the sin of despair, a theme from Christian theology. Rand might have been horrified to hear it thus described—or she may have purposefully echoed Christian theology, and been delighted at, once again, turning a traditional theme on its head. Hope (as in "faith, hope, and charity") is a virtue in Christian doctrine because its antithesis, despair, leads one to feel that it is permissible to sin. If evil is destined to inevitable triumph, why struggle to achieve virtue?

According to Ron Merrill's reading, this is precisely the fundamental premise of Dominique and Wynand. Not believing that good can triumph, they permit themselves to do evil. Wynand uses his 'power' to exalt the banal in human existence, and to crush men who show signs of integrity. Dominique wastes her talents and, like Wynand, leaves a trail of agony behind her, as she does her best to destroy that which she most values, from statues, to Roark, to her own soul. On a more accurate reading of the novel, Wynand and Dominique are not completely convinced that good won't triumph, evidenced by Dominique's decades-long attempt to destroy Roark, and Wynand's practice of breaking people— these are their continual attempts to *prove* that their despair is realistic. Ironically, rather than struggling to achieve virtue, they struggle to destroy their own virtue.

On another level, *The Fountainhead* deals with the twin issues of independence and integrity. One of Rand's objectives in the novel is to show that independence, in the end, must mean intellectual independence. The man who allows others to tell him what to think thereby allows others to tell him what to do. Rand provides numerous examples of this principle, culminating in the illuminating scene where Peter Keating is reduced to abject slavery by Ellsworth Toohey. Rand goes on to show that integrity can exist only in the man who possesses intellectual independence. For the 'second-hander', dependent on others for his beliefs, can never resist their sway.

Rand in *The Fountainhead* returns to her perennial theme: How can the good man live in an evil society? As we shall see, she still could not find a satisfactory answer to this riddle.

The Break with Nietzsche

The Fountainhead is Rand's final renunciation of the morality of Friedrich Nietzsche. Rand clearly intended this theme and she sets up the conflict quite explicitly early in the novel. When Henry Cameron retires, passing on the torch to Roark, he tells him that, of all the evil in the world, Gail Wynand represents what he has to fight. Foreshadowing her plot in *Atlas Shrugged*, the evil represented by Toohey is made powerful only through the virtues—the creative, productive intelligence—of Gail Wynand. One might well interpret the story as an allegorical struggle between Roark—representing, in a primitive form, Objectivist morality—and Wynand, representing Nietzschean morality—for the soul of Dominique— Rand's alter ego.

For Wynand is indeed the very incarnation of the Nietzschean superman. He is in the tradition of Rand's youthful whip-wielding aristocratic heroes. Though he starts out as a slum boy, both of his parents are suggested to have been of 'good family'; his father's nickname, "the Duke", explicitly evokes aristocracy. Wynand rises without help, solely by means of his unique ability and his iron determination. Not for him the 'slave morality'; he regards himself as 'beyond good and evil'. With an explicit childhood decision he devotes his life to the pursuit of power.

Roark, by contrast, is the prototype of the Objectivist hero. It is very clear from a reading of Rand's out-takes from *The Fountainhead* (see *The Early Ayn Rand*) that her vision of Roark was still evolving as she wrote the novel. The Roark who was excised, particularly in the Vesta Dunning passages, retains vestiges of the superman: cruelty, violence, aloofness. The Roark who remains evolves still more during the story. As he matures (and as Rand matured), Roark becomes more emotionally open, more introspective, more willing to relate to, and value, other people.

Dominique Francon, like Rand's other heroines, is an expression of Rand's own personality. Like Rand, she struggles with the problem of existence in a world hostile to rationality. Rand described Dominique as "myself in a bad mood." But Dominique is this and much more; her extraordinarily complex and subtle psychology enriches the novel.

To paraphrase one of Rand's favorite quotations from Aristotle, one might describe Dominique as a neurotic, not as neurotics are, but as they should be. She is a fundamentally rational and even heroic person, driven over the edge by the devastating pressure of an irrational society. At the root of her personality is a moral flaw: despair. She has given up on life. She knows what's good—and she 'knows' that the good has no chance. Building on this single thesis. Rand constructs a complex and consistent personality. Her psychological insight is impressive on its own terms, and astounding when one realizes the extent to which she must have confronted her own internal conflicts to develop such an analysis.

At the beginning of the novel, we see Dominique living solely for amusement—the amusement of teasing and tormenting the people she despises. She has intentionally subjected herself to suppressing her emotions. When she finds a statuette that she loves, she destroys it—not, as she tells Alvah Scarrett, so that nobody else will see it, but so that she herself will not see it—because she cannot allow herself to feel what it makes her feel. After making a promising start as a journalist, she sabotages her own career for fear that she might come to enjoy it too much. She has no friends; she cares nothing for her father; when men embrace her, she feels no desire, nor even revulsion.

The fundamental, thematic conflict in the novel arises from the simple fact that for a woman of Dominique's intense life-force, this emotional control is unsustainable. The crack in her armor is Howard Roark. This is the man who is her proper mate, a fitting hero. But how can she respond to him? Later in the story, Wynand, who faces the same problem, says that love could come to him only in a twisted form. In the same way, Roark can come to Dominique only as a 'rapist'.

The famous quarry sequence shows Rand's literary technique at its best. Dominique's struggle to maintain—or rather to restore—her emotional control is described with masterful psychological insight. Roark, naive though he is at this stage, cannot but recognize her need; "Pressure is a powerful factor. It leads to consequences which, once started, cannot be controlled." It certainly does!

In the wake of her encounter with Roark, Dominique is compelled to follow the logic of her psychological premises. She must, of course, destroy him—not, as she says, to save him from the world's corruption, but to allow her to restore her emotional control. But she also realizes that she is faced with a further task: she must destroy not just Roark but herself. If values have no chance in the world, then her only value—her own integrity—is itself a threat to her. Ultimately she must degrade herself. This she attempts, first by marrying Peter Keating, then by agreeing to be rented (and later sold) to Gail Wynand.

And yet, she cannot succeed. Repeatedly she breaks down—she defends Roark at the Stoddard Temple trial; she warns Peter Keating not to marry her; she tries to torture Wynand, and then to save him from Toohey.

Paradoxically, it is by seeking her deepest degradation that Dominique finds the way out of her morass. Voluntarily prostituting herself for the benefit of a man she despises, she encounters Gail Wynand. There is a parallel here between Kira and Dominique, both of whom initiate romantic relationships with aristocratic 'supermen' by acting as prostitutes. Similarly, in *Penthouse Legend,* Karen Andre's affair with Bjorn Faulkner begins when he attempts to buy her favors for a thousand kroner. Even in *Atlas Shrugged* there is a hint of the same theme, when Rearden and Dagny wish that they had begun their affair in such a way.

Dominique and Wynand are similar in what they value, and in their treason to those values. It is this similarity that draws them to each other. But their marriage traps both of them into confrontation with their fundamental error. Intellectually, Dominique cannot avoid seeing, exposed at close range, Wynand's treason to his own values—and he cannot avoid seeing hers. Emotionally, Dominique cannot avoid responding to Wynand—just as he cannot make of her just another mistress to be toyed with and discarded. But by opening themselves to such emotions they initiate the destruction of their self-delusion of apathy. They lose their ability to delude themselves any longer into believing they don't care for the values they, in fact, deeply love.

Howard Roark's return from exile at just this point destroys the already tottering emotional balance of Dominique and Wynand. They are drawn by Roark back to reality, to the necessity of values and the need to fight for them.

The plot-climax, the dynamiting of Cortlandt Homes, serves to bring to a crisis Dominique's internal conflict as well as Wynand's. Finally they renounce their treason and fight together for Howard Roark and the values he represents. But their crime—treason, the deepest and vilest of crimes which dooms one to freeze in the ninth circle of hell—cannot be expiated so easily. Dominique, in an ecstasy of self-mutilation that virtually compels comparison to religious penitence and mortification, nearly kills herself. Wynand fares even worse; he closes the *Banner* and actually destroys himself. While the book is ambiguous about Wynand's demise, Rand made it explicit with a suicide in the movie version of *The Fountainhead.*

Why is Dominique redeemed but not Wynand? Essentially, because of Roark, Dominique re-centers her values on the man she worships. This gives her a base on which to rebuild her life. But, unlike Dominique, who committed the sin of omission, dropping out of life, Wynand, dedicated his life to power, to controlling other people. He has nothing left when he sees that power is worse than worthless. The superman, with his 'morality of masters', is revealed to be the slave of the masses he despises. His dream of a Wynand Building becomes a mockery and a reproach; he is too old to go back to Hell's Kitchen and start from scratch. And he has done too much evil—how can he redeem himself? For Gail Wynand, as for Johnnie Dawes, he honors the ideal he recognizes and takes the only way out of an irredeemable life.

A Traditional Antithesis

Part of the nineteenth-century literary tradition in which Rand was steeped was the novel based on the contrast of antitheses. We see this in such titles as *Sense and Sensibility, Crime and Punishment, War and Peace*. Rand begins *The Fountainhead* by setting up a comparison of this type: the man of independent thought, Howard Roark, and the intellectual 'second-hander', Peter Keating. This effective literary device, by contrasting the two personalities and society's reaction to them, helps to clarify and define Roark's personal character.

Those who condemn Rand for creating only 'black and white' characters ought to be surprised and pleased by Peter Keating. He is as gray as they come. Keating is a man of no small ability; critics who portray him as an incompetent are missing Rand's point. Keating has the intellectual potential to become a first-rate artist—his original ambition—or even a first-rate architect. But his failure to establish independence arrests the development of his abilities. Achievement and ability, like all other values, require independence.

Keating is a sort of amateur—or let us say, a small-time, petty Gail Wynand. While congratulating himself on his manipulation of other people, he fails to notice that it is he who is being pushed around. He allows himself to be talked out of the career he wants, of the wife he wants, of everything that might bring him satisfaction in life. In a well-known scene in the second chapter of *The Fountainhead*, Keating asks Roark whether he should accept a scholarship in Europe or go to work for leading architect Guy Francon. Roark chides him for asking advice on such a crucial decision, but recommends taking the job. Keating might have done better not to take Roark's advice—had he gone to the Beaux Arts he would have had a second chance to correct his career choice and become an artist. One wonders if Rand did this intentionally; the ironic illustration of her point might have tickled her fancy.

In the end Keating has nothing to show for his life, in spite of—indeed, because of—all the 'practical' compromises he has made.

The Impossible Villain

Rand's depiction of Peter Keating is a classic of psychological insight. He perfectly fulfills his literary role as a foil for Roark. But he cannot for a moment be visualized as the villain of the piece. That role must go to the inimitable Ellsworth Toohey.

Like his embryonic precursor, Walter Breckenridge, Toohey persuades young people to forsake the careers they love, thus depriving them of joy in their work. But compared to Toohey, Breckenridge is a piker. Toohey is a Moriarty of the mind. He uses an arsenal of techniques to destroy his victims. He advises them to indulge in casual sex—and avoid serious romance. He presses Peter Keating to marry for prestige and professional advancement instead of love. He advocates compromise of moral principles as not only unavoidable but desirable. He uses humor as a weapon to ridicule and degrade anything good. He attacks integrity, independence, and reason.

Toohey, the quintessential Randian villain, seems to be a caricature of her philosophical arch-enemy, Immanuel Kant. If one wishes to look at the novel in allegorical terms, one might say that Rand has realized that Nietzsche's approach, exemplified by Gail Wynand, is unable to defeat Kant-Toohey; it is only Objectivism, as embodied in Howard Roark, that can defeat him.

Ron Merrill thought that Rand paid a heavy price for making Toohey such a perfect personification of evil. In Merrill's view, the character ultimately loses psychological reality:

> One meets Peter Keating every day, and one can imagine meeting Roark or Wynand, but one could never meet Ellsworth Toohey. The problem is that Toohey not only is evil, but knows that he is evil. He has no self-delusion in him. Nobody could function in reality on such a basis; in *Atlas Shrugged*, Rand makes James Taggart go mad on being confronted with his own evil. So Rand ends up using Toohey not really as a character but as a personification of evil. He might best be compared to Goethe's Mephistopheles.
>
> Western literature has long displayed a sort of fascination with the personification of evil, and what Toohey lacks in psychological realism

he more than makes up as a brilliant specimen of demonology. He makes a tawdry, contemptible Satan, much more in the style of C.S. Lewis than of Milton or Goethe. But he is all the more effective a tempter for that. (Merrill 1991, p. 52)

This is a common reaction, but a good argument can be made that Toohey is just as realistic as Wynand. Toohey's self-awareness and acceptance of what he is parallels Wynand's. Like Wynand, Toohey believes that the only relationship between men is one of master and slave; he wants to be the master and uses ethical and psychological power to accomplish that goal. Ultimately, he believes the evil of power is necessary and realistic; therefore, in a twisted way, he justifies it as 'good' because it's a recognition of reality.

Intellectual Snobbery

As she delineates Toohey's little games. Rand provides an analysis of one of the most common and frustrating con games of our time: intellectual snobbery. Today more than ever, what passes for high culture is dominated by those who pretend to admire the ridiculous, the incomprehensible, the disgusting, and sneer at those who 'can't understand'.

Any honest young person who has studied Heidegger; or seen Ionesco's 'plays'; or listened to the 'music' of John Cage; or looked at Andy Warhol's 'paintings'—has experienced that feeling of incredulous puzzlement: But this is nonsense! Can I really be expected to take this seriously?

It's necessary for it to be nonsense; if it made sense, it could be evaluated. The essence of modem intellectual snobbery is the 'emperor's new clothes' approach. Teachers, critics, our self-appointed intellectual elite, make it quite clear to us that if we cannot see the superlative nature of this 'art'—why, it merely shows our ignorance, our lack of sophistication and insight. Of course, they go beyond the storybook emperor's tailors, who dressed their victim in nothing and called it fine garments. The modern tailors dress the emperor in garbage. Rand analyzes the purpose of idolizing garbage as a means of making it impossible to recognize greatness. If you are an ant, you can't comprehend a giant.

Rand brilliantly exposes this deception, and her portrait of Lois Cook, an emperor's tailor if there ever was one, provides some of the novel's most entertaining and illuminating scenes.

A Seamless Patchwork

In the first draft of *The Fountainhead* the story focus on Howard Roark was stronger and more personal. Part of this narrative described Roark's first sexual experience, an affair with the aspiring actress Vesta Dunning, which ends when she sells out her ideals to get good parts. By the time Rand finished Part One of the book, technical problems were already apparent. When the publisher asked for cuts, she took advantage of the opportunity to eliminate Vesta and recast the structure of the novel.

By removing the Vesta Dunning passages from *The Fountainhead* Rand effectively conceded her change of the novel's theme. Having dropped her original intention of centering the story on Roark, she had to tighten the story's focus on Dominique as the female protagonist; Vesta had to go. Much of the material removed had Roark on stage, so that the new focus of the story on Dominique was further enhanced.

The primary plot-line of *The Fountainhead* narrates Dominique's struggle with herself. Her internal conflict involves both a moral issue—treason to values—and a psychological issue—emotional denial. Rand intertwines these two strands skillfully to weave the basic thread of the plot.

In keeping with its paradoxically Christian theme. *The Fountainhead's* primary plot is analogous to that of Dante's *Inferno:* The protagonist, having lost the right way, voluntarily enters Hell, confronting the meaning of evil, finally finding the way out at the very bottom. Dominique, in her downward progression, encounters successively more serious sins, from the venial offenses of Guy Francon, through Keating and Hopton Stoddard and Lois Cook, until she is faced with her own crime in the person of Gail Wynand.

This, the 'new' plot, is spliced into Rand's 'old' plot so smoothly one scarcely notices the joining. The original story of the antithesis between Roark and Keating is arranged as contrary motion. In the first section of the book, we see Keating rise and Roark fall. In the last section, their roles are reversed. In between, the 'old' plot is more or less suspended and Dominique's Dantesque journey of self-discovery takes center stage.

The third strand of the story is, quite literally, a plot: Ellsworth Toohey's campaign to take control of the Wynand empire. This line of action serves several functions in the story, the most important of which is the development of the climax—the Cortlandt bombing and the Wynand strike.

The Fountainhead is far more complex in structure than *We the Living*. Rand's ability to develop a multilevel plot structure and tie together several major story lines represents another advance from her earlier work. Her false start was corrected so skillfully one can scarcely see the repair lines.

Acquittal Unsatisfactory

When it comes to Rand's lifelong dilemma—the survival of reason and heroic achievement in a hostile world—*The Fountainhead* fails to present a convincing solution. The novel, as we have seen, treats the issue of the sin of despair. Rand rejects despair, but she has no real answer yet. The book ends on a note of triumph, but Roark's vindication ultimately rests on faith. A jury of 'the common man' acquits Roark after hearing his courtroom speech in defense of individualism. This likely reflects Rand's experience as a soapbox orator during the Wendell Willkie campaign, which gave her an abiding respect for the commonsense rationality of the literal 'man in the street'. The same phenomenon is used in the scene of Rearden's trial in *Atlas Shrugged*. There, however, it becomes merely an incident, rather than a resolution. Rand by then recognized that the common man's response to reason is temporary; when the influence of the rational hero is removed, the common man returns to irrationality. Thus, to the reader, Roark's acquittal fails to convince.

However, *The Fountainhead* does at least give a hint of the solution that Rand will find in *Atlas Shrugged*. By renouncing Nietzsche she comes to the concept of the impotence of evil. Says Roark to Toohey, "But I don't think of you." This is the attitude that Rand's earlier characters aspire to, but can't achieve. Howard Roark is an assertion that the heroic man can defeat the excruciating pressure of society by sheer grit. Unfortunately, in practice this tends to lead to spurning what you love—the trap into which Dominique and Wynand fall. It seems as if this answer did not satisfy Rand, and she returned to the problem in *Atlas Shrugged*.

Ultimately she found her solution in the concept of the "sanction of the victim."

The Embryo of Objectivism

With Roark's courtroom speech at the climax of *The Fountainhead*, Rand decisively cuts her ties with Friedrich Nietzsche. The power-seeking 'superman' is explicitly classed with the altruist as merely another 'second-hander'. The true egoist, Rand has decided, is not the ruler but the creator. Morality is not a chain for slaves but the root of freedom.

But though Rand had finally crossed the border, she had not yet reached the capital of the terrain which was to become Objectivism. That became her next task.

Nonetheless, several of the basic ideas of Objectivism are explicated in *The Fountainhead*. Reliance on reason, not yet a major theme, is clearly adopted. A related idea, the impotence of evil, is explicit in the novel. Roark's final speech is devoted primarily to the key concepts of creativity and self-generated action as the proper life for man. We can see the roots of the Objectivist ethics, but they are still unsupported. During the next thirteen years Rand laid the groundwork in metaphysics and epistemology that would put the Objectivist ethics on a firm footing.

Anthem

Even as she wrote *The Fountainhead* Rand was experimenting with new ideas and new techniques for later use. Among other things, she began to develop a fascination for the idea of the scientist or engineer as hero. In Steve Ingalls she presents us with a new type. She did one more sketch before tackling her greatest scientist-hero, John Galt. This was Unity 5-3000, the hero of *Anthem*.

The novella *Anthem* was produced during another interruption of Rand's work on *The Fountainhead*. This short but powerful story provides a further premonition of *Atlas Shrugged*, particularly in stylistic matters. The narrative makes scarcely a pretense of 'romantic realism'; the style is that of fantasy, sometimes more like poetry than prose, quite unique among Rand's works. The stylistic influence of Nietzsche is evident, particularly in the eleventh chapter, which is strikingly similar to the opening of *Thus Spoke Zarathustra*. The actual events of the story range from improbable to impossible; it is the ideas that count.

Rand adopts a literary technique popular in the eighteenth and nineteenth centuries, the diary-narrative. The story supposedly is an account written by the hero. The text thus consists solely of a sequence of flashbacks; each chapter jumps ahead in the story, maintaining a high level of suspense until the narrative explains what led up to the new situation. Though old-fashioned, this technique can be highly effective and it is still used (for instance, in Kubrick's *2001: A Space Odyssey)*.

The story employs a classically Randian gimmick: In a collectivist, totalitarian world of the future, the very word 'I' has been eliminated from the language. The conflict between individualism and collectivism is thereby reduced to its ultimate fundamentals.

Rand uses this story to illuminate an issue also basic to *The Fountainhead:* the individual as the source of human knowledge and progress. *Anthem,* in contrast to other collectivist dystopias, forecasts no universal electronic surveillance networks, no manipulative biotechnologies, no domed cities or spaceships. Instead, we are shown a collectivist government that has just accomplished, with no small difficulty, the transition from torches to candles. Rand drives home the point by making her hero a self-made scientist, who rediscovers electricity and uses it to make light. The symbolism is effective.

Rand may have intended *Anthem* as a response to the influential Russian dystopia *We,* written by Yevgeny Zamyatin in 1920–1921. *We* was not published until 1924, and never officially in the Soviet Union, though it may have circulated via *samizdat.* Zamyatin lived in Petrograd during the 1920s, at the same time as Rand. He was a leading anti-Bolshevik intellectual prominent in literary circles. Rand must have been familiar with his work.

Like *We, Anthem* uses the device of a naive narrator in a world in which names have been replaced by numbers. But here the similarity ends. Zamyatin's hero, like those of *Nineteen Eighty-Four* and *Brave New World,* revolts against an allegedly scientific and logical society in the name of love, poetry, and emotion. D-503, a scientist of the One State, is led into rebellion under the sexual domination of a female mystic. His evident masochism makes his final submission to authority plausible. Rand, on the other hand, champions reason and science as the enemies of totalitarianism. Her hero, assigned as a street-sweeper, makes himself into a scientist. He is a leader, not a follower, in his rebellion, and his love interest is an adoring and submissive young girl.

The story begins with a superb hook ("It is a sin to write this") and never drags for an instant. Its inspirational and often poetic narrative is interspersed with just the right amount of Rand's distinctive humor (as for instance the heroine's behavior on her first encounter with a mirror). In *Anthem,* Rand's concept of the impotence of evil is enhanced and expanded. The men of evil now are seen as almost comically helpless and incompetent, fleeing like roaches from the light created by the book's hero. Like John Galt, *Anthem's* hero is a scientist and inventor who develops a new source of energy. And the climax, in which he establishes a remote mountain refuge of reason, looks ahead to Galt's Gulch.

'The Simplest Thing in the World'

Also written during Rand's transition period was the short story, 'The Simplest Thing in the World'. The hero of this little piece is a talented—and therefore starving—writer. Winning a struggle with his artistic integrity, he resolves to write a piece of hackneyed formula fiction, just to bring in some money. Rand takes this classic cliché and gives it a twist. Her hero sets out to write a potboiler—and finds he can't do it. Not because of his scruples, but simply because every conventional, boring plot idea suddenly takes an ingenious twist. Rand depicts with a sure hand the petty humiliations of an impecunious man during the Depression, which were so familiar to her. But ultimately the story is frustrating to the reader who would like to hear the full tale that the hero thinks up of the virtuous blackmailer and the other characters that Rand casually tosses off.

6

The Book that Changed
the World

With the publication of *Atlas Shrugged* in 1957 Rand reached the destination of her intellectual journey—the Taggart Terminal. She had purged the last vestiges of Nietzsche's errors from her thinking, and completely integrated her ideas into her own philosophical system, Objectivism.

The great question of her life, the dilemma of the rational person in an irrational society, at last was solved to her satisfaction. The concept of the "sanction of the victim" provided her answer—and provided also the key plot device for her greatest novel: the strike of the men of the mind.

Some think that *Atlas Shrugged*, from a purely stylistic or literary point of view, is inferior to *The Fountainhead*. But there's no doubt that as an intellectual achievement it is far superior. A complete, radically new philosophy is expounded, and with astonishing clarity. The practical implications of philosophical ideas are illustrated on every level, from metaphysics to epistemology to ethics to politics to economics to esthetics. The novel's plot is a miracle of organization. And with all this, the book is a thrilling page-turner.

A Departure in Style

Rand described her fiction style as "Romantic Realism." She regarded herself as a Romantic in that her fiction dealt with ideal people and their pursuit of important values; and a Realist in that the settings of her stories and the issues they dealt with were those of real life rather than fantasy.

This description is appropriate for most of her work. However, *Atlas Shrugged* marks somewhat of a departure. Stylistically, it represents a considerable change from *We the Living* and *The Fountainhead*. Building on the techniques with which she had experimented in *Anthem,* Rand made *Atlas Shrugged* a more abstract, conceptual, and symbolic work than her earlier novels; it might best be described as a work of Romantic Surrealism. The cover painting done by George Salter for one of the editions accurately conveys the mood and style of the novel.

Atlas Shrugged takes place in the United States, and cities such as New York and Philadelphia are recognizable. But Rand goes to considerable pains to create an ambiance that is far from realistic. The United States of the novel has no President, but a "Head of State"; no Congress, but a "National Legislature." Most of the world is Communist, but this word does not appear in the book at all; instead, Communist countries are referred to as "People's States."

The story takes place in no particular time, and in 'realistic' terms is a tissue of anachronisms. The American economy seems, structurally, to be in the late nineteenth century, with large industrial concerns being sole proprietorships run by their founders. The general tone is however that of the 1930s, a depression with the streets full of panhandlers. The technological level, and the social customs, are those of the 1950s. And the political environment, especially the level of regulation and the total corruption, seems to anticipate the 1970s. We are simultaneously in a future in which most of the world has gone Communist, and the past in which England has the world's greatest navy.

With a subtle choice in literary technique Rand adds to the effective mystery of the story. In *The Fountainhead* Rand adopts the universal viewpoint; we see inside the head of almost every significant character and many very minor ones. (The only important exception is Henry Cameron.) In *Atlas Shrugged* Rand uses what might be called a 'half-universal' viewpoint. We are told the thoughts of nearly every significant character, hero or villain—except the strikers.

In further contrast to Rand's other works, *Atlas Shrugged* is permeated with symbols—from Atlantis to Wyatt's Torch, from Galt's motor, which draws on the power of lightning, to Nat Taggart's statue. The symbolic theme of the stopping motor provides a powerful motif throughout the book. And of course there is the famous dollar sign.

Plot, Plot, and Plot

The plot of *Atlas Shrugged* is marvelously constructed, an intricate machine that meshes smoothly with the novel's philosophical themes.

There are, it must be conceded, some notable flaws. For instance, during his affair with Dagny, why does Francisco not tell her about his college friends—Galt and Danneskjöld? Obviously this would make hash of the mystery element of the plot, so Rand simply makes Francisco behave out of character. Later she is forced to make Hugh Akston lie to Dagny for the same reason.

A minor though surprising error occurs in the very first pages of the novel. Since when, at the latitude of New York City, does the sun set before 5:00 P.M. on September 2nd? Surely not even a very irrational government would decree such a weird form of Daylight Savings Time! Another inconsistency appears near the end of the story: With the entire economy in shambles, a few hours before the lights of New York go out, the telephone system is still functioning reliably and Dagny has no trouble finding a working pay phone! It's an ironic tribute to that classic regulated monopoly, Ma Bell.

A more serious problem is Galt's refusal to let Rearden learn that Dagny is alive, after her crash in the valley. As Nathaniel Branden has pointed out, this gratuitous cruelty does not reflect well on Galt—nor on Dagny.[1] Apparently Rand regarded this incident as essential to the plot; Rearden's loyalty to values, as demonstrated by his continued search for Dagny, is a major factor in her motive for leaving the valley. But surely the dilemma could have been dealt with otherwise.

These are minor problems. Overall, the plot of *Atlas Shrugged* is one of the greatest accomplishments of world literature. Not only is it a masterpiece of logic in itself, but it integrates perfectly the needs of the story with Rand's exposition of a series of philosophical principles. And, with an absolutely insolent arrogance, as

---

[1] Branden 1982.

if to show off, Rand neatly organizes this extraordinarily complex book into three tidy, cleanly structured sections of ten chapters each.

To analyze the plot *of Atlas Shrugged* thoroughly would require far too much space. But we may consider the main strands.

The primary sequence is the story of how Dagny and Rearden discover the secret of the strike and are led to join it. On the political level, this is integrated with the account of the final destruction of statist society. On the personal level, it is integrated with Dagny's romantic involvement with Francisco, Rearden, and finally Galt. These three strands are braided into the primary plotline of the novel.

Half-a-dozen subplots are woven into the structure. One is Francisco d'Anconia's Monte-Cristo-like crusade of destruction. Two follow the fates of minor heroes, Eddie Willers and Cherryl Brooks. Three more describe the degradation and destruction of the villains James Taggart, Lillian Rearden, and Robert Stadler. Is this pleasing symmetry intentional? Quite possibly.

The Technique of Philosophical Integration

The unifying principle of *Atlas Shrugged* is the connection between philosophical ideas and their consequences. It is worth examining one passage in detail to study Rand's technique. The primary incident in the chapter, 'The Moratorium on Brains', is the catastrophe at the Taggart Tunnel in which an entire passenger train is annihilated. At least one critic has cited this passage as evidence that Rand took a malicious, sadistic pleasure in killing (fictional) people. What is really involved here?

Rand makes the tunnel accident play an important role in the novel's plot mechanics. It brings Dagny back from her self-imposed exile so that she can receive Quentin Daniels' letter. It interrupts Francisco's explanation of the strike at a crucial point, and sets up the confrontation between Francisco and Hank Rearden in Dagny's apartment. The disaster necessitates the journey that will put her on a frozen train and propel her to a meeting with John Galt.

The sequence also plays an important part in a more subtle aspect of the plot, by beginning the process of final preparation for Dagny to be confronted with the secret of the strike. The first step is Directive 10-289. Dagny's instinctive rejection of this irrational horror results in her resignation from Taggart Transcontinental. But this, to Rand, could not be a satisfactory resolution; Dagny must reach this stage of emotional revulsion, but she could not be Rand's heroine if she made her decision on the basis of emotion. What has been accomplished however is that Dagny (and the reader) have been presented with the solution to the novel's dilemma—the strike.

Dagny's resignation is followed by a month of meditation in the woods, in which for the first time her basic dilemma is made explicit. Then the pressure is turned up. Francisco appears to present her with the key concept of the sanction of the victim. It is at this point that the tunnel catastrophe intervenes. Francisco fails to recruit Dagny—because Dagny, having quit due to emotional revulsion, returns due to emotional revulsion.

Dagny's emotional reaction to the disaster plays a critical role. She is not merely annoyed by a sublime piece of incompetence. She is not just outraged by the destruction of an important item of her railroad's property. She is horrified by the human destruction, the loss of life. Rand is building up here to a major, dual climax in the novel's plot: Dagny's discovery of the secret of the strike, and her meeting with John Galt. The tunnel catastrophe plays a key role in building the tension that will be resolved—partially and temporarily—in Galt's Gulch.

During this chapter Dagny is put under increasing emotional stress, until she nears the breaking point. Directive 10-289 drives her from her job in disgust—and separates her from Rearden (on whom it also puts pressure). Her month in the woods wrestling with an insoluble problem focuses her emotional state. Then there is the astounding revelation that Francisco is in fact faithful to her—a scene interrupted by the report of the tunnel catastrophe. The sequence continues with the confrontation between Rearden and Francisco, which raises the tension of Dagny's sexual relationship with Rearden to a maximum. We can begin to see how masterfully Rand pulls these two strands of the plot together in preparation for Dagny's encounter with Galt.

But the Taggart Tunnel catastrophe is not merely an incident in the plot; it also functions as a demonstration of an important principle: the relationship between political oppression and the breakdown of social responsibility—and the consequent destruction of social function. Rand in this chapter provides us with a vivid picture of the way even everyday activities disintegrate when the men of ability and rationality are driven underground. This is the function of the scene on the book's philosophical or intellectual level.

Rand begins preparation for this scene early and carefully ties it into the other events of the plot. Early in the story we learn of the bad condition of the Taggart track near Winston, Colorado. Accidents happen on this stretch of the road. The need to repair it is casually mentioned. But it is merely a nuisance, a potential problem.

With Dagny's resignation, Rand begins her demonstration. First, the repairs at Winston are cancelled; the rail instead is used on the Florida line, which is more frequently travelled by politicians. This decision is allowed to stand—because Dagny is gone. Then the spare diesel at the Taggart Tunnel is withdrawn, again to please a politician. Eddie Willers attempts to stop it, but with Dagny gone he is helpless.

The process by which the accident happens is, to anyone acquainted with industrial safety principles, entirely realistic. It is exactly the sort of sequence which creates real-life disasters such as the Bhopal and Chernobyl accidents—again demonstrating her amazing prescience.

The petty politician Kip Chalmers, inconvenienced by a derailment near Winston, insists on immediate continuation of his journey—through the tunnel—though no diesel engines are available. Like Dagny, the men of intelligence and integrity, who could prevent the ensuing catastrophe, are gone because of Directive 10-289. The best of those who remain are, like Eddie, of insufficient rank to intervene successfully. One by one, the safeguards set by rational men are violated by political appointees, driven by their fear of political reprisals.

It would take only one man to prevent the tragedy—but that one man is not present any more. The Superintendent of the Division has been replaced by an incompetent. Higher management, with Dagny gone, evades all responsibility. The one man who fights the disaster, Bill Brent, lacks authority. The physical order is signed by a boy who lacks knowledge.

So the inexorable march to disaster continues. The dispatcher knows he is sending men to their deaths. But he no longer cares; his beloved brother committed suicide, his career ruined by

Directive 10-289. It appears that disaster may be averted when the chosen engineer walks out rather than take a coal-burner into the Tunnel—but a replacement is found, an alcoholic who kept his job by political pull and union corruption. The conductor, who might have warned the passengers, has become embittered and cynical; he limits his action to saving himself. Even the switchman might have averted the wreck at the last minute. But in the new environment of the railroad, he fears for his family if he disobeys orders, even to save lives.

So the Comet proceeds into the tunnel. And with magnificent irony Kip Chalmers, having succeeded in scaring the Taggart employees into sending him to his death, proudly proclaims, "See? *Fear* is the only effective way to deal with people!"

Rand's Heroes: The Roots

By her own account, in *Atlas Shrugged,* Rand finally succeeded in portraying her ideal man, John Galt. And indeed, she has met the challenge of showing completely moral persons in a way that she did not achieve in *The Fountainhead*. Dominique and Wynand are, as we have seen, contaminated by Nietzschean morality and the corresponding despair. Roark is morally perfect, but he is not a full ideal because he is naive. He is good without knowing fully why he is good. John Galt, however, has moral stature and confidence, and philosophical knowledge.

Atlas Shrugged has a complex plot involving a number of major and minor heroic characters. Rand takes as her primary heroes the giants of intellect and productivity, particularly business entrepreneurs. The basic fabric of these characters derives from the hero of one of her favorite books, Merwin and Webster's *Calumet 'K'*. Charlie Bannon, an engineer and construction supervisor, a natural leader and compulsive worker who solves problems with effortless ingenuity, is described as skeletally thin. Appropriately, Rand fleshes out this skeleton with full personalities to create her business heroes.

The modern reader may not realize how radical it was, in 1957, to make a businessman a hero. Rand wrote this book in an environment in which 'entrepreneur' was almost a dirty word. However, there was one other significant writer of the period who defended businessmen: Cameron Hawley.

In Hawley's second novel. *Cash McCall* (1955), the theme is
ethical conflicts in business, and the author comes down squarely
for the position that commerce is an honorable activity. McCall is
what would now be called a 'corporate raider', and Hawley skillfully depicts his economic value and productiveness.

Even more relevant to *Atlas Shrugged* is the theme of Hawley's
first novel, *Executive Suite* (1952). This is the story of a struggle
for control of a major company after its CEO, Avery Bullard, suddenly dies. Here is the scene in which the hero, Don Walling, looking out over the company town, decides it is his responsibility to
take over the leaderless corporation:

> They were his . . . all of them . . . the uncounted thousands, born and
> unborn. If he failed them there would be hunger under those roofs
> . . . there had been hunger before when the man at me top of the
> Tower had failed them. Then there would be no food . . . and the
> belongings of the dispossessed would stand in the streets . . . and a
> man in a black coat would come to take the children to the orphans'
> home . . .
>   . . . Did the people under those roofs know what Avery Bullard
> had done for them? Did they realize that if it had not been for Avery
> Bullard there would be no Tredway Corporation . . . that the Pike
> Street plant would never have been built . . . that the Water Street fac-
> tory would have rotted and rusted away like the steel mill and the tan-
> nery and the wagon works . . . that there would be no Tredway jobs,
> no Tredway paychecks?
>   No, they did not know . . . or, if they did, they would not
> acknowledge their belief . . . or, if they believed, they were not will-
> ing to pay the price of gratitude. Had any man ever thanked Avery
> Bullard for what he had done? No. He had died in the loneliness of
> the unthanked.
>   Don Walling accepted his fate. He would expect no thanks . . . he
> would live in loneliness . . . but the Tredway Corporation would go
> on. There would be jobs and paychecks. There would be no hunger.
> The belongings of the dispossessed would not stand in the streets. No
> children would be sent to the orphans' home. (p. 247)

The late Ronald Merrill speculated that Rand might actually have
been influenced by Hawley,[2] but this seems unlikely, as Rand was

---

[2] Merrill 1991, pp. 67–68.

already deeply into not merely planning but writing her story when *Executive Suite* appeared. At one point, I speculated as to whether Hawley had been influenced by Rand through *The Fountainhead* or her earlier work. I called Hawley's widow in Lancaster, Pennsylvania, but she said she had never heard him speak of Rand or her books, and had not seen any in his library. An examination of Rand's unedited notes and records might shed light on whether she read Hawley and if so, what she thought of his work.

Into the gray-suited bodies of her business executive heroes Rand poured the souls of her childhood idols from the melodramas she devoured as a girl, and the great Romantic literature of Hugo, Scott, and Rostand, she so admired. The result: those extraordinary characters who have inspired so many of her young readers—especially the central heroes of *Atlas Shrugged*, Dagny Taggart and the three men who become her lovers: Francisco d'Anconia, Hank Rearden, and John Galt.

Dagny Taggart and the Randian Woman

In Dagny Taggart Rand creates her ideal woman. Her earlier female protagonists are mostly Nietzschean and, as such, tragic figures. Dominique Francon, it is true, renounces her allegiance to Nietzsche, but this decision does not come until nearly the end of *The Fountainhead,* so that we can only project what her life and personality will be like as a fully functioning Randian heroine. Gaia, the teen-aged heroine of *Anthem,* is not a well-developed character. It is only with the appearance of Dagny that we can see how Rand visualizes the 'ideal' woman.

Dagny, like the other heroes of *Atlas Shrugged*, is an incarnation of the virtue of competence. In her mid-thirties she is the *de facto* CEO of the country's largest railroad. Intelligent, decisive, self-confident, she embodies the prime characteristic of the natural leader: she is the person who knows what to do.

As one might expect from Rand's literary technique, Dagny's characterization is rooted in a seeming paradox. On the one hand, she appears neuter, if not masculine, in her aggressiveness and career dedication. Lillian Rearden describes her as "an adding machine in tailored suits". When Cherryl Taggart claims her place as the woman of the Taggart family, Dagny responds, "That's quite all right. I'm the man."

On the other hand, Dagny is an intensely feminine woman. (She is, in fact, the kind of woman who wears a dress and stockings to explore an abandoned factory!) She is attracted to strong, dominant men, and desires to play an explicitly submissive role in her sexual relationships.

The key to the seeming contradiction is that Dagny has suppressed her sexuality in the hostile society in which she exists. Dagny's air of coldness and unemotional, pseudo-masculine behavior are a consequence of her immersion in a society which contains nobody to whom she can respond naturally. This is hinted at in Rand's depiction of the Rearden anniversary party, at which Dagny is described as presenting a challenge which nobody can perceive. There's a vivid contrast between Dagny's unexpressed personality in the statist world and her temperament in Galt's Gulch, where she happily becomes—a housewife! That this was Rand's conscious intention is shown by her notes for *Atlas Shrugged*:

> Dagny, who is considered so hard, cold, heartless, and domineering, is actually the most emotional, passionate, tender, and gay-hearted person of all—but only Galt can bring it out. Her other aspect is what the world forces on her or deserves from her. (Rand 1983b)

Rand herself was profoundly ambivalent on the issue of feminism. She was a strong advocate of careers for women, of course, and said (in her *Playboy* interview), "There is no particular work which is specifically feminine." She endorsed (with some political reservations) Betty Friedan's *The Feminine Mystique*. She was contemptuous of 'housewives' in general. On the abortion issue, Rand took a vigorously 'pro-choice' position.

Yet Rand could scarcely be classified as a modern-day feminist. Though most of her heroines lack interest in marriage and family life, there are exceptions. Gaia, in *Anthem*, shows no ambition beyond following her man, and is pregnant at the end of the novel. Rand sympathetically portrays the anonymous young woman who chooses motherhood as a 'profession' in Galt's Gulch, as well as Mrs. William Hastings, who appears to be a 'mere' housewife.

Rand's notorious statement that a woman ought not to aspire to be President of the United States hardly sounds like feminism. And, in response to a question about her position (at her 1981 Ford Hall Forum appearance) she said, "I'm a male chauvinist."

Rand could hardly have meant by this—in a literal dictionary sense—that she exhibited "unreasoning devotion" to the male sex and contempt for the female sex. She did not say that men in general are superior to women. What, then, did she mean? Consider this:

> Hero-worship is a demanding virtue: a woman has to be worthy of it and of the hero she worships. Intellectually and morally, i.e., as a human being, she has to be his equal; then the object of her worship is specifically his masculinity, not any human virtue she might lack. ('About a Woman President', in Peikoff 1988)

Later in the same essay, Rand says, "[the feminine woman's] worship is an abstract emotion for the metaphysical concept of masculinity as such." It appears that Rand would attach a special, exceptional value to 'masculinity' as 'the fact of being a man', and that she was a 'male chauvinist' in this sense. Rand is explicit that the feminine woman's desire to look up to man "does not mean dependence, obedience or anything implying inferiority."

When we examine Rand's fictional heroines, we find that they certainly exhibit this intense admiration for the masculinity of their lovers. But, despite Rand's stated opinions, her fiction suggests that she regarded men as being inherently superior to women. Gaia, for instance, is far from being an intellectual equal of her mate. For that matter, Dominique does not seem to be quite a match for Howard Roark in ability, nor Dagny for John Galt.

All Rand's heroines are explicitly submissive in a sexual sense. Indeed, it is hard to avoid the suggestion of a certain degree of masochism in the physically vigorous couplings of Dagny and Rearden, in Faulkner's burning Karen Andre with hot platinum, and of course in Dominique's first sexual encounter with Roark.

Rand herself married a man who was far from being a John Galt in intellectual stature. However, Frank O'Connor, sensitive, protective and nurturing, gave her a lifetime of the emotional support and encouragement she needed to pursue her goals. She needed this support while enduring life with the emotional toughness of a man in order to withstand the never-ending conflict her writing and ideas engendered.

But she really didn't want to be a man. Her struggle over the decades compelled her to become mannish in many ways; a 'womanly' woman could never have waged the war Rand fought. Yet through it all she battled to remain a woman.

Perhaps the key to Rand's worship of masculinity is the emotional toughness and protectiveness of the male sex. In the right man, these qualities offer a strong, independent woman a 'rest' or haven from her worst struggles—and Dagny feels as much in Galt's presence. The heroes of *Atlas Shrugged* demonstrate Rand's vision of man at his best.

Francisco d'Anconia

Francisco Domingo Carlos Andres Sebastian d'Anconia is the favorite character of many readers of *Atlas Shrugged*. Like Dagny, he embodies a paradox: He is at once a man of extraordinary *joie de vivre,* gay, light-hearted, sophisticated; and a man of tragedy, frozen, unemotional, implacable.

The light side of Francisco embodies the sense of life that Rand aspired to, the unobstructed, effortless achievement of joy in a totally benevolent universe. As the young boy who can do anything, and do it superbly, who fears nothing and hates nobody, he presents an extraordinarily attractive figure.

The other side of the coin is the tortured but self-controlled man who allows no feeling or suffering to affect him, much less deflect him. His relentless pursuit of his terrible purpose invokes our awe and admiration.

We love Francisco precisely because of the union of these aspects of his personality. It was a stroke of artistic genius to create a character paradoxically embodying these disparate traits, and it is a tribute to Rand's literary skill that she could integrate them into a convincing personality.

Hank Rearden

Hank Rearden is older than the other major heroes of *Atlas Shrugged*. (He is forty-five as the novel opens.) He also presents a different sort of inner conflict. Unlike Dagny, he feels a fundamental sense of guilt, which has been carefully nurtured over the years by his wife, the despicable Lillian. He has responded by emotional withdrawal. Rand does not present Rearden's obsessive fixation with his business as an ideal. On the contrary, his struggle with emotional repression is a key thread of the plot.

We see Rearden, when he is first introduced, as a man who is interested in nothing but steel. He literally falls asleep when forced to deal with any other topic. The only hint that he is anything beyond a stereotypical workaholic is a jade vase in his office.

But this is not the real Rearden. As his affair with Dagny flowers, he expands as a person. Without losing his passionate commitment to his career, he begins to develop the full personality that he had so long repressed. He takes an interest in ideas, begins to express his love of beauty, becomes more relaxed and gay. As this process unfolds, his emotions open up. He finds himself able to love Dagny. He also responds more effectively to his co-workers; his relationship with his secretary, Gwen Ives, visibly expands and becomes more personal as his affair with Dagny progresses. And he is able to de-repress his resentment of, and contempt for, his worthless family.

Much of the novel is devoted to showing Rearden's gradual emotional blossoming, as he responds to Dagny and to Francisco d'Anconia. This is a vital factor in the plot; before he can join the strikers, he must not only deal with his unearned guilt, but he must establish new, interpersonal values so that his mills are not the be-all of his life—otherwise he could not abandon them.

Who *Is* John Galt?

To depict an ideal man in a work of literature is a difficult assignment for any author. Few have attempted it; none have attempted such an ambitious ideal as does Rand.

John Galt, by the nature of the novel's plot, carries a heavy burden. As the leader of the strikers, and the core of the novel's mystery element, he does not even appear on stage (except in disguise) until the last third of the book. We see him for two chapters; then he again disappears until the book's climax. Galt receives so little exposure to the reader that only Rand's superb technique can make him real at all.

Unfortunately, it's not quite sufficient to fully expand his character. John Galt, like Howard Roark, is too perfect to sustain a convincing internal conflict. Indeed, Galt was explicitly intended to represent man-become-god, and Rand deliberately avoided any details of characterization that might have made him seem more 'human' in the usual, self-deprecatory sense of the word. John Galt is Rand's ultimate answer to Nietzsche; he is an assertion that we need not evolve any 'superman', that man can become godlike himself if he so chooses.

But of course, the Randian paradox appears as always. John Galt, the ideal man, the pinnacle of the human species, is condemned to work underground, as a greasy laborer in the Taggart tunnels. This idea, that in a corrupt society the best men will be found at the bottom, plays a part in all of Rand's novels. Kira encounters Leo in a red-light district. In *The Fountainhead* Dominique discovers Howard Roark working, like a slave or a convict, in a quarry. The hero of *Anthem* is assigned as a street-sweeper and does his illicit scientific work in an abandoned subway tunnel—underground.

An interesting inversion takes place in the strikers' valley, Galt, the lowly trackworker, becomes the revered leader of society. And Dagny, the wealthy executive, finds herself penniless and must find work as a maid. And in the chapter 'The Top and the Bottom', villains James Taggart and Orren Boyle are eating in a restaurant at the top of a skyscraper, made to look like a cave, while the disguised Galt and Eddie Willers meet in the basement of the Taggart building, illuminated as bright as day.

Bit-Part Heroes

The story includes a number of heroes who spend but little time on stage: Lawrence Hammond, Roger Marsh, Midas Mulligan, Kay Ludlow, and many others. Rand herself makes a cameo appearance as the writer-fishwife in the valley, who nurses a hopeless passion for Galt.

Some of these characters are relegated to simple supporting roles. Others, such as Dr. Hendricks and Richard Halley, function as vehicles for short speeches on specialized topics. Only a few play a significant part in the plot. Ragnar Danneskjöld, the philosopher-turned-pirate, is of course the most prominent of these. Hugh Akston, Dan Conway, and Ellis Wyatt also play key roles.

It's a tribute to Rand's literary talent that she makes most of these minor characters real and distinct personalities, though none receives more than a few paragraphs of text.

The Villains

Rand also creates an incredible rogues' gallery of villains, and provides them with some beautifully appropriate names: Wesley Mouch, Tinky Holloway, and Cuffy Meigs are classics. Floyd Ferris has just the right ring for the handsome, slick, and vicious scientist-bureaucrat. Robert Stadler's name gives a hint of the statist views, which make him a villain. Perhaps best suited of all is that undistinguished politician Mr. Thompson, an old-fashioned gangster very similar in style to the weapon suggested by his name.

Though Rand has been criticized for creating two-dimensional villains, the fact is that she devotes considerable effort digging into the psychology of evil. Three villains are analyzed in considerable depth: James Taggart, Lillian Rearden, and Robert Stadler.

Jim Taggart is visualized by most readers as short, fat, and ugly; some critics have even attacked Rand for making all her villains physically unprepossessing. This is a tribute to her skill; the actual description of Jim Taggart in the book is as tall, slim, and aristocratic in appearance. It's the reader who unconsciously visualizes him as ugly, giving him a physical appearance to fit his character.

For ugly he is—psychologically. A man of mediocre talent, he inherits control of Taggart Transcontinental. At the opening of the story, he is thirty-nine and a neurotic whose response to the problems of the railroad he nominally heads is, "Don't bother me, don't bother me, don't bother me." Gradually we watch his psychological disintegration, until he ends up as a catatonic. He is unable to face the fact that he is "a killer—for the sake of killing", and psychosis is ultimately his only escape.

Lillian Rearden is a marvelous portrayal. She is a fitting foil for Dagny: intelligent, capable of shrewd psychological insight, and completely dedicated to the relentless pursuit of a single goal. Her campaign to destroy Hank Rearden is masterfully conceived and flawlessly executed. It is only his extraordinary inner strength, and some timely help from Dagny and Francisco, that saves him.

In the story of Dr. Robert Stadler, Rand achieves a Trollopian depiction of temptation and the consequences of surrender to it. When we first see Stadler, he is a great mind, a brilliant scientist, who has compromised with statism for money to continue his research. This initial sin inexorably presents him with a series of moral dilemmas, and each failure to turn back leads him deeper into the morass.

In his first crisis, the State Science Institute issues an attack on Rearden Metal. Though Stadler knows it is false, he dares not contradict it, for fear that the Institute's funding might be reduced. Later Floyd Ferris attacks science and reason explicitly, and even uses Stadler's name in doing so. This time Stadler protests—but not publicly. Ferris goes on to create Project X, using Stadler's discoveries to forge a weapon of terror. And now, under Directive 10-289, the consequences of rebellion are more serious; Stadler faces not mere embarrassment but the threat of starvation. Under compulsion, he publicly praises his tormentors and commends them for their perversion of the knowledge he had created. By the novel's end Stadler has surrendered utterly to corruption, and his last act in life is an undignified scuffle with a drunken criminal for possession of the murderous weapon he had once scorned.

Most of Rand's villains fill bit parts. The mystic Ivy Starnes, the whining Lee Hunsaker, the pretentious Gilbert Keith-Worthing, and many others are portrayed with a few deft strokes and used as needed. Each, however, is used to make a unique point.

Rand is careful, despite her 'black and white' moral code, to avoid any hint of moral determinism. One villain, the "Wet Nurse," demonstrates that it is possible to turn away from evil. Another, the labor racketeer Fred Kinnan, shows a certain blunt honesty that makes him more sympathetic than his colleagues.

The Secondary Heroes

Perhaps the most neglected characters in discussion of *Atlas Shrugged* are what we might call the 'lesser heroes'—people who are morally good, but lack the immense ability of Dagny and the other strikers. Rand treats sympathetically such tiny roles as the police chief of Durrance (who helps Dagny locate the Starnes heirs) and Mrs. William Hastings. Another such character, the hobo Jeff Allen, supplies a key piece of information in the main mystery of the plot. Three of these characters, however, receive considerable attention: Tony (the "Wet Nurse"), Cherryl Brooks, and Eddie Willers.

Tony, the young, amoral bureaucrat who is sent to supervise Rearden's production under the "Fair Share Law," represents the human potential for moral redemption. At his first appearance, he is a total cynic. The very concept of morality has been educated out of him, so that he finds Rearden's integrity disturbing and incomprehensible. Gradually, in the productive environment of the Rearden mills, he develops a desire for an ideal to believe in. Tony begins to feel admiration and sympathy for Rearden. He offers assistance in bribing the bureaucracy to obtain higher quotas, which Rearden of course rejects. Later, when Rearden defies the State Science Institute's order for Rearden Metal, Tony is concerned for Rearden's safety and chides him for taking such a risk. His commitment to Rearden becomes progressively stronger: he cheers Rearden's triumph at his trial; he fails to report Rearden's violations of regulations, and later volunteers to actively conceal them; he asks Rearden to let him quit the bureaucracy and work for the mill, even if only in a menial job. In the end he has accepted Rearden's ideals and fights to defend them; Tony's murder is the final straw before Rearden joins the strike.

Cherryl Brooks is the most tragic character of *Atlas Shrugged*. She is a slum girl determined to rise. She is not brilliant, not an intellectual, has no career ambitions. But she is fiercely honest, idealistic, and courageous. Finding herself married far 'above her station' to James Taggart, she applies her limited ability to the task she considers appropriate to her: becoming a high-society 'lady'. Zealously she studies etiquette, culture, and style to become the kind of wife Taggart, in her vision of him, deserves. And she succeeds; the slum girl from the five-and-dime transforms herself into a sophisticated member of the aristocracy of wealth. Again we see a classic Randian cliché-reversal. Taking off from Shaw's *Pygmalion,* Rand invents an Eliza Doolittle who transforms herself into a lady on her own initiative and by her own efforts—against the opposition of her 'benefactor', who wants her to remain a slum girl. But Cherryl's effort to become a worthy consort for her husband goes for nothing; Taggart is not a hero but a rotter; he has married her, not to ennoble her, but to destroy her.

The most important of the lesser heroes is Dagny's assistant, Eddie Willers, the very first character to whom we're introduced as the novel opens. It's easy to underestimate Eddie Willers. Standing beside Dagny Taggart or Hank Rearden he seems ordinary, not very competent, almost a bit wimpish. This, however, is due merely to the contrast with Rand's extraordinary heroes, as the moon seems dim in sunlight. Hank Rearden, who ought to know, says that Eddie has the makings of a good businessman. In fact, he is a highly able executive. Toward the end of the book, he bribes his way onto an Army plane and flies into a city torn apart by civil war. In the space of a few days; singlehanded, he negotiates immunity with three separate warring factions, reorganizes the Taggart terminal, revitalizes its personnel, and gets the trains running again. Some wimp!

All three of these lesser heroes come to bad ends. Tony is murdered when he defies his masters and attempts to warn Rearden of the plot against his mills. Cherryl commits suicide when she discovers the horrifying truth about her husband. Eddie strands himself in the desert, sobbing at the foot of a dead locomotive. Why is there no happy ending for these characters?

Mimi Gladstein suggests that Eddie's fate is punishment for his refusal to accompany Dagny to Galt's Gulch (Gladstein, p. 67). Certainly it is a consequence of that decision, but it is wrong to see it as punishment for a moral failing. In her treatment of the lesser heroes Rand expresses an important truth. The essence of statism is the destruction of all that is good in the human spirit. The ablest heroes frequently escape, to make new lives for themselves elsewhere. Such people as Rachmaninoff and Sikorsky and Rand escaped from the Bolsheviks. Such people as Einstein and Fermi and Mises escaped from the Nazis. Rand evokes the tragedy of the ordinary people that perished at Vorkuta or Auschwitz. These were the people who attempted to fight, but lacked the ability to do so effectively—like Tony. Or they were the people who died of sheer despair, facing a horror beyond their conception—like Cherryl. Or, they were those who might have escaped, but could not bring themselves to give up their old life and start over again with no capital but their own minds—like Eddie. Rand had known such people; her own father died under the Soviet regime, unwilling to leave Russia and give up the hope that he might somehow get his business back. She pities them, does not condemn them.

Thirty-Six Just Men?

The late Ron Merrill first proposed the theory that Rand built the story of *Atlas Shrugged* on the Talmudic doctrine of the Thirty-Six Just Men (Merrill 1991, pp. 61–62). The idea of the Thirty-Six Just Men derives from the story in Genesis of the destruction of

Sodom and Gomorrah. Lot, who resided in the former city, was warned by God to leave, as the place was condemned to destruction because of the evil of its inhabitants. Lot attempted to avert the catastrophe, promising to find other good men in the place; when he failed, he and his family left and the cities were destroyed.

Contrary to popular misconception, the great sin of the Sodomites was not sexual perversion but collectivism. According to the Talmudic account, Sodom's equalitarian government institutionalized envy, even forbidding private charity because some recipients might get more than others. The judicial system was perverted into an instrument for expropriating the wealthy and successful. The ultimate crime for which the Sodomites were destroyed was placing envy and equality above benevolence and justice.

From the biblical account of Sodom and Gomorrah, Jewish scholars evolved the idea that God would destroy the Earth if ever it lacked some minimum number of good people. The exact number needed to avert His wrath was hotly debated, and finally settled, for numerological reasons, as thirty-six.

In *Atlas Shrugged,* Rand (who was Jewish by background, though not religious) takes as her theme the destruction of civilization when its 'just men' are withdrawn. Merrill was the first to point out in print that exactly thirty-six strikers are specifically identified in Galt's Gulch.[3] A remarkable coincidence?

In support of his theory, Merrill appealed to an incident near the end of the story. As Dagny, Galt, and the other strikers are returning to the valley after rescuing Galt, they pass over New York City. This in itself is suggestive of some special significance, Merrill argued, since New York is nowhere near the great circle route between New Hampshire and Colorado. As they fly over, the lights of New York go out. Dagny gasps, and Galt orders, "Don't look down!"

---

[3] Hugh Akston, Calvin Atwood, the Brakeman/Music Student, the Chemist, Ken Danagger, Francisco d'Anconia, Quentin Daniels, Ragnar Danneskjöld, the Fishwife, John Galt, Richard Halley, Lawrence Hammond, William Hastings, Thomas Hendricks, Owen Kellogg, Kay Ludlow, Roger Marsh, Dick McNamara, Midas Mulligan, the Mine Superintendent, Judge Narragansett, Ted Nielsen, the three Professors (who work for McNamara), Hank Rearden, Doug Sanders, the Sculptor, Andrew Stockton, the Taggart Terminal Manager, Dagny Taggart, the Truck Driver (who works for Wyatt), Ellis Wyatt, the Young Mother and her two children. Though Rand makes it clear that there are far more strikers in the valley, only these thirty-six are specifically identified.

Merrill reasoned that the incident is out of character for Galt, who had said, "Nobody stays in this valley by faking reality in any manner whatsoever," but can be explained as a sly jest by Rand, who wanted to imply that Galt was saving Dagny from being turned into a pillar of salt.

Although the parallels between the sins of Sodom and Gomorrah and the world of *Atlas Shrugged* are intriguingly similar, I remain unconvinced by Merrill's theory. This last bit of "proof" seems questionable, as Dagny is told not to look down instead of not to look back, and I don't see any further evidence in the chapter to support Merrill's view. If there's anything in Merrill's theory of "Judaic symbolism," it could possibly be substantiated by plumbing Rand's notes—a job for a future scholar.

Nathaniel Branden's Critique

Since his break with Rand, Nathaniel Branden has raised a number of criticisms of *Atlas Shrugged*. Though the book, as is inevitable for such an ambitious undertaking, falls short of perfection, several of Branden's points of attack are not justified. Yet he is a perceptive critic, and his objections are worth serious consideration.

Branden criticizes as psychologically unrealistic, and indeed downright reprehensible, Francisco d'Anconia's twelve-year, self-imposed celibacy in faithfulness to Dagny. For a man of Francisco's vitality to accept such a trial verges, in Branden's judgment, on self-sacrifice, considered a vice by Objectivists (Branden 1971).

Branden makes a good point here, and in a later commentary (Branden 1983) points out an even stronger example. How about John Galt? His ordeal is nearly as long as Francisco's, after all. And this perfect man, Rand's ideal hero, is, it appears, a virgin at the age of thirty-seven when he finally consummates his love for Dagny in the Taggart tunnels.

This behavior, both Francisco's and Galt's, is in fact absurd—or rather it would be, if *Atlas Shrugged* were a naturalistic or even realistic novel. But if we look at the book as it is—as a work of romantic surrealism, which is heavily laden with symbolism—we can see that incidents such as this should be taken as the symbols they are, not as literal prescriptions for human behavior. Francisco and Galt exhibit this uncompromising loyalty to values—'price no object'—to reinforce Rand's ethical point.

Branden also criticizes the scene in which Dagny encounters Jeff Allen on the Taggart Comet. She watches indifferently as the conductor orders him to jump off the train, to certain death. Dagny intervenes only when the tramp, exhibiting a "sense of property", tightens his grip on his belongings. This, to Branden, exhibits a brutal indifference to human life.

Branden errs here by taking the scene completely out of its emotional context in the novel. Suppose we look at it not as an isolated incident but as part of a complex plot, an integral component of the sequence we analyzed above.

Dagny, at this point in the novel, is riding the first Comet to run after the tunnel catastrophe. She had resigned in disgust on the issuance of Directive 10-289; but she was unable to maintain her resolve when the disaster demonstrated the consequences of her absence. She has also just received a series of terrible shocks. She has discovered that Francisco is not, after all, the rotter she thought him, that indeed he still loves her and is worthy of her love. Close on this has followed the devastating encounter between Rearden and Francisco. Then follows the news that Quentin Daniels, the last hope of reconstructing the motor, has quit. Pervading all is her despair—trapped, unable either to quit or to enjoy her work—functioning as a slave, and as a slave-driver—the men she had trusted and respected on the railroad gone—the workers, once her friends, now treating her, deservedly, as an enemy—and above all her loneliness. There is no one on the train she can care for or respect, it seems. Francisco's words ring in her head: "But you would not run trains if they were empty."

It is at this point, and in this mood, that Dagny walks in on the conductor and Jeff Allen in the vestibule of her private car. After what she has been through in the last few days, it is not easy to care about these two strangers. So what if a tramp dies? So what if the whole human race dies? But then a simple gesture reminds her that there are human values in the world. Suddenly the context of her life and her values is regained, and she says, "Wait. Let him be my guest."

In fact this short scene, only a few paragraphs, provides an excellent example of Rand's psychological insight and literary skill. With effortless accuracy she portrays Dagny's moment of despair and rage, and her resilient recovery.

Rand and Repression

Branden's strongest criticism of *Atlas Shrugged* is that it teaches the reader to repress emotions (Branden 1983). While acknowledging that Rand explicitly rejects and condemns repression, and indeed provides many examples of emotional openness, he nonetheless insists that the tone of the book, taken as a whole, encourages repression.

This raises a difficult issue. To what extent can an author be held responsible for the misinterpretation of her work by her readers? For this is misinterpretation. To anyone who was a part of the Objectivist movement of the Sixties, it is obvious that many of Rand's readers felt encouraged to repress emotions under the social pressures applied by some of the movement's cadre. Yet— objectively!—*Atlas Shrugged* contains a powerful attack on repression. Over and over again, Rand emphasizes that life in an irrational society creates the danger of emotional repression. One of the key ideas of the novel is that the able and rational person is capable of emotional freedom only in the context of social relationships with others of his kind.

Merrill thinks the entire story of Hank Rearden is a devastating depiction of the dangers of emotional repression. He recalls the scene in which Rearden, walking to Dagny's apartment after a meeting with copper producers, realizes that he has lost his sexual desire for her. At the conference he has learned that new government regulations will devastate the copper industry, and he has failed to find a solution. Worse, he's told that the regulations resulted from a deal involving Francisco d'Anconia. Merrill thinks Rearden represses the pain—his frustration, his feeling of failure, and most especially the apparent betrayal by Francisco—and this causes his inability to respond to Dagny. While Rand's depiction of Rearden's psychological journey—its causes—its consequences— and its removal—is psychologically accurate, I'd offer a different interpretation. Rearden feels helpless and hopeless at this point and these are common causes of a lack of desire to do anything.

Rand uses character after character—Ellis Wyatt, Quentin Daniels, and especially Francisco d'Anconia, to demonstrate the contrast between the frozen, embittered, restricted emotional states of heroes trapped in the evil 'outside' world, and the openness and freedom of their behavior in the valley. I don't think, strictly speaking, that Franciso exhibits repression, *per se*, because he is perfectly aware of his feelings; he *suppresses* them. If anyone still feels that *Atlas Shrugged* promotes emotional repression, let him read the scene in which Dagny encounters Ken Danagger immediately after he has joined the strike. Unfortunately, some people, in emulation of Rand's heroes, may have tried to control their emotions by repressing them.

Now admittedly, much of this goes right over the head of even a very intelligent teenager; but is Rand at fault? We may, if we wish, accept Branden's testimony that Rand herself, and the circle around her, encouraged emotional repression in her students. But, on the evidence, *Atlas Shrugged* does the opposite.

Could the vision of extraordinary emotional control presented by Rand's heroes inspire young people to pay too little attention to their emotions? The danger, alas, seems remote. As Jane Austen's Mr. Bennet sarcastically put it, "You may well warn me against such an error; human nature is so prone to fall into it."

If we are to criticize Rand's influence on young people, let's look at a different issue. Rand repeatedly depicts heroes who choose their careers in early childhood and never deviate from their course. Even the brightest of children lack the experience needed to make a rational career choice as teenagers. More of Rand's readers have suffered through trying to emulate her heroes by committing themselves to ill-chosen vocations than through becoming emotionally repressed.

But any such objection to Rand's characterization of her heroes, including this one, is fundamentally unfair. Unquestionably a great part of Ayn Rand's appeal to young people flows from her presentation of heroes they can admire and emulate. The present generation of youth are starved for such heroes, just as were Branden's generation, and mine. Let them get from Rand what they need. Some, no doubt, will fail to understand the full context of her characters and will adopt inappropriate behavior; that danger is inherent in emulation. But better to take that risk than to have no heroes at all.

The Randian Lovers

Finally, Branden has made some strong criticisms of Rand's depiction of love and sex, based primarily on analysis of *Atlas Shrugged*

(Branden 1983). Unlike some critics, Branden does not see Rand's "male chauvinism" (as she herself called it) and preference for male sexual dominance as "a sexist issue." Taken in the context of the story, he considers these attitudes appropriate for her heroines. For similar reasons, he does not criticize the famous 'rape' scene in *The Fountainhead*.

Branden sees as positive aspects of Rand's love scenes two factors. First, Rand presents admiration as a key ingredient of romantic love. Second, as a corollary, Rand promotes dignity in the treatment of romantic partners.

However, Branden emphatically denies the root concept of Rand's theory of romantic love: that a person is determined by his philosophical premises and that sexual desire and love are responses to those premises.[4] Instead, Branden says, sexual psychology is very complex and there are many factors involved in arousing sexual desire for a certain person.

If Branden intends to say that these other factors *in addition to* basic values determine romantic choice, it is hard to quarrel with his argument—and it's not clear that Rand would. After all, she did not portray Dagny as being sexually attracted to all the strikers equally, though presumably they all share the philosophical values of John Galt. It would seem obvious that there must be something more than philosophical premises determining romantic choices. Perhaps Rand should have added another speech to the novel to explain these factors in more detail? If, however, Branden believes that response to values is not important in romantic choice, one would like to hear him expound his theory more fully before rejecting Rand's.

Branden's major criticism of Rand's attitudes toward love and sex, as exhibited in *Atlas Shrugged,* is "lack of psychological realism." As well as citing the celibacy of Francisco and of Galt as totally unrealistic, Branden suggests that Rearden and Francisco's lack of sexual jealousy and depression when Dagny becomes Galt's lover shows a psychological resiliency, which is not just superhuman but inhuman.

However, it's possible that Rearden and Francisco were reserving the expression of those feelings, similarly to the gentlemanly

---

[4] Barbara Branden also vigorously disagrees with Rand on this issue (Barbara Branden 1990).

way in which nineteenth-century men handled their feelings about their love affairs, according to the ethic that one's feelings are one's own responsibility.

Branden also complains that Rand fails to show intimacy and warmth between her lovers. To Branden, this lack of realism amounts to the projection of unattainable ideals which may lead readers (particularly young readers) to dismiss romantic love as being impossible to real people.

If Branden's analysis is taken as a warning to readers not to unthinkingly adopt the behavior of Rand's characters as a literal prescription, one can scarcely fault it. But as a literary critic, Branden, in accusing her of demanding too much of her readers, is himself demanding too much of the author. Branden is by implication demanding that every idea must be worked out not just in broad strokes, but in detail. Each character must, like an over-ambitious actor pestering the director for more lines, have the chance to display every facet of his personality. The plot must include not just the essential action but enough to make sure that even the most naive reader will not mistake the meaning of events.

It is simply too much. Dr. Branden expressed the desire to write a novel himself. Would he wish to be held to the standard he sets for Rand? We would welcome a demonstration.

Paradox Resolved

It is indeed ironic that Rand should be accused of advocating emotional repression. The struggle for spontaneity and the free expression of emotions dominated her art no less than her personal life. She recognized that the true individualist has the most to contribute to society, and can benefit the most from being one of its members—another classic Randian paradox. As we have seen, her career was an agonized struggle to confront her alienation from a hostile society. Consider her description of the Halley Fourth Concerto:

> It was a "No" flung at some vast process of torture, a denial of suffering, a denial that held the agony of the struggle to break free. The sounds were like a voice saying: There is no necessity for pain—why, then, is the worst pain reserved for those who will not accept its

necessity?—we who hold the love and the secret of joy, to what punishment have we been sentenced for **it,** and by whom?
      . . . It was her quest, her cry.

So it was. And, after decades of struggle, Ayn Rand, like Dagny
Taggart, finally found an answer that satisfied her: the sanction of
the victim.

It was Objectivism that led her to the answer. If reason is an
absolute, if the good is the rational, then evil is irrational—which
means: illogical—which means: unworkable. Evil, being based on
a contradiction of reality, is inherently self-destructive; left to itself,
it must disappear. How, then, can evil even exist?

There can be only one answer: Evil is made possible only by the
generous but ill-advised support and assistance, the sanction, of the
good. If good people were completely consistent, completely uncompromising, completely intolerant of evil, evil could not endure. Here
is the root of a key theme of *Atlas Shrugged*. Rand pitilessly exposes
the essence of envy—the hatred of the good for being good. And she
exposes altruism as the tool and weapon of evil, the false morality that
teaches its victims to hate what is good in themselves.

The discovery of this concept of the sanction of the victim
marked, like the renunciation of Nietzsche, a major turning-point
in Rand's life and thinking. It changed the way she thought about
society—about politics—about her relationships with people. It lay
at the root of her attitude toward her enemies—and her attitude
toward her supporters. The triumph and tragedy of the Objectivist
movement grew out of Rand's conviction that she must deny sanction to evil at all costs.

Beyond the Taggart Terminal

Atlas Shrugged is one of the most complex novels ever written, and
its analysis poses hundreds of fascinating problems which will occupy
scholars for decades. We could only touch on a few of them here.

Atlas Shrugged is not merely a novel to be read for entertain-
ment, enjoyable though it is. Nor is it a treatise to be read for
enlightenment, instructive though it is. The reader will benefit
most who regards the book as a sort of magical box full of tightly
folded intellectual *origami*, each of which should be carefully
opened, contemplated, and cherished.

7

Rand the Philosopher

The publication of *Atlas Shrugged* in 1957 marked the end of Rand's career as a writer of fiction. During the next decade she devoted herself almost exclusively to the task of extending, elucidating, and publicizing the ideas she had developed. This she did through several media: *The Objectivist Newsletter* and later *The Objectivist; a* series of books collecting her essays from these publications; pamphlets and lectures provided through the Nathaniel Branden Institute. Although much of this material was devoted to political issues (to be discussed in the next chapter), her primary emphasis during this period was on defining Objectivism as a coherent philosophical system, culminating in the publication of a small formal treatise, *Introduction to Objectivist Epistemology,* in 1970.

However, it is a capital error to attempt to fit Rand into the context of academic philosophy. She herself never entered or tried to enter into the world of standard scholarly discourse. She never submitted a paper to a philosophical journal, nor did she even read many such papers—if any.

Rand desperately wanted recognition from other intellectuals, and became angry and depressed when she failed to get it. But if she never achieved the respect of professional philosophers, it was because she was not willing to enter their world or debate on their terms. She was not, nor did she aspire to be, a scholarly or academic philosopher. Yet neither was she a mere popularizer, re-writing and simplifying the ideas of others. Rand fits into a different tradition, that line of active thinkers who have learned from life and speak clearly to any intelligent man or woman.

Objectivism Versus Academia

Although Rand did not publish professional papers in philosophy, some of her followers have done so. A running debate appeared in the pages of the journal *The Personalist* in the 1970s. Nathaniel Branden and Tibor Machan presented the Objectivist ethics and rights theory, while Robert Nozick was the most prominent of the opposition.[1] To read these arguments is frustrating; the two sides are simply not communicating. The opponents of Objectivism, steeped in the tradition of academic philosophy, display their superior debating skills while adroitly dodging the real issues. There is a tone of rather tolerant amusement, as of a chess-master demolishing a naive opponent. It seems never to occur to them that Objectivists might not regard philosophy as a game.

Ayn Rand stated repeatedly and emphatically that she regarded philosophy not as an academic exercise but as a critical need for every human being. Her interest was in the application of philosophy to the problems of real life. Furthermore, Rand was Aristotelian not only in the content but in the approach and objective of her philosophical thinking. Like Aristotle, Rand regarded it as her task to *help people to know*—to make it possible to find knowledge and certainty. Most modern philosophers have been more attracted to the opposing approach, the tradition of Socrates. They are critical and not uncommonly skeptical, and see it as the duty of philosophy to make people question their beliefs and realize that they know nothing.

Thus academic philosophers, who ought to have been Rand's allies in helping young people to knowledge, proved instead to be her enemies.[2] Philosophy courses, with some honorable exceptions, seem designed to leave students with the impression that philosophy means never having to say you're certain. Young people who seek knowledge to guide them in life are presented with a smorgasbord of contradictory doctrines. Take your choice, they are told—none of them is *really* true. Philosophy *does* not achieve, and indeed cannot even aspire to, the kind of certainty offered by the sciences.

---

[1] Major papers in this debate are: Branden 1970; Machan 1971; Nozick 1971; Lugenbehl 1974; Dwyer 1974; Machan 1977; Den Uyl and Rasmussen 1978.

[2] For an eloquent indictment of the professoriat, with some 'horror file' material to back it up, see Peikoff 1983.

Take for instance *Philosophy: The Basic Issues* (edited by Klemke *et al.*), which is by no means atypical of philosophy texts. This book provides readings on both sides of major philosophical questions. The only doctrine unchallenged, for which only one side is presented, appears in the Introduction:

> [A scientific question] can be settled "once and for all," or at least with a high degree of probability. [A philosophical question] cannot, or at least it is not immediately apparent how it could be. (p. 8)

Another text of readings (Jones *et al.*, *Approaches to Ethics*) offers the student this warning up front (p. 14):

> What can the student expect to learn from the study of ethics? He must not expect to absorb a conception of the good life, or a ready-made code of conduct, in the manner that the student of physics can absorb a knowledge of Newtonian mechanics and the differential calculus.

The traditional dialectical teaching method affects to be neutral among philosophical doctrines. But the dialectical method itself smuggles into the student's mind the doctrines of which it is an expression: that no truth is ever certain, that no question is ever settled, that no argument is irrefutable. All too often the superficial commitment to free inquiry conceals a covert intellectual intimidation. Under the cover of a quest for rigor is conveyed the subtle message that skill at debate makes right. And so everything is uncertain, for perhaps a faster gun will come along tomorrow. It is no accident that the dialectical method of instruction is the normal mode in law schools.

The fact is that teachers of philosophy, in their obsession with critical and analytical skills as opposed to construction and synthesis of knowledge systems, have failed their students. This is not a new criticism. Mortimer Adler—himself a distinguished academic philosopher—saw, and illuminated, the problem in his 1940 essay 'This Pre-War Generation'. Following up on his critique more recently, he says:

> Is there any wonder that subjectivism and relativism should have been prevalent among college students exposed to such indoctrination by their professors in the 1930s and 1940s? That indoctrination has continued right down to the present. The moral skepticism among the

students is the same as it was then and its cause is the same, though the vocabulary in which it is expressed may have changed in detail. (Adler 1988, p. xxix)

But the students themselves have not always been so passive as Adler seems to imply. In the NBI era, thousands upon thousands of college students spent evenings in cramped, stuffy rooms listening to tape recordings about philosophy—and paid NBI's not inconsiderable fees for the privilege. Their thirst for knowledge was that intense—a thirst that the universities they were attending during the day failed to satisfy, but Ayn Rand did. It is her focus on substantive problems, her anti-skeptical approach, and her assertion that one can attain knowledge and certainty on fundamental issues, which make her philosophy so attractive to intelligent young men and women. A lot of bright people are turned off by being told that true philosophical understanding means knowing that you know nothing. One might as well sign up for a lobotomy; at current college tuition rates, the surgical route to this insight would be cheaper, too.

Objectivism, with its confident assertion that philosophical problems *can* be solved once and for all—that there are two sides to every question, the right side and the wrong side—is profoundly antithetical to the philosophical tradition of the twentieth century. What's more. Objectivism cuts through or brushes aside many of the field's historical controversies as irrelevant or meaningless. Naturally this does not sit well with most professional philosophers. Objectivists appear to them as dogmatists who casually dismiss the work of famous thinkers without so much as reading it.

Objectivism's distinctive approach and style must be kept in mind as we examine Rand's philosophical thought. Her approach to philosophy, like it or not, was simply not 'scholarly'. Regarding philosophy as too important to be left to the philosophers, she focussed her attention on crucial human problems, especially in ethics, and paid little attention to the more subtle and abstruse issues that concern modem professional philosophers. If, as a result, her thinking has a certain naivety, it also has a certain freshness.

Metaphysical Roots

Rand repeatedly expressed her debt to Aristotle for his formulation of the laws of logic and his development of a metaphysics of objective reality. She never attempted to make a significant contribution to metaphysics herself, but adopted the essentials of Aristotelian metaphysics without modification as the basis of her own philosophy. (She rejected, however, Aristotle's cosmology and other peripheral aspects of his metaphysical theories.)

Metaphysics has developed a whole series of new problems and challenges with the development of modem science. Some of the most exciting questions deal with, quite literally, 'meta-physics': Why do the laws of physics take the form they do? That is, to what extent, and in what ways, do metaphysical considerations such as self-consistency or causality put constraints on the laws of nature? And what are the implications of modem physics—especially quantum mechanics—for concepts of causality and volition?

Rand paid little attention to these controversies, although many of them had already emerged in the latter part of her lifetime. It seems unlikely that she could have made any contribution to them, in view of her ignorance of mathematics and the natural sciences.

However, Rand contributed a great deal to the popularization of metaphysics. Rand took the viewpoint—by no means universal among philosophers—that philosophy is hierarchical. One's conclusions about metaphysics constrain, if not determine, one's conclusions about epistemology; which in turn constrain one's views on ethics; which in turn constrain one's views on politics and esthetics. She was thus led to place a very strong emphasis on correct metaphysics as the root of philosophical thought.

This emphasis is most obviously evident in *Atlas Shrugged*. Rand's three previous books are very definitely political novels on essentially political themes. *Atlas Shrugged* is a philosophical novel—and more, it is explicitly a novel of metaphysics. At all levels, from its passages of philosophical argument to its symbolism, *Atlas Shrugged* is concerned with the metaphysical roots of ethical, political, and even esthetic choices.

As an Aristotelian, Rand not only asserts the existence of an external, objective reality, but emphasizes that existence is identity. "To exist is to be something." This has the advantage of obviating the need to construct an endless chain of explanations for the universe, for in this viewpoint the 'what' of an existent *is* its 'why'.[3]

---

[3] For a more extensive discussion of this position, and paraphrases from Aristotle and several other philosophers, see Den Uyl and Rasmussen 1984, pp. 4–5.

This underlies Rand's eminently practical approach to philosophical questions. She insists on avoiding intellectual fibrillation by examining philosophical queries for meaning and self-consistency before tackling them. In this way she is able to discard whole libraries of pointless argument and cut through to what is real and important.

An Epistemological Radical

Although Ayn Rand was most obviously controversial in her ethical and political views, the case could be made that it was her epistemology that was most radical. What has really driven opposing *philosophers* up the wall has been less her individualism or her egoism than her claim to certainty. Vital to the structure—and attraction—of Objectivism is its promise of a route to knowledge—real knowledge, certain knowledge. The importance of this attraction is pointed up by the title of Leonard Peikoff's 1989 Ford Hall Forum talk: 'Certainty and Happiness'.

Objectivists have had no difficulty rebutting direct attacks on their claim of certainty. Told, 'Nothing is certain', an Objectivist, like any other Aristotelian, can quickly respond with, 'Are you sure about that?'

Neither do Objectivists have much to fear from the 'How do you know you know?' line of argument. An essay on the subject by Leonard Peikoff takes the position that, once a conclusion is supported by a logical argument, carefully constructed and examined, the burden of proof is on the skeptic. He may not attack it simply by pointing out the possibility of human error; some specific objection must be raised (Peikoff 1981).

Yet, surprisingly, there does not seem to exist anywhere in Rand's writings a definition of 'certainty'. There are a number of questions along this line that Objectivists need to ask themselves. What is certainty, and why does man need it? What does it really mean to say that one is 'certain' of some conclusion? Are there different kinds of 'certainty'? By what criterion can one decide whether some particle of knowledge is certain or tentative? What can one do with certain knowledge that one cannot do with knowledge of which one is merely pretty sure?

Rand, as we have seen, was the ultimate anti-skeptic. In her journal she wrote in 1958, "All the evils of philosophy have always been achieved via epistemology—by means of the 'How do you know that you know?'" (Rand 1984). The absence of a positive theory of certainty is a striking deficiency in her philosophy.

Though Rand did not take up the question of certainty as explicitly as one would like, she does offer very strong justification for her view that we're capable of knowing reality beyond any reasonable doubt. She succeeds because she adopts an approach that at first may appear to be merely a matter of style.

For the past hundred years, writings on epistemology have been permeated with discussions of 'propositions' and 'predicates' and 'logical inference'. Commonly knowledge has been seen as the outcome of a process of *proof*. Ayn Rand's terminology reflects a different viewpoint. She talks in terms of 'concepts', 'abstraction', and 'integration'. Her emphasis is on *understanding*.

Rand obviously acknowledged the role of proof in reasoning; she did, after all, glory in the appellation 'Mrs. Logic'! But she was less interested in how one establishes the truth of particular propositions than in how one develops a complete structure of interrelated knowledge. Thus her epistemology is centered, not on a methodology of logical inference, but on a theory of concepts.

Rand's Theory of Concepts

The closest thing to a formal, academic paper on philosophy in Rand's work is her mini-treatise, *Introduction to Objectivist Epistemology*. The title, as she indicates at the start of the work, is literal; the book is only an introduction, specifically a discussion of the theory of concepts.

Introduction to Objectivist Epistemology begins with a description of the way in which concepts are formed from percepts. Rand builds a theory of concept-formation based on an analogy with mathematics, in which 'units' and 'measurements' become the raw material for constructing concepts.

This approach leads naturally into a discussion of the Aristotelian structure of definitions in terms of *genus* and *differentia,* corresponding exactly to Rand's theory of concept formation— not surprisingly, as she very likely worked backward from the structure of definitions.

Rand now gets into the real meat of her subject: the question of 'essence' and the debate between 'nominalists' and 'realists'.

She pays little attention to issues and distinctions that most philosophers would consider important here. For instance, the term 'nominalist' has actually been applied to a variety of related but distinct positions, as has 'realist'. The question of 'essence' also has a metaphysical component—circles exist (though perhaps no perfect circle), but does 'circularity' exist, and if so what is the manner of its existence? Rand more or less ignores such questions to concentrate on what she sees as the crucial aspect of the problem.

To abbreviate Rand's already simplified summary, the problem may be stated as follows. Is there such a thing as a 'correct' definition for some particular concept? The most commonly held modern view is that there is not; a definition is an arbitrary convenience. This 'nominalist-conceptualist' or Humpty-Dumpty school of thought holds that definitions need only be consistently maintained during a particular discussion. Just as Americans drive on the right side of the road, and British on the left, a concept such as 'bird' may be defined as a feathered animal, or as an egg-laying animal. As long as everyone who is using the definition (or road) agrees to accept a particular procedure, the exact procedure chosen is of no importance.

Opposed to this is the 'realist' school of thought, in its pure Platonic or diluted Aristotelian variants, which hold that there is only one correct definition for a given concept. What, though, could give this 'essence' of the concept its special validity? The 'essence' is real in this view—it actually exists, as a Platonic form or some such entity.

Rand rejects both these approaches. As she describes it, the nominalist regards definitions as arbitrary; there is no 'essence' of a concept. The realist postulates the actual existence of the essence; essence is metaphysical. For Rand, definitions are not arbitrary—there is an essence—but the essence is not metaphysical but epistemological. Though concepts are in the mind, they are not arbitrary because they reflect reality; concepts identify real attributes of reality, organized in the best manner for the human mind; the correct relationship between the mind and reality is the objective.

Now, why should anyone bother with all this? Rand's answer would be that philosophy is practical. The nominalist view assumes that thinking is a matter of detached, abstract debate. It is a game, and the only requirement for the rules is that they be self-consistent and agreed to by all the players.

But for Rand, thinking is man's means of survival, and its rules are absolutely critical. If you pick the wrong way to define a concept, it may not just be 'Well, that's an interesting way to look at the subject'; it could kill you.

The same practical considerations prompt Rand to reject the realist position. Thinking must be contextual. As a practical matter, one cannot wait to learn everything there is to know about a concept, so that one can discover some 'ultimate' essence. Even in the context of limited knowledge, one must have some essence—something to think with, until one learns more.

Take for example the concept 'critical mass'. Many know roughly what this means, but for nuclear physicists, developing an exact definition was, shall we say, critical. When one is working with plutonium assemblies, one cannot afford the casual attitude of the nominalist; one's definition of 'critical mass' had better correspond as exactly as possible to reality. To use an arbitrary definition makes thinking more difficult, and increases the possibility of a mistake in reasoning which may have rather serious consequences. The realist's approach is also defective. The first approach to the concept of critical mass may be primitive—for instance, failing to take into account the dependence on the shape of the object; a sphere of plutonium has a lower critical mass than a cube. But if one waits, avoiding reliance on the concept of critical mass until everything about fission is completely understood, difficulties are likely to mushroom during the early experiments. A concept such as 'critical mass' can be valuable, even essential, to learning, although only imperfectly understood.

Rand's view of essence, one should note, brings her epistemology into line with her metaphysics and her ethics and achieves a uniform consistency in her conception of the human mind. Here, as elsewhere in her work, she decisively rejects the mind-body dichotomy. For Rand, mind is part of reality. In metaphysics, she holds that consciousness is neither illusory, nor a projection of some special, mystical plane of meta-reality; consciousness perceives reality and is part of it. This leads to her conclusion, in epistemology, that concepts, the working fluid of consciousness, are also real—neither arbitrary constructs, nor 'forms' in some meta-reality, but part of ordinary existence. In ethics, Rand's principle leads her to emphasize the complete integration of the human mind and body as the basis of the Objectivist ethics.

Returning to Rand's exposition of epistemology, we find that she goes on to deal with another difficult problem: axiomatic concepts. These concepts—existence, identity, and consciousness—are the broadest possible abstractions. Because they identify the most fundamental aspects of reality and knowledge, no other concept can be formed without use of them. It is in this sense that they are 'axiomatic'.

The Analytic-Synthetic Dichotomy

It should be noted at this point that the Objectivist theory of concepts completely nullifies Kant's 'analytic-synthetic dichotomy'—a sophistry which has confounded and confused generations of college sophomores. A valuable essay on this subject by Leonard Peikoff is appended to Rand's text. Though the Objectivist refutation of the dichotomy is not the only challenge to Kant on this issue, nor even perhaps the most cogent, it is probably the clearest and most easily understood.[4]

Kant's distinction divides propositions into two classes: 'analytic' statements, which are, directly or indirectly, true by definition; and 'synthetic' (strictly speaking, 'synthetic *a posteriori*') statements, which state empirical facts. 'Analytic' statements are 'logically true', but provide no information about reality, since they are in essence just restatements of the definitions of the terms used in them. 'Synthetic' statements, on the other hand, cannot be logically proved; they can only be inferred from what we happen to observe and thus are uncertain, subject to change as we gain new experience. It is therefore impossible for reason to generate knowledge which is both certain and about reality. Kant himself thought that there were 'synthetic *a priori*' judgments which were built into the human mind and allowed us to know things without the need for experience or reason. This view, however, has not been widely accepted by philosophers; what has achieved immense influence is the use of the analytic-synthetic dichotomy as an argument for epistemological skepticism.

---

[4] The analytic-synthetic dichotomy has also been criticized by some academic philosophers, including Willard Quine, John Wild, Morton White, and Wallace Matson.

The Objectivist counter to this dichotomy argues that concepts subsume all the characteristics of the entities to which they refer, not just those included in the definition. Thus 'men are rational animals' is no more analytic than is 'men are featherless bipeds'; the latter, as well as the former, can be derived by 'analysis' of the concept. And the former is no less synthetic than the latter, since the definition of man is based on experience and is not arbitrary in the manner of the nominalists.

The analytic-synthetic dichotomy is merely a more subtle formulation of Hume's assertion that neither deductive reasoning nor inductive reasoning can provide us with real—that is, non-tautological and also certain—knowledge. Deductive reasoning, we're told, can prove nothing that is not already implicit in the postulates assumed; inductive reasoning is at best statistical inference and can never be certain in its predictions.

Objectivism simply rejects the dichotomy. Reasoning, for Rand, is a means of comprehending reality. Inductive reasoning derives concepts from observations of facts; deductive reasoning subsumes new instances under known concepts. Like the two blades of a pair of scissors, these modes of thinking do together what neither can do alone.

Epistemology in Practice

In her closing chapters, Rand surveys a few important practical issues in epistemology. In particular, she attempts to deal with what she regards as an attack on scientific knowledge by the logical positivists. The position she opposes had become the dominant paradigm of scientific epistemology following the 1962 publication of Thomas Kuhn's brilliant and extremely influential book, *The Structure of Scientific Revolutions*. This is the view that scientific progress involves a series of 'paradigm shifts', in which an existing theory is gradually overwhelmed by new facts or insoluble problems, forcing development (or acceptance) of a new theory. The older theory, and the concepts on which it is based, are thus invalidated. Kuhn's model has been widely used to attack the very concept of scientific knowledge; according to these Kuhnists—perhaps we should call them 'vulgar Kuhnists'—nothing may be considered certain, for everything we know is subject to reversal by some future 'paradigm shift'. Or, as Rand puts it, "On such a premise, every advance of knowledge is a setback, a demonstration of man's ignorance" (Rand 1990, p. 67).

Rand does not specifically mention Kuhn. I bring his name into the discussion because his work (which is erudite and full of important insights) has been used so widely to attack science's claim to certainty. His model of scientific progress fits precisely the line of argument which Rand criticizes in this passage. Kuhn suggests:

> We may . . . have to relinquish the notion . . . that changes of paradigm carry scientists and those who learn from them closer and closer to the truth. (Kuhn, p.170)

In defending himself from critics Kuhn later (p. 206) makes his position quite clear. Science *does* make a meaningless sort of progress in that its repertoire of "puzzle-solutions" grows. But it is *not* the case that "successive theories grow ever closer to, or approximate more and more closely to, the truth" (p. 206).[5]

Rand points out the philosophical roots of this error. She emphasizes that concepts are open-ended and subsume all information about their referents, including that not yet discovered. Thus new facts and unexpected discoveries extend or expand our concepts; they do not invalidate them. Unfortunately Rand passes over this subject quickly; a scientist could wish that she would deal with Kuhn and his followers in more detail, for they have done great damage to scientific epistemology.

In general it's regrettable that Rand's ignorance of the sciences left her unable to contribute directly to scientific epistemology. Many of the most crucial modern problems in epistemology are raised by work in the sciences.

If the reader wonders what could constitute a really 'practical' epistemological problem, here is an example. It not infrequently occurs that we must choose between two theories. One theory, let us call it A, is internally self-consistent, but there are some experimental facts that contradict it. The other theory, call it B, is consistent with all the facts but contains internal contradictions. No better theory is currently available, but one must make decisions, and right now—to design a spacecraft, to plan a campaign against a deadly epidemic, to prevent an explosion in a refinery. One must

---

[5] For a thorough discussion of the issues raised by Kuhn, see Laudan 1990.

act, and on the basis of one theory or the other. Which should be chosen, A or B? This is an epistemological problem. The solution is left as an exercise for the reader.

The Objectivist Ethics

Rand's most substantial contribution to philosophical thought lies in the field of ethics. It was Ayn Rand who, after centuries of failed attempts, finally proposed a viable solution to the fundamental problem of ethics: deriving normative from factual statements, or, less formally, deriving 'ought' from 'is'.[6] Philosophers have long recognized this as a major problem. Arguably Ayn Rand's most important accomplishment was producing a solution to this problem. In response, her opponents have concentrated their fire primarily on her ethical reasoning.

Every human society has had ethical precepts, claims that one 'ought' to do, or not do, certain things. How can such claims be justified? The historic justifications have been such as: 'You ought to, because I say so.' Or: 'You ought to because God, speaking through me, says so. Or: 'You ought to because all the rest of us took a vote and the majority says so.' Or: 'You ought to because if you don't we'll burn you at the stake.'

At least in modern times we would not accept any of these modes of argument to settle a factual question such as, say, whether the earth revolves around the sun. Why should we accept them in determining moral questions? But if we don't, just how should we determine the truth of a moral dilemma?

Rand attacks the problem of ethics by going to the root, to a question of 'meta-ethics'. Instead of asking, 'Which morality is correct?', she asks, 'Just what *is a* "morality", anyway?' There are many possible moralities which might be correct: Christian ethics, the Ten Commandments, 'Seek the greatest good of the greatest number', 'Do what thou wilt is the whole of the Law', and many others have been asserted. But what do they all have in common? What is a morality?

---

[6] This is a modern formulation of the problem of ethics, dating from relatively recent philosophical skeptics such as Hume. The ancients would not have recognized the 'ought-from-is' problem as a problem. A number of philosophers besides Rand have rejected Hume's argument, for example Searle 1964.

A morality—any morality—is a set of rules to guide the actions of an individual human being. This—and only this—is what all possible moralities have in common. This is the definition of a morality. (Rand puts it: "A code of values to guide man's choices and actions (Rand 1961, p. 13).

Well, given this, asks Rand, why should there be any morality at all? This is of course a normative question, so let's rephrase it in factual terms: What would happen to a man who practiced no morality?

A man who practiced no morality would be a man whose behavior was guided by no rules at all. Even the English occult mystic Aleister Crowley's morality has a rule ('Do what thou wilt') but our hypothetical literally amoral man could not follow even his whims consistently. He would have to behave as if his brain were connected to a random number generator. What would happen to him? He would of course quickly die.

This suggests that the connection between factual and normative statements is man's life. Man needs morality to live. Man ought to do certain things, because they are necessary in order for him to be. He 'is' because he does what he 'ought'.

The skeptic might say, 'You are assuming that I ought to choose life—what if I don't?' It's tempting to reply (as, in effect, John Galt does), 'Fine. If you prefer death, shut up and die.' But this is inadequate. It is not enough merely to demonstrate that altruism is a morality based on a premise of death. We need to make a positive argument to show that morality must be based on the standard of human life. To Merrill's mind Rand's argument for this position is insufficiently rigorous. However, her line of reasoning is basically sound and can be put on a very strong footing.

Ethics and Values: Two Lines of Argument

Rand defines a 'value' as "that which one acts to gain and/or keep" (p. 147). A value is an object of human action. According to Rand, a value is not something one desires or wants, but something one acts to achieve. One wonders whether Rand was familiar with the work of Ralph Barton Perry. He conceived of 'value' along the same lines as Rand, and was led thereby to propose a "bio-centric" theory of value (Perry 1926).

Thus we might rephrase the fundamental question of ethics as, 'What values or goals ought one to choose?' For a given person in a given context at a given instant, correct ethics must specify some value to pursue. So it's only logical that if we are interested in ethics we ought to examine the concept of 'value' and ask what that concept implies. The fundamental argument of the Objectivist ethics is the assertion that value (in the ethical sense) is both *practically* and *conceptually* dependent on life. Rand uses two parallel lines of argument for her case.

There is what might be called the 'metaphysical' line: that all values are dependent on life as a practical, metaphysical matter. Rand asserts that only living creatures have, or can have, values. More, she claims that there can be no meaningful values except those which are aimed at the preservation of the individual's life.

But Rand also uses a separate, 'epistemological' line of argument, which relies on use of the 'stolen concept' approach. As has been pointed out by other writers,[7] Rand makes an argument for human life as the standard of ethics which is analogous to the argument for the validity of logic in epistemology. Just as one cannot demand a proof of the validity of logic, since the concept of 'proof' already assumes the validity of logic; so one cannot challenge life as the standard of ethical value, since the concept of 'value' already assumes that one is talking about a living being. In this line of argument, the concept of value is seen as epistemologically dependent on the concept of life.

Ron Merrill was hesitant to lean on the epistemological line of argument because it appears endangered by circularity. Rand's definition of life is "a process of self-sustaining and self-generated action," a process of pursuing values. This sounds very much as though she is implicitly using the concept 'value' to define 'life'. How could one explain "self-sustaining action" without the concept of action to "gain and/or keep" something? But if 'life' is, directly or indirectly, defined in terms of 'value', then in what sense is the latter conceptually dependent on the former? However, the solution to Merrill's problem lies in the metaphysical fact that life is a circular process. The process of life is to keep the process of life in existence, a kind of perpetual motion. Life is a process of valuing.

---

[7] Hospers 1967; Lugenbehl 1974.

Now let's consider this point in more detail.

The Randian Argument

In line with her usual epistemological style, in Rand's copious writings on ethics she is mostly concerned with building a conceptual framework. She never attempts a formal proof of the basic principle of the Objectivist ethics. However, at one point she does outline the basic structure of her argument explicitly.[8] We may summarize the key steps as follows;

   i. **Living beings, and only living beings, have values (goals).**

   ii. **Man, being volitional, must choose his values.**

   iii. **Values—goals—may be means to an end, but must lead to some ultimate end. An infinite chain of means leading to no final end would be meaningless and impossible.**

   iv. **Life is an ultimate end, and furthermore it is the only 'end in itself'. Life by its nature is an end in itself: it is a process of keeping itself in existence.**

   v. **Therefore, the only meaningful or justifiable values a man can choose are those which serve to sustain his life.**

The logical inference which leads to the conclusion is sound enough. Premises i, ii., and iii., though occasionally challenged, hardly seem open to serious attack. It's sometimes argued that non-living entities, such as target-seeking missiles, have 'goals', but this position is refuted by Harry Binswanger (Binswanger 1990). With missiles, it is human goals they are fulfilling.

So the fight is over premise iv. Is life an'end in itself'? And if so, is it the only possible end in itself?

---

[8] Rand 1974, pp. 16–17. An article by Eric Mack (Mack 1971) attempts to exploit the 'ultimate end' approach and further points up the difficulties involved in doing so.

Ends and Ends in Themselves

The classical philosophical tradition in ethics, tracing back to the Greeks, seeks an 'ultimate end' of human action. The argument typically runs as follows:

Consider a goal, alpha. This goal actually is a means to an end, another goal, beta. But beta is itself a means to another goal, gamma, and so on. Can we find some ultimate goal, call it omega, which is an end in itself, not a means to any other end? If we can, and if we can show that every goal is ultimately a means to omega, then we have a basis for ethics.

Suppose, for instance, that we could establish that every human action is aimed at the individual's happiness. We're compelled to assume this proposition in strong form: A person does nothing, and can do nothing, purposeful unless the purpose is to serve his happiness. Even if he thinks he is doing something for other reasons, his real objective is and must be his own happiness. Then ethics reduces to a matter of engineering, so to speak; one need merely determine the most efficient way to serve one's happiness.

The proposed ethical 'end-in-itself' has been variously identified as justice, love, equality, the greater glory of God, and many other things. But in the end nobody has been able to satisfactorily establish that all goals are means to some end-in-itself.

Has Rand found the answer? It looks problematic at first glance. *Is* life an end-in-itself? Do humans *never* regard life as a means to an end? One thinks of Tony, willing himself to live for one more minute, then one minute more, until he can find someone to carry his urgent warning to Rearden. And is life the *only* end-in-itself? Do humans *never* seek any other value for its own sake? Critics have seen this premise as the crucial weak point of the Randian argument.

Rand's chain of reasoning will not hold unless she can show that, as a matter of metaphysical fact, there is no 'end in itself' other than life. What if there are other ultimate ends, unrelated to, and perhaps even incompatible with, life or survival? Then it will *not* follow that all values must serve to sustain life. So Rand in adopting this argument requires herself to prove a negative.

At best this is going to be difficult, and probably it will be impossible. Take just one prospective counterexample: reproduction. Even with modern medicine a woman faces a noticeable risk of death in having a child. Taking into account economic and other costs, one can scarcely argue that reproduction makes a net contribution to the survival of the parents. It certainly seems plausible to assert that people value their offspring as ends in themselves, and not just as means to the survival of the parents.

If we look at the more general context the situation becomes even worse. Reproduction is extremely hazardous for many animals, and fatal for some. Consider insect species in which the male is eaten by the female immediately after, or even during, copulation; or those in which the female's body becomes the initial food for her offspring. These cases—fortunately!—have no direct relevance to human ethics, but they certainly make hash of Rand's general claim that an organism's survival is the only possible 'end in itself'.

In general Rand and her followers have tiptoed around the question of reproduction and human valuing of children. Binswanger does approach the issue, very obliquely, in dealing with a problem of teleology—How can an action, the effect, precede the goal, the cause? (Binswanger 1990, pp. 156–58, 165–66).

But, if "life is a process of self-sustained and self-generated action,"—Rand's non-technical definition—it is not specified as an individual entity's life. And we can argue that the person who chooses to be a parent values actualizing that aspect of their functioning existence as inherent to the meaning of life. In other words, they're fulfilling their need for achievement and a meaningful existence by having and raising children because, for humans, their psychological existence is as important as—if not more so than—their physical existence.

Before we can deal with the problem we have identified, we must recognize that Rand is not using the term 'end in itself' in its traditional sense:

> Metaphysically, *life* is the only phenomenon that is an end in itself: a value gained and kept by a constant process of action. (Rand 1974, pp. 16–17)

Clearly this is not the usual conception of an 'end in itself'. But just what does it mean, then? Here's a paraphrase by Harry Binswanger: "only life is an action directed toward the perpetuation of itself" (p. 165). And illuminating this in more detail:

A common misconception is that of thinking of 'survival' as if it were some single vital action that occurs after all the other actions [necessary to life] have been completed. 'Survival', however, means the continuation of the organism's life, and the organism's life is an integrated sum composed of all those specific actions which contribute to maintaining the organism in existence. In this sense in living action the parts are for the sake of the whole: the specific goal-directed actions are for the sake of the organism's capacity to repeat those actions in the future.

An ultimate goal, if it is truly ultimate, must be an 'end in itself'. An 'end in itself' gives the appearance of a vicious circle: it is something sought for the sake of itself. This circularity vanishes when we regard *life* as an end in itself: actions at a given time benefit survival, which means they make possible the organism's repetition of those actions in the future, being then again directed toward survival, which means their repetition, and so on. (pp. 64–65)

What Rand and Binswanger seem to be saying is that life is an 'end in itself' in an unusual and very special meaning: Life is an ordered collection of activities, which are means to achieving an end, which is—simply those activities. Every action taken to sustain life is simultaneously a means (because it supports life) and an end (because life is by definition simply the collective of such actions).

This conception of life is not only accurate and perceptive, but enormously fruitful for ethics. What's more, it offers a way to escape from the need to prove a negative in the argument for the Objectivist ethics.

The Means Test

We can reformulate Rand's argument in a way that leads to the same conclusions, without encountering the difficulty that we discovered above. All we need do is recognize that Rand's idea of 'life' as a sort of self-contained vortex of values which are simultaneously ends and means allows us to reverse the traditional program, as follows.

Consider a goal, Z. Attaining this goal is dependent on another goal, Y, which is a means to Z. Y in turn is dependent on another means, X, and so on. Is there some ultimate *means*, A, which is a means for all other goals? There is indeed: Life is a prerequisite for pursuing any other goal.

We are now in a position to ignore the problem of competing 'ends in themselves'. Let us argue as follows: Man must choose what values to pursue. But can something be a value if its attainment would be such as to eliminate or reduce one's ability to pursue values? To seek an end while rejecting an essential means to that end, is to act (means) to gain and/or keep a value (end) while not so acting—which is a contradiction. So whatever ultimate ends there may be, one can seek them only if, and to the extent that, one values that which serves one's own life.

Whether or not life is the *only* ultimate end, it is an end which is a necessary means to any and all other ends of a living being. The Aristotelian flavor of this approach becomes evident if we phrase the argument this way:

This goal is a means for all other goals, and not for some special genus apart from others. And all men value it, because it underlies all values. For a value which everyone must hold, who values anything at all, is not arbitrary. Evidently then such a value is the most certain of all; which value this is, let us proceed to say. It is the life of man *qua* man.

This line of argument offers the prospect of putting the Objectivist ethics on a truly solid logical footing.

Rand and the Aristotelian Legacy

Jack Wheeler argues that Aristotle anticipated the Randian ethical argument in key ways, and he makes his case well (Wheeler 1984). We need not deny the originality of Rand's accomplishment in conceding, as Wheeler puts it, that she sees farther because she stands on the shoulders of Aristotle. I would take the position, though, that Rand's perception of the crucial connection between values and life is a major innovation and allows her to ground her ethics solidly in a way which is quite impossible for Aristotle, and indeed for the neo-Aristotelians such as Henry Veatch.

To fully illuminate certain aspects of the Objectivist argument it is helpful to refer to the opening of the *Nicomachean Ethics*. Aristotle begins his analysis by attacking the question, "What is the good?" After explaining the notion of an ultimate end, the "highest good," he surveys various suggestions for identifying this highest good. Then, to open discussion of his own view, he invokes an analogy.

We understand, says Aristotle, what is the 'good' in the sense of a good physician or a good general or a good carpenter. The 'good' for each of these is the goal of his profession—a healthy patient or a won battle or a well-constructed house. And a 'good' professional is thus one who is effective and skillful in pursuing the end appropriate to his art. If we then ask what is the highest or most general good, to which all humans ought to aspire, it must be to live most fully that life proper to man; and the 'good' man is one who lives this life.

Well, to the modern or post-Hume philosophical mind, this argument depends on a false analogy, a truly stunning non-sequitur. How can we identify 'good' (= 'skillful') with 'good' (= 'moral')? Would we say that a surgeon is morally good simply because he is skillful at his craft? Of course not!

Let's see how Ayn Rand's line of argument can deal with this kind of ethical skepticism.

From Is to Ought: Is There Aught or Is All for Nought?

It's a truism of modern philosophy that statements about 'good' and 'bad', in the moral sense of these terms, differ essentially from ordinary statements of fact. 'Normative' statements, it is said, cannot be proved; they are a matter of personal preference, or social rules, or religious prescription (Hume 1990, p. 469).

It is this truism that Ayn Rand challenges. She asserts that the Objectivist ethical code constitutes a valid, verifiable morality, in which the distinction between 'good' and 'bad' is not arbitrary or intuitive but logically derivable from the facts of reality.

To preview Rand's approach, consider the following response to the Humean argument. The argument may be exemplified by contrasting two statements:

'You are a human being.'

'You ought always to tell the truth.'

Hume's argument says that the first statement is factual, the second normative, and that these two types of statement fall into entirely disjoint categories. Furthermore, there is no way to derive normative statements from factual statements.

This position is superficially plausible, but what happens if we look at it a little more closely? Consider the following statements:

'You ought to format a new disk before attempting to write a file to it.'

'You ought not to open with 1. g4.'

'You ought to first examine the equation to see if the variables are separable.

To which type do these statements belong? Clearly if they are not normative statements, they are at least phrased as if they were. Yet they are factual statements, and they can be logically derived from observation in the same way as any other factual statement. Thus we see that rules can be factual statements. If expanded, they have the form, 'In order to accomplish X, it is necessary (or at least helpful) to do Y'. In the examples given, X is (respectively) operating a personal computer, winning a game of chess, and solving a first-order, first-degree differential equation.

So, if we can agree on what morality is to accomplish, we can develop moral rules as factual statements. For normative statements would then be merely factual statements about means and ends (Machan 1985, p. 186). Here is how we can get from is to ought.

But, of course, at this point we will be challenged. We are making precisely the same error that Aristotle made in using the word 'good' in two different meanings. Everybody knows that 'ought' in the operational sense, as we have used it above, does not mean the same thing as 'ought' in the normative, or moral sense of the term. We are simply drawing a false analogy. Who would be silly enough to assert that there is something moral or virtuous about formatting a floppy disk, for God's sake!

But we need not give up at this point. Let us take a bold step. First, though, we must suspend operations for a moment while I resort to another analogy.

Physicists have long known that gravity produces effects similar to those of acceleration. An astronaut in outer space, whose rocket is accelerating at about 10 meters per second squared, will find himself feeling the same sensation of gravity he would experience were he simply standing on the surface of the earth. But of course, in Newtonian times, everybody knew that these two phenomena were not really the same, and that the apparent similarity was merely coincidental. Then Einstein tried making the assumption that the effects of acceleration and of gravity really *are* indistinguishable in every way. The result was the Theory of General

Relativity, and experimental test confirmed that Einstein's radical conjecture was indeed correct.

Now Rand does much the same sort of thing, and let us see if we can follow her. Let us simply assert that 'ought' in the operational sense and 'ought' in the normative sense are after all equivalent, and challenge the critics to prove that they aren't! For, once Mr. Hume is on the defensive, we see at once that he has a glass chin. If the skeptic agrees that the normative 'ought' is equivalent to the operational 'ought', then the whole problem of 'deriving ought from is' instantly evaporates. If he does not we may ask, just what *is* the meaning of the normative 'ought'? If he invokes tradition or religion, or his emotional feelings about right and wrong, the Objectivist will happily agree that such an 'ought' cannot be derived from 'is'! The skeptic is reduced to saying that the Objectivist ethics isn't 'really' morality, even though it can provide a prescription for any specified moral dilemma. But this is merely to say that if he doesn't agree with the rules, it isn't morality.

So we may now feel that the Objectivist argument has given us a firm footing and that we can get from 'is' to 'ought' by a logical procedure. Morality, we will say, is a process of selecting goals; the appropriate goals are determined by the principle of sustaining human life, based on the facts of human nature—the 'is'; and moral rules—the 'oughts'—merely identify the connections between the ends and the means.

But there's a price to pay for bridging this philosophical chasm. In saying that 'ought' has only one meaning, and not two, we are compelled to defend the proposition that formatting a floppy disk *is* an act of moral significance. In fact, any set of procedures, from the rules of football to a recipe for beef stew, may become part of our structure of morality. This does seem a bit heavy-handed, and hardly in accord with the way we normally think about morality. And since the argument above, as I have presented it, is a very loose paraphrase indeed of Rand's reasoning, one may reasonably ask if her argument is being fairly represented.

A quotation from *Atlas Shrugged* may perhaps indicate whether Rand would care to defend this position. Here is Francisco d'Anconia explaining to Hank Rearden the moral significance of—a steel mill.

> "If you want to see an abstract principle, such as moral action, in material form—there it is. Look at it, Mr. Rearden. Every girder of it,

every pipe, wire and valve was put there by a choice in answer to the question: right or wrong? You had to choose right and you had to choose the best within your knowledge—the best for your purpose, which was to make steel—and then move on and extend the knowledge, and do better, and still better, with your purpose as your standard of value . . . Nothing could have made you act against your judgment, and you would have rejected as wrong—as evil— any man who attempted to tell you that the best way to heat a furnace was to fill it with ice." (p. 451)

And when, a couple of pages later, Francisco says, "You knew what exacting morality was needed to produce a single metal nail," the point is driven home. From her books—as well as from her personal behavior—we can deduce that Ayn Rand did regard essentially every human choice as a moral choice, in the most fundamental sense. Consistency, and price no object, was her policy, and here we see it again. It is not an easy way of life into which logic has led her, and one can now more clearly understand the lament of Dr. Stadler:

"You're asking the impossible! Men can't exist your way! You permit no moments of weakness, you don't allow for human frailties or human feelings! What do you want of us? Rationality twenty-four hours a day, with no loophole, no rest, no escape?" (p. 1118)

And indeed that is exactly what Rand wants of us, or rather what she demonstrates we ought to want of ourselves. Her principle unifies thought and life and everything clicks into place. 'Ought' in the operational sense *is* normative ought. 'Good' in the sense of skillful and well-done *is* moral good. 'Right' in the sense of logically correct *is* morally right.

'Aha! So a skillful bank robber is acting morally!' That would be to confuse efficacy with efficiency. To be skillful, a surgeon must not only make incisions well; he must make them in the right places!

What Is the Meaning of 'Life' Anyway?

We still have one step to take if we are to put the Objectivist ethics on a firm footing. Rand demonstrates that life is the root of all value; but then she goes on to specify the standard of value as "the life of man *qua* man." Somehow we have made a transition from 'life' meaning pure biological survival to "life of man *qua* man" meaning something like Aristotle's good life. When Rand invokes "the life of man *qua* man" as a moral standard, the critic may protest that something other than life (that is, survival) is now being added. Rand's standard may now be characterized as 'biological survival with some added quality'; the critic may demand identification, and justification, of this apparently hazy added quality that makes life the "life of man *qua* man."

Rand's answer is simple: there's no real distinction between the 'simple biological survival' of a human being and the "life of man *qua* man." She applies an Aristotelian metaphysical principle: To exist is to have identity. To survive as a living organism *is* to live the kind of life appropriate to that type of organism. To survive as a man *is* to live the life of man *qua* man. There is no such thing as generic survival which comes in a plain white box and may be taken in combination with any lifestyle one wishes. Reality offers only a package deal: the brand-name product, *LIFE MQM*, is the only box on the shelf.

To survive requires a complex, organized structure of action. A human being cannot survive by acting like a dog, a hippopotamus, or a philodendron. Those strategies are not appropriate to, or effective for our species. Still less can a person survive by using no strategy at all. When a man says, 'I will survive', he is saying, 'I will act as a human being'.

Some difficulties, though, do arise when we try to put Rand's standard into application. Rand will approve of suicide under certain circumstances. In *Atlas Shrugged*, for instance, the Sheriff of Durance says that he will not pass judgment on the man who kills himself because of unbearable suffering. Cherryl Taggart commits suicide rather than live in a world of Jim Taggarts, and Rand expresses no disapproval. John Galt explicitly states his intention to kill himself if Dagny is used against him as a hostage. Can this be consistent with Rand's argument for life as the standard of value? Several of her critics have cited it as a contradiction. If sustaining the "life of man *qua* man" may, under certain circumstances, require one to seek death, then "life MQM" must be a rather peculiar type of life.

Once again we face a real difficulty, but one that can be dealt with. We can resolve the apparent contradiction if we look at Galt's argument with Mr. Thompson. "Don't you want to live?" asks the latter. Galt replies, "I do want to live. I want it so passionately that I will accept no substitute."

Now we're getting to the key. Rand once again is challenging us to look at a fundamental question: What is life? What does it mean to live? Philosophers and scientists have long haggled over the definition of life, but one thing is sure: Essential to every known or conceivable form of life, be it a man, an aardvark, a virus, a Martian, or a sentient super-computer, is goal-directed behavior. And goals imply—indeed by Rand's definition essentially are—values. So there is an ineradicable connection: living beings, and only living beings, have values. Those who have no values, or no possibility of acting to achieve values, are, in effect, dead. In fact, it might be helpful to establish a trichotomy: life, death, and 'negative life'—analogous to negative numbers—a status in which a person can achieve no values and in which any action merely makes the situation worse.

So Galt will kill himself if Dagny is tortured. "There would then be no values for me to seek." Or, as he puts it to Mr. Thompson, "The offer not to kill me is not an inducement." Life is *not* merely the absence of death.

Rand's writings on ethics tend to present life as a binary, on-off, either-or status of an organism. But this is not really compatible with Rand's concept of life as a complex collection of survival-sustaining actions. What is the meaning of 'life'? Consider a steer in the slaughterhouse, a second after it has been killed. A biologist would say, of course, that the animal is dead—as a steer. Yet virtually all of the billions of individual cells in its body are at this point still alive and functioning. Indeed, many cells will still be alive when the ground round arrives in the meat section of the supermarket. So even from the strictest biological point of view there is a sense in which 'life' is more than a binary or 'on-off' attribute.

The definition of 'life' raises some fascinating and important questions. Are the electromechanical devices described in *Vehicles* by Valentine Braitenberg, which in spite of their simple construction are capable of amazingly complex goal-directed behavior, 'alive'? We may say they are not, since they are human constructs, not organisms. But then what of a new micro-organism constructed by gene-splicing?

We must make a distinction between 'life' as a characteristic of an organism, and 'life' as a biological phenomenon in general. It is the first sense of the term that we have used in the context of our discussion of ethics. But also relevant is the second sense. A widely accepted definition of 'life' in a biological context is that proposed by Jacques Monod. He cites three essential characteristics of living organisms: goal-directed behavior; self-constructing action; and reproduction. This definition of life in biological context does have implications for objectivist ethics; if we accept that reproduction is part of the concept of 'life', we have a tool with which to remove the objectivist ethics' difficulties with moral issues involving children.

If life is defined in terms of an organism's exhibition of goal-directed behavior, then we must visualize the possibility that it can exist on a multitude of levels, an Aristotleian hierarchy. On what we might call the 'hamburger' level, cellular behavior is very primitive, consisting of a small set of rather simple tropisms. The 'warm body' level, in which all or at least some organs are functioning, represents a higher level of complexity. When the organism—a human being, in the case we are concerned with—is able to perceive and to act, then the range of goals accessible to him expands enormously, and it is only at this level that we would regard him as 'completely alive'. And yet, need we stop here? If our subject is more alert, more intelligent, more healthy, more strong, is he not more able to select goals and pursue them, and is he therefore not more alive yet?

It can be confidently asserted that this concept of life is perfectly valid from a biological point of view. Indeed, many of the modern controversies of 'biomedical ethics' are confronted on the shadowy borderland which is now seen to lie between the traditional domains of life and death. It also accords with the way in which we as human beings regard our own existence and that of our comrades. It is a commonplace to regard those dull, lethargic people who seem to have been defeated by the challenges of existence as being less than fully alive. And who has not awakened on a Spring morning, full of zest, and said, 'Ah, I feel very alive today!'

We can now see that life should be regarded not as a discrete but as a continuous quantity. If one increases one's values and one's ability to attain them, one actually becomes more alive. If one decreases one's options, one becomes less alive. A healthy person is more alive than a Karen Ann Quinlan. A free man is more alive than a slave. And above all, a moral man is more alive than an immoral man. Let's reformulate Rand's argument: morality consists not just of preserving life (MQM), but of maximizing life (MQM). The objective of ethics is not simply to maintain one's ability to pursue values, but to optimize it. In taking this step, we don't abandon the 'either-or' dichotomy between life and death. The dichotomy between 'nothing' and 'something' remains, even when we recognize that there may be different levels or quantities of 'something'.

So, the Objectivist ethics may be seen as a set of rules to guide human action, which is based explicitly on maximizing life. Any 'anti-Objectivist ethics', which chooses values hostile to life, then must be self-contradictory because it would involve destroying or eliminating values by attacking that which makes values possible. Furthermore, the acceptance of anti-life 'values' contradicts the basis which makes the concept 'value' meaningful. Any 'non-Objectivist ethics', which chooses values neither favorable nor hostile to life, may be challenged to give a cause for its selection of such values.

Some Objections to Objectivist Ethics

The Randian argument in ethics is controversial and has come under attack from philosophers. The most effective criticisms are those which either attack Rand's 'ultimate end' premise or exploit the concept of life as 'pure survival'. These objections are cogent but can be met effectively by modifying the Randian argument in ways that do not affect its basic structure or its conclusions.

A number of critics have asserted that the Objectivist ethics is simply a disguised or variant form of Thrasymachan or Nietzschean or Stirnerian 'might makes right' egoism, or even that Rand advocates some sort of Nazi-like attitude. Sometimes real or alleged deficiencies in Rand's personal conduct are cited to suggest that she displayed such behavior in practice as well as advocating it in theory. Some characterize Objectivism as identical to Social Darwinism, generally depicting the views they dislike in terms that indicate that they have read nothing from either school of thought. Since such assertions don't address the real nature of the Objectivist ethics in the first place, it is neither possible nor desirable to answer them.

From Leaking Lifeboats to the Asteroid Test

It used to be fashionable to attack Objectivists with 'lifeboat dilemmas'. 'Suppose you are on a lifeboat and the only way to survive is to murder your companion . . .' As Rand has pointed out, by assuming a situation so far from the normal human condition, one has invalidated the 'normal' prescriptions of Objectivist ethics (Rand 1974, p. 47). At this point we have moved outside the context for which the ethics was constructed. We can still have an Objectivist ethics—we can still try to maximize our life—but the specific rules would change. In fact, since an emergency may be defined as a situation inherently hostile or dangerous to human life, the first rule of emergency ethics would be 'Take action to end the emergency!' So any such exceptional cases may be regarded as rare, temporary, and unimportant to the real task of ethics.

Incidentally, in real-life emergencies the 'push the other guy out of the lifeboat' technique is seldom if ever advisable. Historical examples show that those who survive do so by co-operating with their comrades in misfortune, not murdering them. When Rand said that "normal ethics don't apply in an emergency," she was addressing the issue of giving and receiving aid. By the Objectivist Ethics, normally, a person is expected to support himself or herself, and is proud to do so. But, in an emergency, it is perfectly acceptable to support others as long as one doesn't sacrifice one's own life and goals to do so. In such circumstances, it is also acceptable to receive aid.

Another challenge along the same lines is the 'invulnerable criminal dilemma'. 'Suppose you knew for sure that you could get away with robbing a bank. Why not do it? It would be selfish.' This is a little more subtle. The essential answer is that ethics demands not only attaining values at the range of the moment, but maximizing one's ability to attain values in the long run. Go back again to Rand's fiction. There is a continual stress laid on the importance of what one *is* rather than what one *has*. The hypothetical invulnerable bank-robber doesn't act in his self-interest; he diminishes his capabilities by wasting time and effort (if nothing else) on nonproductive work; he diminishes his options by putting other people in power over him (since he must lie, at least, to conceal his crime). And of course, in reality—as opposed to some imaginary universe—bank robbery is a distinctly hazardous affair.

Eric Mack claims that Bertrand Russell was immoral by Objectivist standards and therefore "has been a problem for disciples of Rand" because he lived to a very ripe old age (Mack 1984). This is invalid even by the most literal interpretation of Rand's wording. Suppose, in fact, that pure survival were to be the ethical criterion. Ethics would then tell us, for instance, 'cross a street only with the "walk" light'. Statistically, those who obey this rule will live longer, but one could certainly find examples of those who consistently jaywalk and get away with it! Russell was lucky, that's all.

This in fact illustrates an important point: Rand was very much aware that life is, so to speak, a stochastic achievement test. Sometimes the moral person, in spite of all efforts, will encounter a run of bad luck, fail, and die. Sometimes the evil person will encounter a run of good luck and prosper to a ripe old age. No matter how rational or intelligent one may be, one cannot always attain certain knowledge of the consequences of one's actions. (It's partly for this reason that Rand so strongly emphasizes the difference between irrational behavior, which is immoral, and action based on an error of knowledge, which is not.) This uncertainty, which is an inherent part of life, does not change the principles of moral action. The race is not always to the swift, or success to the rational—but that's the way to bet.

Again, Mack asserts that a "looter" is not necessarily likely to live less long than a productive man, so the choice of productivity is only a matter of taste. Is it? The looter is a parasite. He destroys or at least damages his victims. Every time he is 'successful', he reduces his future opportunities. The productive man, after each success, is richer not just in wealth, but in experience, skill, and knowledge, better equipped to succeed next time. Instead of victims wary of further attack, he faces partners and customers eager to do business with him again. Furthermore, he's spent his life exercising his abilities to make life better—an essential aspect of being human, since humans survive by changing the world to fit themselves. Theft, looting, and deceit exercise the ability to manipulate others based on their ignorance and fear, very different abilities than those needed by the productive.

And is it true that looters do well? Have the thugs of totalitarian states led, on average, long lives? The fact is that for every Deng who lives into old age, there are dozens of Berias and

Roehms and Trotskys who fail in the struggle for power and meet with untimely and unpleasant ends.

It's instructive here to take one more example, which archetypically illustrates this general line of argument. This is a case proposed by David Friedman which is aimed, not specifically at Objectivism, but at any attempt at moral grounding for human rights. Friedman postulates the following moral dilemma:

- The earth is going to be destroyed tomorrow by an asteroid strike (!)

- This can be prevented by use of a piece of equipment costing $100 (!!)

- Of which there happens to be only one unit in existence (!!!)

- And the owner refuses to let go of it because he'd just as soon he and the rest of the human race were killed (!!!!)

So: Should one or should one not steal it?

Here we have a real beauty, almost a caricature of this sterile mode of ethical argumentation, once again using an emergency scenario. It brings out very explicitly the essence of this approach: to attack the Objectivist ethics by saying, 'But suppose reality weren't what it is? Then your rules would get you in a mess.' The Objectivist reply is simply, 'So what?'

The Objectivist ethics is based on a context of the full reality of human life. Human beings—real human beings—are not hypothetical constructs who can somehow live and thrive by cheating, theft, and murder. And in fact, when it's not Rand who is saying this, the statement isn't even controversial. 'The wages of sin is death.' 'Crime doesn't pay.' 'Evil deeds do not prosper.' The contrary is difficult even to imagine. Writers of fiction reward their heroes and punish wrongdoers, not just as moral propaganda, but because it's hard to make the reverse believable. Could even the talent of Dostoyevsky make us believe in a Raskolnikov who gets away clean and lives happily ever after?

Well, some philosophers will defend—or at least affect to defend—the proposition that crime does pay. They assert that it really is in the self-interest of at least some people to live as parasites and seek values by the destruction of other people. At this point, though, we may sign off, because we have left the realm of pure philosophy. The practicality of crime as a mode of life need not be a subject of speculation or analysis; it can be, and has been, and is studied empirically. Most of us know what conclusions result.

The Galt-Like Golfer

King invokes a somewhat more subtle dilemma to attack the Objectivist ethics (King 1984). What about a highly productive man who, rich at thirty, retires and spends the rest of his life playing golf? Has he really done anything wrong? Yes, he has, by the standards of Objectivist ethics. Again, it's not what he has that counts, nor even what he does, but what he is. By living in idleness, he is diminishing his productive capacity and ability, and thus acting against his own life. In reality skills decline if not practiced—business skills, not just golf! Knowledge is forgotten or becomes obsolete if not used; ability and ambition decay if not presented with new challenges. And that matters, because—in reality—fortunes are vulnerable to inflation, depression, and confiscation.

This and many other objections to the Objectivist ethics fail to understand an essential principle involved. We're accustomed to thinking in terms of one of the two moral modes basic to Western culture. The Judaic ethical mode is legalistic; you are good or bad based on what you do. The Jew has made a covenant—a contract—with God. He has merely to live up to its terms to be good. The Christian ethical mode puts actions in second place, and judges you by what you think. Under Christian morality your actions are of secondary moral importance, and it is your intentions and even emotions that determine your moral stature. This is exemplified by the well-known warning that 'lust in your heart' is sufficient to make you guilty of adultery.

Objectivism takes an entirely different approach. Rand utterly rejects the Christian conception. One need not feel guilt over thoughts or feelings. "There are no evil thoughts except the refusal to think." Neither can one take credit for good intentions not carried out in action. "If one of my blast furnaces goes down, can I keep it going by feeding your intentions into it?" But Rand also refuses to wholly accept the Judaic approach. Although Objectivist ethics characterizes actions as right or wrong, the morality of actions is secondary. To Rand, it matters not what you intend, and only indirectly what you do; the real moral essence is what you are—what kind of person you choose to be, one honestly striving to follow the truth and do what's right.

Robert Nozick Versus the Count of Monte Cristo

No philosophical disputation would be complete without an example of the classic meaning-switch cheapo, and in the debate over Objectivist ethics Robert Nozick has provided the most ingenious application of this traditional technique (Nozick 1971).

Nozick asserts that one cannot derive an ethics from the fact that life is a prerequisite for all other values and cites a counter-example: Being cured of cancer is obviously a value. But having cancer is a prerequisite for being cured of cancer. Does this mean that having cancer is a value?

Well, let us take this sophomore stumper in the spirit in which it is intended and have some fun with it. A dedicated dialectician could dance a pleasant polka with Nozick by taking the affirmative of the question. For instance: Who has not on some occasion abstained from eating before a special meal, in order that hunger may sharpen the appetite and the enjoyment? Perhaps we should go all the way with the Count of Monte Cristo. He asserted that nobody could know true joy who had not experienced the ultimate depths of suffering, and went so far as to let a friend think his fiancée had died so he would be really happy when he learned she hadn't. A professional philosopher no doubt could convince us that it really does make sense to beat your head against a brick wall in order to enjoy the sensation when you stop.

But we must be moving on. Let's point out that Nozick has dropped the context that gives meaning to the value he is invoking. 'Being cured of cancer' is a value only to someone who has cancer. Modern cancer cures range from unpleasant to devastatingly painful; nobody would consider the cure a value in itself.

In short, there is an obvious distinction, which Nozick is fogging, between the circumstances which make something a value, and the means used to attain that value. When we say that Philosophy 101 is a prerequisite for Philosophy 102, we mean that the student will need the information, concepts, and skills taught in the first course in order to profit from the second. We may also say that a certain amount of ignorance of philosophy is a 'prerequisite' for Philosophy 102, in the sense that if the student already knows the material he won't benefit from taking the course—but now we are using 'prerequisite' in an entirely different meaning of the term.

Human Nature and Its Consequences

Rand adheres to a biocentric approach by examining the essential attributes of human nature. She asks in effect (to use modem biological terminology), 'What is the ecological niche of *Homo sapiens*?' Put this way, the answer is clear: Man is the animal that lives by its mind.

Human beings live, not by sharpness of tooth or claw, but by sharpness of mind. In a way, biologists make a mistake when they classify humans as mammals; we differ from other mammals so greatly in mode of existence that humans might well be considered to be, like the first proto-amphibian that crawled up out of the sea, representatives of a new class of vertebrate. The possession of the ability to think in concepts and to communicate these concepts to other members of our species is a fundamental difference from other living creatures; it is comparable to the development of wings by birds, or of warm blood by mammals.

Since man's mind is his biological means of survival, the first and most fundamental of the cardinal virtues of Objectivism is rationality. The human mind is the primary tool by which a man is enabled to pursue values, and therefore its application and development are a primary value. As a virtue, 'rationality' must be defined in a very broad sense. The casual reader of Rand's nonfiction often receives the impression that rationality is simply a matter of choosing to 'focus' one's mind—or making decisions based on logic, rather than being ruled by emotional whims. This is correct as far as it goes, but inadequate. Rationality in its fullest sense is maximization of one's ability to think, as well as the fullest possible use of this capability in solving life's problems. "Reason is the faculty that identifies and integrates the material provided by man's senses" (Rand 1974, p. 20).

Another distinctive characteristic of the human species is its dependence on productivity. The vast majority of plant and animal species exist essentially as consumers, by pure exploitation of their environments. A few species make significant modifications of the environment to create resources for themselves; for instance, beavers dam streams to create ponds in which to live. Through most of its existence, the human species has existed as hunter-gatherer bands, differing in degree but not much in kind from beavers. Modern man, however, operates on a vastly larger scale, making massive changes in his environment to make it suitable for himself. He no longer exists by simple exploitation of existing resources, but by the creation of resources. This way of life, though it has its own special perils, is immensely more successful than the primitive mode. In terms of the Objectivist ethics, the pursuit of values by creation ('production') is infinitely more efficient than simply picking things up. And the higher the scale of capitalization that can be achieved, the more efficient the production is. Productivity, like rationality, is a prime Objectivist virtue because it increases one's options and one's ability to pursue values.

Rand selects as the third cardinal virtue of Objectivism 'pride'. In doing so, she makes explicit the crucial importance she attaches to improving one's abilities and options. There are no less than eight definitions of 'pride' in the Objectivist literature, but primary is: "moral ambitiousness" (Rand 1974, p. 22). Nathaniel Branden amplifies this: "Moral ambitiousness, the dedication to achieving one's highest potential, in one's character and in one's life" (Branden and Branden 1962, p. 30). Thus 'pride' for the Objectivist denotes a constant effort to improve oneself. This translates to a concentration on increasing one's capabilities. The Objectivist must not only be competent; he must make a commitment to self-education and self-improvement, to the constant expansion of his competence to deal with reality.

The Ethics of the Future

Rand's development of the Objectivist ethics was, in its practical significance, her greatest and most lasting intellectual accomplishment. Our generation, and the future generations of mankind, owe her an enormous debt for the guidance she has provided.

Yet there is much work yet to be done in the extension of the framework Rand constructed. There are major gaps in Rand's prescriptions for human behavior. She has almost nothing to say, for instance, about ethical questions in man-woman relationships, marriage, and raising children. Partly, of course, this reflects her own lack of personal experience with family life. But, intellectually, it results primarily from her acceptance of the doctrine of biological plasticity of human beings.

The famous 'nature versus nurture' argument of the twentieth century left its mark on Rand's thought. In rejecting Nietzsche, she rejected the notion that the abilities, character, and unique personality of a human being are hereditary in origin. Thus she makes a particular point in *Atlas Shrugged* of showing a James Taggart springing from noble stock, of Ragnar Danneskjöld arising from a decadent line, of John Galt appearing from undistinguished lineage in the boondocks of Ohio. Emotionally, Rand never quite lost her respect for aristocratic bloodlines; consciously and rationally, she emphatically rejected it.

Yet Rand only partially accepted the counter-trend of environmental determinism. Ethically and politically, she rejected the idea that you are what you're taught, that you are a product of your environment, which determines your thoughts, your character, and your ability. But—though Rand vigorously attacked Behaviorism and the related ideologies of environmental determinism, she accepted the error which lies at their root: the idea that human beings are born with no inherent characteristics.

If we're born formless minds, blank slates on which our personalities are written (whether by our culture or by our wills), if biology has nothing to say in defining the sexes or creating individual differences, how can a biocentric ethics give us guidance? Further, if we have no 'instincts' or inherent biological need to reproduce, whence the tendency? Why go to the trouble and expense of having children at all?

During the last decade of Rand's life, the scientific basis for a full expansion of the Objectivist ethics began to be built. The new field of 'sociobiology' (now more often called 'evolutionary psychology'), though starting from biology rather than philosophy, converges on the same goal Rand pursued: describing how human ethical values can be explained by, and derived from, the distinctive biological nature of human beings.

Going beyond primitive notions of 'nature versus nurture', evolutionary psychology attempts to construct an integrated view of man, in which the mind-body dichotomy is rejected. This discipline promises to provide empirical data, and to some extent a theoretical framework, for 'biocentric' moral rules that could contribute in a major way to the future development of the Objectivist ethics.

From Theory to How-to

Nathaniel Branden has pointed out the need for something beyond ethics as traditionally conceived. It is not enough, he suggests, to develop a set of rules for action, to tell people *what* they ought to do. Ethics is not complete until it provides rules or prescriptions to advise people *how* to be moral. Most of us know the difference between right and wrong—but do we always do what is right? Branden calls for a field of study that would extend ethics into 'how-to' methodology for people who want to be moral.

Naturally psychotherapy or psychology is a logical candidate for this field of, so to speak, para-ethics. (Indeed, Branden's original 'Objectivist psychotherapy', which he has since repudiated, was characterized in exactly these terms.) Most moralists have been inclined simply to rely on human will-power (supplemented by reward and punishment), and thus have not much to contribute. Unfortunately, psychologists have not to date contributed much more. Traditionally they have been prone to assume that if the patient only understands the roots of his behavior he will change it. As Arthur Koestler pointed out in *Arrival and Departure,* this theory doesn't work. Nathaniel Branden (along with a few other psychologists, notably Alexander Weinberg) deserves credit for not only raising this issue, but making an effort to develop some useful techniques. The research and developments of the Positive Psychology movement in the past twenty-odd years, in the work of Martin Seligman, Mihály Csikszentmihályi and others, goes far to discover the principles and practices needed. These psychologists have found that Aristotle's ethics best coincides with the way happy, succesful people live.

Objectivist Esthetics

Rand attempted to do for esthetics what she did for ethics: put the field on a firm logical foundation, and make it possible to make esthetic judgments on the basis of objective standards. There are many aspects of her esthetics that need expansion, but the basic principles are useful in understanding the appeal and importance of art.[9]

Rand defines art as, "a selective re-creation of reality according to the artist's metaphysical value-judgments." Rand does not attempt to connect esthetics to ethics. Though she does not hesitate to evaluate a work of art as being good or bad in ethical terms, for Rand 'good art' or 'bad art'—esthetic judgment—is not ethical in basis but metaphysical. "The basic purpose of art is not to teach but to show" (1971, p. 22).

The Objectivist esthetics is thus organized into three subdivisions: 1. The nature and purpose of art, and how it is related to metaphysics on the one hand, and human psychology on the other hand. 2. The ethical evaluation of art, which for Rand boils down to the conflict between Romanticism and Naturalism. 3. The esthetic evaluation of art, which is a matter of judging effective craftsmanship and technique.

Central to the Objectivist esthetics is the notion of 'sense of life'. This is the individual's subconscious view of the nature of the universe and life. It expresses itself in terms of 'metaphysical value-judgments'. Unlike ethical value-judgments, metaphysical value-judgments refer not to evaluations of good and bad but to evaluations of important and not-important. Is challenge important or is safety important? Is success important and failure merely an occasional nuisance—or is it the other way around?

The creator of a work of art expresses his sense of life—or at least a sense of life. Barbara Cartland expresses the sense that romantic love is all-important; Stephen King that fear and horror are fundamental to existence; Mickey Spillane that conflict and violence are the essence of life. Horatio Alger expresses the sense that justice is ultimately decisive in human affairs; Jean-Paul Sartre that it is not. These are the metaphysical judgments of one-dimensional writers; the judgments of Jane Austen, or Victor Hugo, or Ayn Rand, could not be so briefly summarized.

How is a sense of life projected by a work of art? Rand's approach is epistemological: Just as a concept is formed by dropping the concrete examples and retaining the essence which characterizes them,

---

[9] An elaboration of many aspects of Rand's esthetic theory is provided by Torres and Kamhi 2000.

art expresses the creator's sense of life by dropping that which he regards as unimportant and retaining only the important.

According to Rand, the reader or viewer or listener responds to art on the basis of the level of agreement between his sense of life and that of the artist. This seems open to challenge; many people deliberately choose art which expresses the sense of life they would like to have, rather than the sense of life they do have. Consider Ayn Rand herself. Rand's sense of life, as projected in her novels, is one of a world in which men can accomplish great things, but only by means of a violent, tortured struggle against desperate odds. Yet in her own esthetic tastes, exemplified by her choice of music, she sought a sense of life which was free of all challenge or threat, pure undiluted happiness.

The ethical component of art, for Rand, is expressed most clearly in the conflict between the 'Romantic' and 'Naturalistic' schools of art. By her definition: "Romanticism is a category of art based on the recognition of the principle that man possesses the faculty of volition." Naturalism, in contrast, is the esthetic expression of determinism.

Thus Romantic art exhibits certain characteristics: ethical themes, since volition implies choice which implies a potential for moral conflict; strong plot, since volition implies purposeful action; larger-than-life characters, since volition implies values. Connected to this view of Romanticism is Rand's adoption of a principle from Aristotle: that fiction is more important than history, for fiction can show men and events as they ought to be, rather than as they are.

Rand cautions that esthetic judgment, literally defined, is not a matter of evaluating an artwork's sense of life, nor its ethical content. She instead asserts that esthetic judgment should be purely technical: How effectively does the creator express the sense of life and the theme of his work?

In the field of esthetic technique, Rand deals only with the area of literature, which perhaps is not surprising. She provides, as one would expect, some superb insights into the writing process.

Esthetic Difficulties and Definitions

Anyone who is interested in esthetics on any level should read Rand's essays on the subject in their entirety and give them careful study. Her analyses are permeated with deep insight and useful ideas. Yet though she makes a major contribution to the field. Rand's esthetics presents some serious problems.

Ayn Rand's views on the esthetics of music are symptomatic of serious confusion. Anyone who can assert that Beethoven had a "malevolent sense of life," or that Wagner "destroyed melody"[10] clearly cannot be relied on as a guide to musical evaluation. To be fair, Rand conceded that she was unable to present an esthetic theory for music. This is not surprising, for if one accepts Rand's definition of art, it is not clear how music can qualify. It scarcely seems to be a "representation of reality" in the sense that the definition is used for literature or the visual arts. However, music is a representation of emotional states and, in that respect, of internal reality.[11]

This leads us further: What of non-representational art in general? 'Modern' (non-representational) painting and sculpture challenge the Objectivist esthetics also. Are they not art? Certainly not by Rand's definition. Many people would say that non-representational paintings are not important art, that they might better be classed as decoration. Even so, they can convey a sense of life, albeit only in a mild and very generalized form.

Rand indeed deals briefly with the decorative arts (p. 74). and in effect (though she does not say so explicitly) seems to regard them as a 'borderline case'. Rand included architecture in the fine arts, although it has a utilitarian function. However, she didn't treat it in *The Romantic Manifesto*, referring to *The Fountainhead* for her views. This has led to some confusion among her followers, but, clearly, good architecture can evoke deep emotion so that, despite its utilitarian function, it is a fine art.

How about dance? Rand interprets dance as a 're-creation' of human body movements, capturing the grace and fluidity by omitting the unessential (p. 66). She argues that music gives dance its deepest meaning.

---

[10] Rand's views on Beethoven are reported by Barbara Branden (1986, pp. 243, 311). Her views on Wagner were expressed in conversation with Ronald Merrill.

[11] For an extensive examination of Rand's hypothesis about how music evokes emotion, see Enright 1995, available at <http://fountainheadinstitute .com/con-molto-sentimento>.

8

Rand's Politics

Ayn Rand, like any rational person, wanted nothing more from politics than to ignore the subject. But from childhood she was confronted with the great political issues of the twentieth century, and in her work she could not avoid dealing with them. Rand's radical individualism inevitably made her one of the most controversial political thinkers of her time. She wrote copiously on political problems, in both her fiction and non-fiction work. This included a few stints as a political activist.

A Political Odyssey

The starting point for Ayn Rand's political journey was her fervent anti-Communism, born of personal experience. She emphasized, quite correctly, that *We the Living* was an anti-collectivist novel, an attack on the totalitarian vision as such, rather than merely Soviet Russia or Bolshevism. Even so, she never had much to say about Nazism; much as she opposed it, it seems never to have inspired her with the same visceral hatred that she felt for Communism.

During the 1930s and 1940s the cause of freedom was at a low ebb politically and especially intellectually; the dominant ideologies of the day were communism, socialism, and fascism. In American practical politics, the New Deal prescribed taking these collectivist toxins in homeopathic doses to prevent a more serious outbreak. It was in this hostile environment that Ayn Rand fought her first political values.

She began as a political naif, even voting for Roosevelt in 1932. Though the exigencies of survival during the Depression left little time for the struggling writer to spend on inessentials. Rand conscientiously studied economics, conservative political theory, and current events. Even so, she remained innocent enough to become an enthusiastic supporter of Wendell Willkie's 1940 presidential bid. Rand and her husband lived off their savings for months as they worked full time in the Willkie campaign.

The US presidential election of 1940 revolved around fundamental issues. In domestic policy, there was the potential for a referendum on the New Deal and the 'mixed economy'. The question of America's entry into World War II was prominent, and even in 1940 it could be seen that intervention would probably imply, in the end, at least a *de facto* alliance with the Soviet Union. Finally, Roosevelt's quest for a third term, following on his scheme to pack the Supreme Court, suggested the danger of a major weakening of constitutional protections. If there was ever a need—or an excuse—for political involvement, this election was the time for it.

Willkie sought the Republican presidential nomination along the traditional path—the Right. He appeared to many, including Rand, as a crusader for capitalism and traditional American freedoms. Joining his campaign. Rand quickly graduated from typist to propagandist, setting up an 'intellectual ammunition bureau' to assemble arguments against Roosevelt. Then through sheer merit she moved up to public speaking, in spite of her nearly impenetrable Russian accent.

But Willkie, once he had the nomination, followed the customary Republican strategy of 'moving to the center' for the general election. As he compromised one after another of the ideals he had pretended to stand for, Rand became increasingly disillusioned. Though she stuck it out to the end of the campaign, Willkie's support melted away and he lost the election.

In the aftermath, the New Deal was consolidated and even extended by wartime controls, with the government gaining unprecedented powers over the economy. A series of important court precedents irreparably breached important bulwarks set up in the constitution. And the war resulted in a world in which a nuclear-armed Communist empire presented a threat far greater than Hitler ever had.

A handful of right-wing intellectuals clung to one another in the resulting environment like survivors of a shipwreck. Among them for a while was Ayn Rand. Her participation in the Willkie campaign brought Rand into contact with a number of important conservative and libertarian thinkers: Albert J. Nock, Isabel Paterson, Rose Wilder Lane, and others. Disillusioned with politicians, Rand attempted to organize the intellectuals. Her grand scheme quickly disintegrated, as she found them timid, defeatist, and philosophically ungrounded.

Rand became friendly with Isabel Paterson, author of *The God of the Machine,* in spite of fundamental philosophical differences, particularly over religion. Rand learned much about history and politics from Paterson, but eventually the relationship broke up. Ironically, the precipitating cause was Paterson's offensive behavior to some of Rand's other conservative friends. Barbara Branden's account (Branden 1986, pp. 203–05) shows Ayn Rand in a novel role as conciliator; it's amusing to watch Rand playing the nervous hostess, desperately trying to keep the volatile Paterson from fighting with her fellow guests.

During the 1940s, Rand also met Henry Hazlitt and Ludwig von Mises. After her move to California, Rand became known as an outspoken anti-collectivist; she even testified before HUAC on communist influence in Hollywood. But as she began work on *Atlas Shrugged* and developed her unique philosophy and politics, she increasingly distanced herself from the conservative movement. The latter was beginning to recover and grow, nourished by the outbreak of the Cold War. In spite of her fervent anti-Communism, Rand could not join in a movement which, she now saw, was based on a foundation not only different from, but fundamentally incompatible with, her own philosophy.

The Radical for Capitalism

Rand's break with conservatism became mutual with the publication of *Atlas Shrugged* in 1957. Conservatives abhorred much of her doctrine—the rejection of religion, the call for pure laissez-faire, and the repudiation of altruism and traditional ethical values. What's more, her open advocacy of "selfishness" threatened to discredit the movement and supply ammunition to its enemies. It became important to the conservative intellectual leadership to destroy Rand, or at minimum to repudiate her as a conservative[1]

William F. Buckley, editor *of National Review,* assigned the book to Communist-turned-Quaker Whittaker Chambers. Ironically, for a Quaker, Chambers reviewed *Atlas Shrugged* with a viciousness that surpassed the efforts of even the most virulent liberal critics. In scarcely disguised phrases he portrayed Rand as a Nazi, likening her to the SS monsters who perpetrated the Holocaust—an accusation calculated to maximally offend a Jew. Rand never forgot this libel; and her enemies on the Right, in accord with the principle that one never forgives those one has wronged, pursued her with relentless hate.

The Goldwater Debacle

In spite of her intellectual distaste for conservatism, and her personal distaste for Buckley and his minions, Rand continued to back conservative candidates. In the *Objectivist Newsletter* of October 1963 Rand advised her readers to register as Republicans and vote in the presidential primary elections for Barry Goldwater. She based this advice primarily on the need to prevent "an intellectual coup d'état" by Nelson Rockefeller—a takeover of the Republican Party by welfare-state liberals. Her endorsement of Goldwater was tentative, though she cited his position on Cuba and his opposition to the Nuclear Test Ban Treaty as encouraging. A few months later (March, 1964) Rand endorsed Goldwater more strongly, explaining that "Freedom is his major premise." She described him as "singularly devoid of power lust."

One of the longest articles Rand ever published in the *Objectivist Newsletter* was '"Extremism" or the Art of Smearing' (September 1964). Provoked by the furor over Goldwater's refusal to repudiate the support of the John Birch Society, this essay analyzed the controversy at the Republican Convention in epistemological terms. Rand introduced the idea of the 'anti-concept', a useful tool in understanding political propaganda. Terms such as 'extremism' (or 'isolationism' or 'McCarthyism'), she pointed out, are designed to fog out and obliterate real concepts, such as con-

---

[1] For a discussion of the conservative reaction to *Atlas Shrugged,* see Nash 1976, pp. 156–58.

servatism. She congratulated Goldwater on his handling of this attack.

But by October, Rand was sounding a warning to her students, predicting that Goldwater would likely be defeated because "his campaign has been conducted so badly." If Rand still retained any hope of a Goldwater victory at this late date she was far behind other political analysts. All but the blindest of Goldwater's partisans had written off his chances even before he was nominated. Still, many of the Objectivist movement's younger adherents had campaigned for him enthusiastically. They needed an explanation.

The December 1964 issue of the *Objectivist Newsletter* carried an article which had crucial influence on the course of the Objectivist movement—and, perhaps, on the course of American politics. Entitled 'It Is Earlier than You Think', this essay reaffirmed Rand's analysis of the Goldwater campaign. She ascribed his defeat to the lack of any rational intellectual basis for conservative ideas. Rand went on to assert that the debacle had at least cleared away the old-guard conservatives, leaving the way clear for consistent supporters of capitalism to fight more effectively. But Rand warned that it was too early for direct political action. Instead, she urged her supporters to work in the intellectual sphere: "The battle has to be fought—and won—in colleges and universities, before it can be carried to the voting booths."

This article began a period in which the Objectivist movement became, quite explicitly and self-consciously, hostile to the very idea of political action. Those who were unwilling to renounce activism were read out of the movement. There was an indirect effect on the conservative movement also. The youth wing of conservatism had been heavily penetrated by Objectivist college students, resulting in a gradually escalating conflict with the 'trads'. The sudden withdrawal of Rand's followers settled this conflict decisively. Although libertarian elements hung on in organizations such as Young Americans for Freedom for several years, without the impetus of Objectivism behind them they could make no progress and gradually diffused out. A threat to the traditional right's control of the conservative movement was thereby averted.

Hundreds of young Objectivists have attempted to penetrate Academia, but with much difficulty, although some valiant troops have made it—mostly as Academic ninjas. In recent years, various organizations have revealed the leftist bias of the Academy; any

hint of alliance with anything perceived as "the Right" and some
reason is found to make things difficult for a graduate student or
turn down a young professor's tenure, no matter how bright and
accomplished. But the most reviled and feared are those who
admit any agreement with Ayn Rand. This bias has driven an enormous increase in independent, libertarian think tanks, offering a
true diversity of ideas lacking in the Academy. The best thing
about this blacklisting of the new Right by the Academy is that it
bespeaks their huge fear of competing ideas.

Rand no longer indulged in any political activity. She reluctantly and with many qualifications endorsed the presidential cam-
paigns of Richard Nixon and Gerald Ford; she wouldn't even do
that much for Ronald Reagan. Rand had finally given up on conservatism. She had never accepted libertarianism. But—another
Randian paradox—having retired from active political struggle, she
wrote thereafter increasingly on political, rather than philosophical, subjects.

Roots of the New Conservatism

The postwar intellectual renaissance of the Right contained three
strands. Foremost was what is now called conservatism.

The conservatives of earlier eras—even the 1930s, let alone the
nineteenth century—would scarcely have recognized modern conservatism. After the political disasters of the New Deal, conservatives revived their movement only by means of a quite thorough
housecleaning. As a result, modern conservatism shares little with
its predecessors beyond the classic emphasis on tradition and social
stability, religion and morals. Many key principles of the old conservatism were abandoned or even reversed. Antisemitism was qui-
etly repudiated, and racist notions of black inferiority and the
'yellow peril' were toned down to an occasional whisper.
Protectionism was reluctantly abandoned. In the realm of foreign
policy, the traditional isolationism was completely reversed with
the adoption of a program of active intervention to oppose
Communism.

The founders of the new conservatism smelted it from a mix-
ture of ideological ores which did not always fuse into a stable
alloy. For a base they adopted—with reservations—the classical liberal critique of the State, in particular the argument of Friedrich

Hayek's *The Road to Serfdom*. Long the defenders of strong central government, conservatives had finally learned during the New Deal what it was like to be at the wrong end of the big stick. To add intellectual tensile strength it was essential to mix in 'Austrian' economics with its advocacy of laissez-faire capitalism, repellant though this was to their traditional big-business constituency. The consistency of the melt was thickened with a fervent anti-Communism. Finally, to add luster and sheen to the surface, the Southern Agrarian tradition with its European aristocratic cachet was added.

With the resulting material, weakened though it was by its internal contradictions, conservatives felt strong enough to go on the offensive against the dominant liberal ideology. Yet for thirty years conservative political generals managed to snatch defeat from the jaws of victory—just as Rand predicted all along. Scarcely an issue of *National Review* appears that does not bemoan the great problem of conservatives: they can't seem to actually make any changes in government, even when elections give them the 'power'. Conservative politicians somehow fail to implement their right-wing views. (For eight years conservatives muttered darkly about advisors who wouldn't 'let Reagan be Reagan'.) American foreign policy remains left-liberal in trend no matter who is President, and appeasement of collectivism, whether in the form of Communism, fascism, or through state efforts or non-state terrorism, continues no matter whom he appoints as Secretary of State. Conservative Supreme Court nominees strangely become 'moderate' or even 'liberal' justices as soon as they take their seats. It would be fascinating to see what Rand would have said about the "war on terror." Her analysis of complex issues, especially political, were rarely predictable, yet always penetrating. I'm sure she would have come up with something nobody's thought about.

Rand's Critique of Conservatism

Rand's most trenchant and specific attack on conservatism was developed in her essay 'Conservatism, an Obituary' (in Rand 1967).

At this time (1960) she had already clearly identified the weakness of modern conservatism and foreseen its inevitable impotence to reverse or even halt the trend to statism. Though she took up this theme again in her articles during the Goldwater campaign, during the next decade Rand concentrated her fire on the liberals, most notably in her articles on the 'consensus' politics of Lyndon Johnson.

Rand, obsessed with consistency, saw all along the defect in conservatism: its internal contradictions. Despite the ingenious efforts of Michael Novak and George Gilder, it is difficult to reconcile the Judeo-Christian morality of altruism with laissez-faire, a system based on self-interest. A reverence for tradition tends to conflict with the goal of imposing American cultural and political forms on other countries. The belief that it is the duty of the State to supervise the moral education, sexual behavior, and reading habits of the people is scarcely compatible with opposition to strong government. Since to be a 'principled' conservative is a logical impossibility—the principles of conservatism being mutually contradictory—any conservative who achieves political office will inevitably adapt himself to the expediency of the moment—which means groveling to the special-interest groups.

The process by which such contradictions corrupt the political process was described by Rand in her *Objectivist Newsletter* article 'The Anatomy of a Compromise' (January 1964). Half a century later, her predictions have been amply born out:

> It is precisely those ends (altruism-collectivism-statism) that ought to be rejected. But if neither party chooses to do it, the logic of events created by their common basic principles will keep dragging them both further and further to the left. (Rand 1967, p. 146)

With time the conservative movement has absorbed some ideas from—Ayn Rand. For example, during the 1980s 'entrepreneurship' came into vogue not only in business management, but in the political literature. The leader in this apotheosis of the business founder was George Gilder, a thinker who admits to having been influenced by Rand's writings. Gilder led the way in celebrating the importance of the entrepreneur in economic growth and increasing employment—ideas that are central to (though not original in) *Atlas Shrugged*. Gilder also makes much of the "essential altruism" of the entrepreneur, the fact that he creates far more than he is ever compensated for. This is a primitive distortion of Rand's insight that great innovators leave mankind a legacy so great that they can never be fully repaid.[2] These are the people to whom it is impossible to 'give back', but who most deserve ever-lasting gratitude.

Having rejected conservatism. Rand might have been expected to embrace the political philosophy described by the rather awk-ward term 'libertarianism'. But she didn't.

The Evolution of Libertarianism

Developing in parallel with, but more slowly than the conservative movement, there appeared what is now referred to as the libertar-ian movement. Again, much of the basis for this ideology was pro-vided by the Austrian economists, especially through the mediation of Murray Rothbard. But the movement drew greatly on early individualist thinkers such as Lysander Spooner, Albert J. Nock, Frank Chodorov, and Rose Wilder Lane.

Although the conservative movement is scarcely monolithic, we can discuss American 'conservatism' with a reasonable notion of a specific set of ideas to which one is referring. The same cannot be said for libertarianism. Unlike modern conservatism, libertarian-ism's only consistency is agreement to the 'non-initiation of force' principle. The term is use very broadly, often to include the views of Objectivists, but most libertarians do not accept Objectivist phi-losophy, particularly the ethics, to undergird their political views. Much of the movement consists of limited-government advocates who in essence agree with Ayn Rand's political position. Represented by *Reason* magazine, they are sometimes derided by more radical anarchist types as 'coffee-table libertarians'. Then there are various flavors of anarchists, ranging from the 'vonuists' who try to eliminate their vulnerability to government oppression by hiding in the woods or joining a truly 'underground' economy by living in caves, to radical pacifists like Robert Lefevre.

The Essence of Libertarianism

Can we find any unifying factor—any 'essence'—that will give us a useful definition of libertarianism (as distinct from classical

---

[2] Another source is the revival of the ideas of the Austrian economist Joseph Schumpeter, which has given a major boost to modern theories of entrepreneurship.

liberalism)? If we can define libertarianism at all, we will do best to characterize it as a spectrum of political philosophies which regard the State as inherently an evil. Some libertarians may regard it as a necessary evil, or an unavoidable evil. But anyone who sees government as capable of being intrinsically good is often not considered a true libertarian. If we accept this concept of libertarianism, then we may say that in its purest or most radical form it must advocate the actual abolition of government. This in fact is what the line of thought usually referred to as 'anarcho-capitalism' aims at.[3]

It's important to get at the root of the anarcho-capitalist position, because it deals with the most fundamental question of political theory: the origin of the State. The radical libertarian critique of politics gives us a new perspective from which we can more clearly understand the problem which Objectivism must deal with.

As soon as political theory moved beyond primitive 'might makes right' or religious justifications of the State, the basic issue of politics was re-opened in new form. What is, or could be, the origin of the Just State? Why ought citizens to accept its authority?

Roots of the Political Conflict

Most commentators see the fundamental debate of the modern era as a continuing clash between the ideas of two political philosophers, Hobbes and Locke.

For Hobbes, human beings are inherently vicious and, left to their own devices, will live without society in a war of all against all. As his most famous phrase puts it, man's life in a "state of nature" (a situation without a government) will be "solitary, poor, nasty, brutish, and short." Fortunately, the State relieves mankind from this unpleasant condition by curbing and taming humanity's evil tendencies and enforcing society and co-operation. In this vision the State is inherently good and just; even if oppressive, the government does not make its subjects' lives as terrible as they would be if the State did not exist. In other words, anything is better than anarchy.

---

[3] For thorough-going defenses of the anarcho-capitalist position, see Tannehill and Tannehill 1970; Perkins and Perkins 1971; Rothbard 1973; Friedman 1989a; Skoble 2008; Lester 2012.

Locke takes a somewhat more optimistic view of human nature. People may not be perfect, but they have reason and a great capacity for decency and are inclined to choose good rather than evil. Life in a 'state of nature' is less than optimal, but men can, and if given the chance will, form a government in order to better their condition. A government constituted in this way—and only such a government—is just because it develops out of the voluntary choice of the people it governs.

Hobbes's approach assumes that government is inherently good, and thus just, because it benefits the people. Locke's approach assumes government may or may not be good; it is just only when it is the choice of the people to protect individual rights. Hobbes relies on an appeal to security and welfare; Locke on the concept of rights.

Hobbes never lost his hold on intellectuals in continental Europe, and the primary political tradition there is the primacy of the State. The default, so to speak, is with the government: It may be good to have some limits placed on the State (such as the Magna Carta), but in general the government may do anything that is not specifically prohibited to it. In the political arena of twentieth-century America, this position has been most commonly associated with what *Americans* call 'liberalism' or 'progressivism'. However, it has also had a strong attraction to conservatives. Indeed, perhaps the most eloquent American spokesman for the primacy of the State was the conservative jurist, Robert Bork.

Locke, however, took hold in revolutionary America. His political philosophy assumes that the right lies with the individual: The government may do nothing except to execute those functions specifically allowed to it by the people who created it. This view was virtually universal among the Founders, whether Federalist or Anti-Federalist. For years, support for it gradually eroded, so that only a small minority of Americans accepted it explicitly. But the financial upheaval of 2007 and Obama's Progressivist response to it has stirred up deeply individualist sentiments and a large revival of interest in the Constitution, US political history and a rebellion against Progressivism, expressed in encounters such as Obama's with Joe the plumber. While only Objectivists and libertarians consistently support Lockean philosophy, the ideas are being revived in many quarters, most notably among Tea Party members.

What, then, do Objectivists and libertarians have to argue about? A naive observer might find it difficult to understand why these two groups should be at each other's throats. The writings of the two sides seldom address the real issues clearly, but on analysis we can see that both have a case to make.

Objectivism versus Libertarianism: The Case for the Plaintiff

Libertarianism, which even more than conservatism, is an ideological mélange, was scarcely likely to impress Ayn Rand as the vanguard of the future.

By the time this ideology appeared on the scene in its modern form, Ayn Rand was a very mature thinker with deep insight into the ethical roots of politics and a shrewd understanding of practical politics as well as ideology. The intellectual flowering of anarcho-capitalism in the 1970s produced more enthusiasm than practical thinking, and with her usual ability to put her finger on the key problems, Rand turned out to be right in essence if not in detail.

There are a number of practical objections which might be raised to anarcho-capitalist models, and Rand quickly zeroed in on the apparent absurdity of the idea of 'competing governments' or what the anarcho-capitalists designate 'competing defense agencies' since each person chooses a way to defend himself.) What are the consequences, she asks, when agents of one defense agency attempt to arrest a subscriber to a different, competing defense agency? ('The Nature of Government', in Rand 1974)

On examination, this objection seems to lose force. How is the same problem handled now? For we have competing governments right now; they simply don't share the same geographical territory. In fact, there are cases where two governments have existed within the same geographical area without conflict. Perhaps the best example is Hong Kong, where for over a century there have been two separate legal systems, one for Chinese and one for British inhabitants. Of course, technically these systems are subordinate to a single government, but functionally they are themselves governments. They do not, however, 'compete' in the sense discussed by anarcho-capitalists, since in general a citizen has no choice as to which system governs him.

Another example is provided by the situation in the United States, where state and local police sometimes become involved in jurisdictional disputes with the FBI, our national police force. Similarly, there is much debate and occasional conflict over the jurisdictional privileges of state versus federal courts.

If an American citizen is accused of a crime against a Canadian, the Canadian government asks for his extradition. Of course, a service business might be reluctant to extradite one of its customers! But after all, a national government is generally reluctant to extradite a citizen, and the political imperatives can be just as strong as economic motives. The extradition problem is not a serious objection from a practical point of view. However, in raising it Rand hints at her real reason for opposing competing governments: If governments are Just, they must be based on the same universal principles of individual rights.

A more substantive objection, much debated within the libertarian movement, is the 'free rider' problem. A government's services, particularly defense against foreign aggressors, are hard to individuate. A 'defense agency' that protects one subscriber in, say, Seattle from nuclear attack can hardly do so without protecting the whole city. Most inhabitants of the area are likely to refrain from subscribing to such a costly service, since they will get the benefit for free anyway. They are 'free riders'.

But in Rand's analysis, the radical libertarians fail on epistemological grounds. The anarcho-capitalist position is a politics based on subjectivism. In essence, their argument is, 'There's no objective basis for controlling the use of force. Your belief that you're using force to protect yourself is just an opinion; what if it's my opinion that you are violating my rights?' Thus the anarcho-capitalist invokes 'the market' as a sort of mystical, godlike force that will somehow, automatically, solve the problem of justice in a way that is beyond the capabilities of individual humans.

There is also a deep problem of a "market" in force, since a market assumes that people agree on whose property is whose and how to resolve disputes in order to allow for significant trade. Over history, most peoples have recognized limited personal property and participated in limited amounts of trade. But these arrangements simply are inadequate for the development of a robust and worldwide market involving complex inventions, organizations, and property. Works such as Hernando de Soto's *The Mystery of*

Capital examine the developmental limitations posed by the inadequate recognition and development of property rights.

The Objectivist argument against libertarianism has been summed up in an essay by Peter Schwartz. "Libertarianism," he says, "is a version of moral subjectivism." It is a political ideology with no moral or philosophical grounding; this is shown by the widely varying, and violently contradictory, moral theories of its adherents. When Murray Rothbard, Robert Poole Jr., Walter Block, and Milton Friedman are all accepted as libertarians, the ideology must be considered eclectic, to say the least. But if there is no moral basis for politics, then how is one to understand political conflicts? Only by introducing a libertarian version of 'class warfare', in which those who benefit from the State oppress those who pay for their benefits. So the logical conclusion, says Schwartz, quoting some 'radical' libertarians, is violence. If ideas are not the source of ideology, then 'education' is useless, and only a resort to armed force can overcome the State ('Libertarianism: The Perversion of Liberty', in Peikoff 1988).

Schwartz has a field day depicting libertarians as monsters, adducing 'horror file' quotes from thinkers across much of the libertarian spectrum to support his points. He forestalls the protests of those libertarians who *don't* believe that the US is the world's foremost oppressor or that pederasty should be legalized by pointing out that libertarianism must be thought of in terms of its essential characteristics. And by his definition, the essence of libertarianism is nihilism.

Certainly the critique of libertarianism developed by Rand and elaborated by Schwartz has a great deal of force. It is perceptive, and fundamentally correct, in stating that the key problem with libertarianism is its aversion to grounding political principles in moral philosophy. The detachment of politics from ethics, the attempt to make politics as *wertfrei* (value-free) as Austrian economics, is doomed to failure—and dooms its adherents to failure.

However: While agreeing that the hierarchical structure of knowledge requires that political philosophy be based on ethics, can we accompany Schwartz the rest of the way? In his eagerness to condemn the people, he has incorrectly defined the idea. Moral subjectivism is certainly a characteristic of most libertarian thought—but it is not the essence. In epistemological terms, it is merely an 'accidental' characteristic. The true essence of libertarianism is that it challenges the idea that government can be a good in itself. This idea may be wrong—but it is not nihilism. Anarcho-capitalists say that, in some way, market forces can produce justice better than a government can, just as they can produce shoes better than a collective can. This is not the same thing as saying that there is no such thing as justice, or that justice is undesirable.

Objectivism versus Libertarianism: The Case for the Defendant

The anarchist stream within the libertarian movement has its own case to make, and it is a cogent one. The root of the anarcho-libertarian argument is, in effect, a critique of the concept of the 'social contract'. I am here using 'social contract' primarily in the sense of an agreement between citizens and government. Perhaps 'political contract' would be more accurate.

The American political tradition derives from the natural rights theory of Locke and states that "to secure these rights, governments are instituted among men, deriving their just powers from the consent of the governed." To this the anarcho-libertarian replies, 'Wait a minute! When did *I* consent? Show me this social contract—where's my signature?' For the social contract is not really a contract, since it is imposed by force. The terms are dictated, not freely chosen. Of course, they may be reasonable terms. 'It takes money to pay for policemen and courts and an army to protect you; if you want to be a citizen you must pay taxes, or some equivalent, to fund these services.' But in practice the terms tend to become somewhat less reasonable. 'We have to have an army to deal with foreign aggression, and no amount of money will hire enough soldiers, or the right kind. So if you want to be a citizen, you must accept being drafted.'

The strong point of the anarcho-capitalist critique is that Locke's compact between government and citizen is not really voluntary. The State, like Don Corleone, makes you an offer you can't refuse. The individual must sign or, at minimum, be forcibly ejected from the country of his birth. (This was the choice faced in very practical terms by Tories during the American Revolution.) So Locke's Just State is nothing of the kind, for its basic moral justification—voluntary acceptance by its citizens—does not really exist.

As Murray Franck has argued in 'The State, the Market, and the Morality of Taxation', it's well-nigh impossible for humans to live outside of a social group; therefore humans are always under some form of government or another. The choice, the 'contract' the individual can make is under which government he chooses to live—and to actively engage in the political process if he wants it to be different. Ironically, since anarcho-capitalists believe in 'anarchy', they do not see that they are free to 'compete' at any time; the fact that they don't attempt to compete with large governments shows the fundamental problem with attempting to defend oneself without organization.

The anarcho-capitalists reject the social contract as a group contract. They demand an arrangement under which each person can voluntarily make an individual social contract. But, in their view, if government is a monopoly, then those who reject its terms have no viable options. The 'consent of the governed' is extorted, not truly voluntary. So government must be a function of the market, just like any other service, with competing 'defense agencies' providing police, military, and judicial services.

In this interpretation, the anarcho-capitalist position must be conceded to have great force. Many practical objections (such as the 'free rider' argument mentioned above) have been raised. However, let us bypass issues of this sort and stick with the key issue: What is the origin of the Just State?

Objectivism and the Theory of Government

Having examined Rand's interpretation, and critique, of conservatism and libertarianism, we are now entitled to ask what positive vision she offers. What is her own theory of politics, and what does she offer as a model of the Just State? Rand's 'limited government' is consistent with her approach to epistemology. Justice is objective and knowable. Man can, by logical analysis, determine what justice is and construct a government which will enforce it. What is missing—and it is a crucial omission—in the Objectivist politics is a positive theory of the origin of government. What is government? What justifies it? Why should rational men submit to it? How does it, or should it, originate?

Rand's essay 'The Nature of Government' begins with the same approach she used in the Objectivist ethics essay: Define the topic—and ask why it should exist at all. A government is an institution that holds the exclusive power to enforce certain rules of social conduct in a given geographical area. Do men need such an institution—and if so, why?

Rand goes on to summarize her theory of rights (which is essentially plain vanilla natural rights theory, though based on Objectivist ethics rather than God). But she soon moves on from this topic to the question of the need for government. Her argument is that retaliatory use of force is necessary to prevent the individual from being left at the mercy of thugs. Anarchy is unacceptable:

> The use of physical force—even its retaliatory use—cannot be left at the discretion of individual citizens.
>
> It is therefore necessary to develop objective laws, objective rules of evidence, and an institution charged with implementing and enforcing those laws. Government places the retaliatory use of force under objective control.

So far we may follow Rand without difficulty. But now comes the hard part. Though she quotes with approval the American principle that the source of government authority is "the consent of the governed," Rand fails to consider how that consent is to be obtained. If she rejects the anarcho-libertarian approach—that the individual may freely choose whether to give his consent to be governed—what alternative does she propose?

What is the source or origin of government? Rand simply dodges this issue. She says 'society' is to provide organized protection against force. Doesn't sound much like Ayn Rand's usual mode of thought, does it? Where is the Ayn Rand we are used to—the one who would ask, 'Just who is this "society" and how is it decided what "geographical area" the government may properly police?' 'Society' as used here is just the sort of floating abstraction that Rand so vigorously attacked in her other work.

Having bravely stepped into this intellectual quagmire. Rand found herself sinking deeper when she took up the issue of government financing. Her essay, 'Government Financing in a Free Society' (in Rand 1974) begins to flounder in the first few paragraphs. Sounding perilously similar to the socialists who tell us that problems with their system will be solved 'somehow'. Rand says that the question of government financing is a "very complex one" and that getting down to specifics is premature. She immediately concedes that taxation is an initiation of force and therefore impermissible. But, though avoiding this sinkhole, she is unable to find a path through the morass.

Tentatively she suggests a possible solution: a stamp tax. Of course she doesn't call it that; it is characterized as a fee for the service of enforcing contracts. And in fact this fund-raising mechanism, which is also advocated by many libertarians, would not be a 'tax'—except that Rand states that "only a government" can enforce contracts. Government fees are ultimately taxes (Franck 1994). Even in the present-day US, most contracts depend on non-legal sanctions. With rare exceptions, both industrial and consumer agreements are enforced not by threat of lawsuit but by threat of refusing to carry out or renew transactions. In the cases where this informal sanction fails, private arbitrators and other mechanisms are taking a growing amount of "business" away from the government courts. Yet ultimately, private arbitration depends on the context of government law—and enforcement if the parties do not abide by the arbitration.

Rand's other suggestion—a government lottery—runs into the same problem. Would she outlaw private lotteries? If not, how would a socialized lottery compete in the market? The difficulty is general. Any proposal that the State 'earn its keep' must face the historical fact that governments are not good at running businesses.

What about other government services? Exactly how could one charge the users of police services, let alone military services? Developing an answer, she says, "has to be regarded as a goal for a distant future" Here, I think we must give Rand the benefit of the doubt: first, that she was not primarily a political philosopher interested in working out all the details and second, that any such minimal government would only exist in the far future.

Rand's evident problems with the government financing question arise from the fact that it involves the literal implementation of the 'social contract'. To specify exactly how citizens will be charged for government services, we must first consider the terms of their contract with the government and how they were reached. This is precisely the question that Rand failed to resolve.

Rand's View of Man and Society

Objectivist political theory is vulnerable to the anarcho-libertarian critique because Rand's work in this area failed to delve to the roots of the subject and deal with the inherent weakness of Locke's concept of government. But cannot the situation be retrieved? Let's ask how we might proceed if we wish to build a positive theory to justify Rand's 'limited government' position.

There are strong implications, especially in Rand's fiction, that she was groping toward what might be called a 'super-Lockean' approach—or, more precisely, a return to Aristotle. Aristotle's famous assertion that "Man is a political animal" is in fact a mistranslation. Converting it literally from the Greek gives, "Man is an animal whose nature it is to live in a *polis* [a city-state]." For Aristotle, man is naturally social, and it is his nature and good for him to live in society, just as it is the nature of antelope to live in herds or monkeys to live in trees.

Modern political philosophy is based on a radically different view of man. It begins with Hobbes and Locke, though Hume, Rousseau, Mill, and many others have contributed to it. Throughout their many vigorous disagreements, political theorists of the modern tradition have united in their belief that there is a fundamental conflict between the good of the individual and his entry into society. Men's interests, in this view, are naturally in conflict; the function of society is to suppress this conflict, by forcibly repressing the self-interest of the individual. Locke was the least pessimistic of these philosophers. His view was that an intelligent, rational man could perceive that it was in his long-run self-interest to join society. Although, even for Locke, men's interests are inherently in conflict, the individual will gain from his co-operation with other men more than he loses by renouncing the chance to attack them, thus developing a net profit from his socialization.

Where would Rand fit into this debate? Since politics is a corollary of ethics, we find Rand constrained very tightly by her ethical egoism. This compels her to take the position that there is no conflict of interests among rational men (Rand 1974, pp. 50–56).

The classical philosophical 'refutation' of ethical egoism is an attempt to reduce it to absurdity as follows: 'Suppose the egoist wants some particular thing—say, to marry a certain woman. How would he counsel another man who would benefit by marrying the same woman? If he tells him to court her, the egoist is going against his own self-interest; if he tells him not to court her, he is advising the other man not to be an egoist. Thus egoism contains an inherent contradiction.'

Rand simply cut the Gordian knot. She asserts that there is not, and cannot be, any conflict of interests among rational men. Thus she makes a point of challenging this argument explicitly in *Atlas Shrugged* by embodying precisely the example given in the competition between Rearden, Francisco, and John Galt for the favors of Dagny Taggart.

Rand repudiates the basic idea of modern political theory, for she does not believe that seeking values by force is practical or 'selfish'. Thus she goes Locke one better; man's entry into society is, or at least ought to be, pure profit. In giving up the chance to live as a predator, the individual is losing nothing. It is not commonly appreciated that this is one of Rand's most radical positions. In a typically Randian paradox, this quintessential individualist counters the philosophical tradition that men are merely isolated individuals.

As we saw in Chapter 6, a key theme in *Atlas Shrugged*, derived from Aristotle, is the idea that man is naturally social. Statist government creates not society, but a perversion of society, which drives the best men into isolation and cuts them off from human intercourse. What Rand saw as an ideal society, her "Utopia of Greed" in Galt's Gulch, is one in which government is so unobtrusive as to be almost invisible. Her heroes have no laws, only customs and an arbitrator to settle any disagreements—of which there are none. Rational men, living together, have no conflicts of interest. It is ironic indeed that the one example of ideal society which Rand shows us is a culture with no government.

Unfortunately, this approach to politics is, in a very literal sense, utopian: Its implementation would require a society made up exclusively of rational men. The logic of Rand's position forces her to focus on morality, for a moral citizenry is a prerequisite for her political system. The modern political tradition aims at a social structure which will, at minimum, function with an imperfect citizenry, and preferably result in their moral improvement. Rand's position seems to imply that she does not regard this as possible; morality produces good government, not the other way around. But a deeper look at her essays shows that she recognizes the corrupting or improving possibilities of the social milieu, including the law.

In this she is at one with America's founders who, following Montesquieu and a tradition going back to ancient Rome and further, believed no republic could operate successfully unless its citizens valued rectitude above all. As an inscription in Oregon's State Capitol puts it:

> In the souls of its citizens will be found the likeness of the State; which, if they be unjust and tyrannical, then will it reflect their vices; but if they be lovers of righteousness, confident in their liberties, so will it be clean injustice, bold in freedom.[4]

In the end Rand's position is that morality provides not only the intellectual but the practical foundation of politics. No political theory can be sound unless it is thoroughly grounded on the basis of the Objectivist ethics. And, it would seem, no just government can survive unless the citizens exhibit Objectivist virtues; to what degree is the question.

The problems with the foundation of Objectivist politics remain unsolved. Rand's position seems, for the most part, to defer to Locke's justifications. However, at least Merrill has clearly delineated where it fits into the debate. To provide a simplified summary:

- Hobbes justifies the State on the basis of its benefit to the people.

- Locke regards the State as just provided it protects rights and reflects the choice of the people.

- Rand's Objectivist Just State is to merit its authority because it implements objective, knowable moral principles in regard to how people deal with each other.

- For the anarcho-libertarians, the State by definition is imposed without the consent of the individual, and so nothing can justify government.

Libertarians are not unnaturally wary of accepting the principle that government can be justified because it enforces morality. History provides too many examples of the abuse of this justification—from the theocracies of old to modern totalitarian states. Yet

---

[4] This is said to be a quote from Plato's *Republic*.

libertarians need a stronger counter-argument than moral subjectivism. For what is the argument from the 'consent of the governed' if not a moral argument? When they assert that neither Objectivism nor any other morality can be logically justified, they cut the ground from under their own feet.

The Final Decline

Rand's last writings, the essays she published in *The Ayn Rand Letter*, are her weakest. During the 1970s, while she was writing this material. Rand suffered from lung cancer. The effects of ill-health are evident in the frequent publication delays and, unfortunately, in the content of the articles. Rand's analysis, in these essays, is less fundamental and more derivative of her earlier principles, but still original nonetheless.

Rand's last series of essays exhibited a frequent choice of current rather than timeless subject matter. The writer who once dealt with the rise and fall of philosophies and civilizations was now analyzing *New York Times* editorials and discussing the significance of Boris Spassky. *The Ayn Rand Letter* might better have been titled *John Galt's Breakfast*.

Still, almost to the end Rand was producing useful insights, intermittently delving into deeper philosophical issues. Her critique of Rawls's A *Theory of Justice* is incisive, though not up to her best work. In another essay on the fall of Vietnam, her comparison to the Russian Civil War is perceptive and illuminating.

At the end, Rand's last article in *The Ayn Rand Letter* sounds tired and disillusioned. She seems to feel that her work has had little influence on American and world politics, though she cites some possible counter-examples. Her tone, if not her words, is pessimistic. One may ascribe this simply to the fact of her age and illness. Or, perhaps one should credit her remarkable intuition; this last letter was written on the eve of the Carter era. Caught between the Scylla of Carter and the Charybdis of Reagan, Rand could favor neither. Nor could she throw her support to the nascent libertarian movement. With NBI destroyed, the Collective mostly excommunicated, and the Objectivist movement reduced to a minuscule, inbred clique, where could she see any hope? Only by reverting to her emphasis on the realm of the intellect, the importance of philosophy.

The final essay in her posthumous book, *Philosophy: Who Needs It,* is titled, 'Don't Let It Go', echoing Eddie Willers's cry as he futilely attempts to re-start the last of the Taggart engines. It is a cry of despair. Yet she did predict the future once again when she described the "American sense of life": "An American is an independent entity. The popular expressions of 'Don't push me around' and 'Isn't my money as good as the next fellow's?' capture this.

> . . . emotionally, an American has no concept of service (or of servitude) to anyone. Even if he enlists in the army and hears it called "service to his country," his feeling is that of a generous aristocrat who *chose* to do a dangerous task. . . . Americans admire achievement; they know what it takes. . . . *Initiative* is an "instinctive" (i.e. automatized) American characteristic; in an American consciousness, it occupies the place which, in a European one, is occupied by *obedience*. . . . The American attitude is best expressed by a line from a poem: "The world began when I was born and the world is mine to win." (Rand 1982, 253–55)

She said that it would be the American sense of life—combined with the philosophy that is "the conceptual equivalent of America's sense of life" (p. 262) which would save the country. With the surging interest in and influence of her ideas, are we seeing that liberation now?

The Path Less Traveled

The libertarian movement, following the line initiated by Rand's article 'It's Earlier than You Think' has adopted the 'educationist' approach. If only we can convince the population, spread the correct ideas, they will vote for the right candidates and changes will be made. But any changes which result will be superficial and ephemeral. One recalls Hank Rearden's belief, after the John Galt Line triumph, that "all that stuff will be swept away." As Rand had recognized as early as the 1950s, politics doesn't work that way.

Rand's political thought converged with the basic principle of the American Founders (not original with them) that good government flows from the virtue of the citizens. Good leaders are available in any generation—but will they be elected? A shrewdly designed constitution may be written—but will it be obeyed? The electorate may be educated in economics and political philosophy—

but will that induce them to vote against their own subsidies? For Rand, as for those who founded this country, practical political results flow from moral choices.

Many libertarians revolted against Rand's unification of 'ought' and 'is' and rejected her insistence on making politics the hand-maiden of morality. Instead, some of them sought to broaden their support by appealing to the New Left and other discontented por-tions of society. The most obvious feature of libertarian political propaganda has been the appeal to moral tolerance: Vote for us, and you can smoke marijuana, live in a commune without being hassled, or work as a prostitute. This approach has not proved suc-cessful in arousing fervent enthusiasm in large numbers of people. It is hardly appealing to the middle class, who tend to embody the Founders' virtues of hard work, achievement, prudence, honesty, honor, and responsibility to family and friends.

Rand's insight remains valid: Political success is more likely to result from taking the moral high ground, even if only small forces occupy it, than from leading a large mob into the swamp. For, in the area of political strategy, Rand leads us in a direction diametri-cally opposed to modern libertarian theory. As we discussed above, the essence of the libertarian approach is to entice supporters by offering tolerance. This seems quite logical; what we are offering, after all, is the removal of government restrictions. How can we expect potential allies to join us in the fight for freedom if we con-demn them as evil or immoral? How can we have political toler-ance without moral tolerance?

Ayn Rand saw it differently. Political freedom, she asserts, can exist only in an atmosphere of moral intolerance for certain kinds of social action. Those cultures which have been distinguished by limited government, close to laissez-faire economies, and few legal restrictions on personal freedom, have also exhibited strong social and moral restrictions on their people. Victorian England provides a good example.

If we are to implement Rand's approach to government, we must return to her key idea of "the sanction of the victim". Her insight was really very simple: statists are, in essence, bullies. Whether they are Nazi Brownshirts breaking up an opposition rally, 'New Left' activists shouting down Edward Teller at a physics lecture, environmentalists disrupting a corporate stockholders' meeting, or 'Occupiers' breaking shop windows, the psychology is the same. They are, like schoolyard bullies, cowards at heart. Present them with firm and principled opposition, and their facade of confidence breaks up.

As Rand knew from her early experiences under Communism, *the thugs thrive on weakness and compromise.* Like dogs, they watch a potential victim intently, seeking even the slightest sign of uncertainty, the slightest hint of willingness to compromise—and if they find it, they attack. So, she concluded, the only solution was a complete withdrawal of moral sanction. One must give one's opposition nothing; one must offer no compromise; one must allow no tolerance.

Withdrawing the sanction of the victim is at the heart of Rand's political strategy. The actual strike which she presented in *Atlas Shrugged is* merely one variation on this theme. For Ayn Rand the only solution to government oppression—whether for the individual or for society—is the withdrawal of moral sanction.

Rand's insight is compelling—but not without its dangers. Moral intolerance carries, as a tactical implication, the hazard of infighting and schism. This drawback must be dealt with if the Objectivist political program—or, indeed, Objectivism itself—is to have a future.

More recently, libertarians and even some more conservative organizations like the American Enterprise Institute have recognized that their battle against the Left and for a freer society will never succeed without a moral defense of capitalism.

After years of characterizing their views as "free market" (presumably to avoid the negative connotations of the word "capitalism,") they have now turned to a positive and active advocacy of capitalism. They've gone on the offensive. And it's about time, perhaps just in time, as the American people, in true Tocquevillian fashion, have woken up to rapidly advancing statism and socialism, and begun to figure out how to defend the freedom they've long taken for granted.

9

Ayn Rand's Revolution

In the battle for the mind, the ideas of Ayn Rand are winning.

And yet they are winning in a way which no one back in the 1960s or as recently as the 1990s was able to foresee. And no doubt more big surprises are in store.

A Second Crusade?

To convinced adherents of Rand's philosophy, the dream of reviving the exciting days of NBI in the 1960s—the vision of Objectivism as an intellectual and moral crusade—still beckons. What of Objectivism as a unified movement?

Rand's own thinking on this question evolved. At first she did not envision an organized movement at all. She saw Objectivism as gradually becoming predominant in the field of philosophy and spreading through the intellectual structure of civilization—like any other idea, only better. She seems to have hoped that Objectivist philosophy would take over from what she perceived as the dominant Kantian philosophy; but at that time she probably would not have thought of an Objectivist 'movement' any more than she would have recognized a Kantian 'movement'.

With the success of NBI, her thinking began to change. In spite of her skepticism, a movement did indeed form. Objectivism became more than a set of ideas. Nathaniel and Barbara Branden developed an organization with a mission, assembling a group of like-minded people, and serving a social as well as an ideological function. Rand realized—and she seems to have found it rather disconcerting—that her ideas were now unifying a significant social force of young people. She felt compelled to take the lead.

In the process, her ideas of intellectual progress were modified. Up until the early 1960s, Rand seems to have accepted the process by which her ideas were incorporated piecemeal by other thinkers. Though another intellectual might not be consistent in his agreement with Objectivism, if he took some of it, his thinking would at least be better; the next generation could take even more, and eventually the contradictions would be eliminated and Objectivism as a fully consistent philosophy would be accepted.

But as she became involved with NBI and *The Objectivist*, Rand's attitude changed. Now Objectivism was a movement. And as an organized movement, it had new imperatives. There was yet another possible reason Rand became focused on who was and who wasn't to represent her ideas. A movement must know who is part of it and who is not. There must be a party line. There must be a mechanism to prevent corruption of the party line. There must be enforcement procedures to prevent schisms, by crushing dissent before it can become strong enough to threaten the unity of the movement. Rand would have understood all this.

Her followers, for the most part, did not understand it. Many accepted the new policy blindly. Others, including Nathaniel and Barbara Branden, while enforcing the policy, became somewhat disquieted with Rand. The doctrinaire approach, the 'excommunications', the viciously insulting statement, "Our job is to tell people *what* Objectivism is; your job is to tell them *that* it is"—all these were discomfiting to many.

Rand seemed to have adopted the manner of a power-luster. But this evaluation isn't exact. Rand's policies were influenced by her concept of "the sanction of the victim" and her commitment to systematic moral intolerance. Rand's implementation of her enforcement procedures was crude, inefficient, and often cruel. But, to keep control over the ideas, some such methods must be used by anyone who wishes to continue an organized 'Objectivist movement'—and they are. She understood that it was not easy to be an Objectivist, especially in an irrational society. Rand accepted from Nietzsche the idea that personal moral and intellectual growth is often painful, and that helping someone to grow means in a sense to be cruel to him. Finally, she knew from experience that no one can achieve unbreached rationality without a commitment to consistency, and so she came to believe that those who only partly agreed with her would be, in the end, worse than useless. She saw the NBI structure, one suspects, as a support system for young converts, a set of training wheels to keep them from falling away from Objectivist principles until they were competent to maintain integrity by themselves.

The problem which arises, though, is that a movement requires leadership—not only intellectual leadership but managerial leadership, and indeed in a broad sense political leadership. Someone must not only develop and police the ideas but develop and police the people. Rand was only fairly well suited to performing the first function, and not suited at all to performing the second. Still, her leadership was accepted because of her evident genius.

Or the Ivory Tower?

And what of the approach suggested by Rand's analysis in her essay 'For the New Intellectual'? Develop a new generation of Hugh Akstons who will conquer the philosophy departments of academia; then Objectivist thinking will trickle down to the masses.

Rand, as noted before, disdained to present her philosophy in the standard academic forums. But she developed a few disciples, notably Leonard Peikoff and Harry Binswanger, who have attempted to carry Objectivist ideas into the ivory tower of the professional philosophers. Others, including Tibor Machan, John Hospers, and David Kelley, have joined in the work. In 1987, Allan Gotthelf and George Walsh established an Ayn Rand Society within the American Philosophical Association. Even so, it appears that the members mostly talk to each other (and often not even that!); they don't seem to have made any impression on other philosophers. They are outsiders, in their interest in Rand and her ideas.

A few noted modern philosophers have taken Rand, or at least some of her ideas, fairly seriously. Robert Nozick analyzed 'The Randian Argument' in a well-known article. And lately there has been an apparent revival of Aristotelian philosophies in general, including the growth of Virtue Ethics. In the 1990s a substantial intellectual journal, *Objectivity*, was published by Stephen Boydstun.

Yet it seems likely that Objectivism will have minimal direct influence on academic philosophy for the foreseeable future. It is not so much that academic philosophers are hostile to Objectivist ideas (though they very definitely are) as that they just don't think in that way. After a century dominated by Analytic philosophy in the English-speaking world, which emphasizes details and devolves into nit-picking, the kind of Aristotelian fundamentalism Rand offers is an entirely alien way of thinking. Further, Rand's mix of deep philosophical thinking with passionate polemic is hard for some to accept as serious philosophical writing. Objectivism did not grow out of the academic mainstream, even as a revolt against it; if it had, it might have been better received. Rather, Objectivism is totally alien, an outsider; it is nearly incomprehensible to the current philosophic mainstream in its focus, its approach, and even its terminology. Above all, academia finds Objectivism totally indigestible because of the philosophy's inherent and aggressive anti-relativism.

Will the day ever come when Objectivism gets a place in the philosophy curriculum? When Ayn Rand is taken as seriously as Plato or Kant or Mill—when textbooks devote a chapter or so to her ideas—when students learn about Objectivism and carefully compare and contrast its tenets to those of other schools of thought: that will be the day when professors will no longer fear Objectivism—because it will be, like Aristotle, so completely incorporated into the ideas of the culture that most will accept many of its premises without realizing it.

Academia may be taking its first steps towards recognizing Rand's importance. After twelve years in privately-funded publication, *The Journal of Ayn Rand Studies*, edited by New York University scholar Chris Matthew Sciabarra, is now published by the Pennsylvania State University Press and the JARS Foundation and the content archived by Stanford University. More accomplished professors, known to be Objectivists, are teaching in colleges and universities. Stephen Hicks and Shawn Klein at Rockford College, James Lennox at the University of Pittsburgh, Mimi Reisel Gladstein at the University of Texas at El Paso, and John McCaskey at Stanford University are a few. Chairs have been established at a number of institutions by John Allison's BB&T charity and the Anthem Foundation for Objectivist scholars and Tara Smith at the University of Texas at Austin and C. Bradley Thompson at Clemson University are two of the scholars who have benefited.

In the long run, we must aim for a goal consistent with Objectivism's premises. If we truly believe that reality *is,* and is *knowable,* then we can ultimately accept nothing less than that philosophy should be treated as a science—which means: the total rejection of relativism.

Can we achieve this? Can we foresee an environment in which the university philosophy curriculum gives as much time to Plato's Forms as the chemistry curriculum does to the Philosopher's Stone? In which a philosopher who accepts Kant's metaphysics will be no more employable than a mathematician who believes he can square the circle? In which those who deny the possibility of a rational ethics will be taken as seriously as Flat Earth enthusiasts? For if we are really Objectivists, we must know that Objectivism, *as represented by its basic principles,* is not just one of many contending schools of thought; it is—the truth.

Merrill did not see much prospect that Objectivism would overcome the academic world's passionate commitment to philosophical relativism any time soon. It is still safer, on campus, to advocate Nazism, or even the abolition of tenure, than to assert that one's philosophical opponents are objectively wrong, out of court, and that their positions are not credible enough to be taught. But I wonder whether we're at a philosophical tipping point now.

Professional philosophers of an Objectivist bent are doubling their efforts, and it is well that they should. But academia is a formidable redoubt, in spite of the ivy that covers it. However, there's a great change coming in education, mostly as a result of technological developments, but partly due to the bubble caused by out-of-control government funding of education. This could be a game-changer. The Tower could crumble on its own, leaving people to seek a new paradigm.

Given the huge influence of Rand's ideas on the public, the day of reckoning may be sooner than we think.

The Schoolroom or the Polling Booth

Perhaps a more broad-based education approach would be effective. Can we enlighten opinion leaders or even the masses directly? Or perhaps even get into practical politics? This has been the strategy adopted by libertarians. How well has it worked?

The Libertarian Party has had little direct success in elections, which is no surprise. It is not impossible but extremely rare for a third party to displace one of the two major parties under the US federal system. However, it is much more common for a third party to influence the policies of one or both of the two major parties, and we do observe, since the financial crisis of 2008, that the libertarian Ron Paul has made an impact on the Republican Party.

But what of other advances? Are not libertarian ideas and libertarian policies making progress? Numerous expansions of personal freedoms have been made in the past fifty years. Owning gold is now legal, lawyers can advertise, and an unmarried couple can share a hotel room without signing the register 'Mr. and Mrs.' There has been partial deregulation of the transportation and communication industries; tax reform, with a big drop in the nominal top rate; the end of military conscription, and, most recently, the decriminalization of marijuana, the acceptance of gay marriage, and the re-affirmation of gun rights in places where they were abrogated for many years.

Nonetheless, an objective observer would have to conclude that American freedoms have, overall, declined precipitously in recent decades. Government agencies have grown like weeds at every level, and businesses now face a regulatory environment that makes Directive 10-289 look downright sensible. The Bill of Rights is under assault on a broad front, and judicial protections dating back to Colonial times—such as the presumption of innocence for those accused of crimes—have already been abridged, especially because of the drug war and the use of RICO. Government has grown by leaps and bounds, both through the War on Terror and through the response to the 2008 financial crisis.

But has there not been a resurgence of libertarian ideas? Indeed there has. Communism as a major force is dead, despite small revivals in places like Venezuela. Poor countries everywhere are seeking to expand their markets, with China leading the charge—although it remains only too authoritarian in its government. But we face a formidable challenge from sophisticated statist ideologies such as environmentalism. Environmentalism alone has justified inordinate numbers of impoverishing regulations. And regressive, religiously authoritarian regimes have risen in the Middle East.

Fortunately, the long-term educational efforts in economics are beginning to bear fruit. Within the economics profession, there has been a dramatic expansion of free market thinking. New, exciting areas of analysis, such as experimental economics, are blazing trails. And now, instead of merely producing the same dreary critiques on yesterday's issues such as criticism of the FAA or farm subsidies or auto import quotas, work is moving in the direction of fundamental questions and out-of-the-box developments such as Free Cities and Seasteading.

The late Ronald Merrill published the original version of this book in 1991—just before the World Wide Web and all its power was born. He didn't foresee the hugely beneficial effects it would have on the spread of Ayn Rand's ideas and their children and relatives (libertarianism, the rise of free-market economics, and some aspects of conservatism). All the technological fields, but especially those involved with computers, are rife with individuals influenced by Rand. The very existence of the Internet has been a great boon to individualism, as it supports the flow of free thought and allows people to learn and connect in their own time, by their own interests.

Back to the Future

If Objectivism is to have a future, we must return to the insights Rand gave us years ago. The ultimate objective is not political, nor even intellectual, but personal and cultural change. Ayn Rand teaches us that government is not a primary. We cannot succeed as long as we think of political reform as our primary task. Society is a three-legged stool which rests on its political system, its economic system, and its social values and organization. All three components must be in some amount of harmony. This goal is at once our greatest challenge, our greatest opportunity, and our greatest danger.

We must develop a vision, not just of a free economy, but of a free society. What are we really aiming at? The sort of nihilism so characteristic of modern ideologies, including much of libertarianism, aims at abolition of the society we have, but offers in return nothing but a vague image of a world in which 'everybody can do his own thing'. There is no such thing. Every society constrains its members in some way—free societies, by custom and law; the others by law and force.

And here is the irony, a final, posthumous Randian paradox: libertarianism has failed by its success. For libertarian ideas *have* triumphed to a great extent—not in the political, but in the social sphere. The moral consensus and corresponding social customs that once restricted Americans' behavior have been demolished. And this has been a major driving force for reduction of freedom in the political sphere. Today teenage girls can bear illegitimate babies without the terrible stigma that once attached to it. Now cities are filled with fatherless children and the welfare state has grown to support them. Taking drugs became a matter of personal choice, not subject to moral censure. Now the public supports a police state to get rid of the crack dealers. Citizens demand—and it is not an irrational demand—that society be orderly, safe, and humane. Remove the 'oppression' of custom and morality, and you get the far worse oppression of government. The principles of social tolerance and moral relativism that Rand saw as evils in libertarianism have triumphed. Now the defenders of the indefensible face the political backlash. A voice from the grave says, "Brother, you asked for it!"

Ayn Rand offers us a vision, incomplete though it is, of a society oriented to achievement. In her "Utopia of Greed", law is imperceptible; but the invisible hand of custom guides every member of society in the same direction. Whoever has a purpose to achieve—whether building a railroad, writing a concerto, or raising a child—is not only utterly free, but honored and supported. It is a free society—but not a tolerant one. In it the purposeless, the idle, the self-destructive have no place. They need not be criminals—but they will be outcasts. Here is a society both unfettered and orderly, a society with rules but no rulers, reigned over by an aristocracy of character which yet is open to anyone who chooses to enter it. The task of Objectivism is to clarify, to elaborate, to fully understand this vision of society—and then to build it.

What Is to Be Done?

The ultimate triumph of Objectivism depends on the process by which individuals absorb the philosophy into their lives. There is no royal road to Galt's Gulch, and society will not be re-formed by teachers or treatises. Objectivists can accomplish more by example than by instruction.

The full strategy and tactics of the coming struggle comprise a book which is yet to be written. Ayn Rand, in her life's work, barely started on the problem. We have only a few insights to give us a starting point.

To begin with, Objectivist intellectuals need to nurture their independence, self-confidence, and courage. They have too often been timid, stodgy, and conservative. Where today do we find the boldness, the radical originality, and the sheer zest that were so characteristic of Ayn Rand? Half of the genius of Ayn Rand was that she saw what everybody saw, and said what nobody dared to say. We need once again to become intellectual leaders, to have the courage to approach the cutting edge of new thought. If this means submerging our longing for acceptance and 'respectability', so be it.

Objectivists surely would accomplish more if they could agree to disagree on peripheral issues. Far from rebuilding and extending a culture of rationality, those who owe allegiance to Objectivism all too often repulse all attempts at reconciliation. Those who treat altruists, collectivists, and mystics with impeccable personal courtesy sneer and spit at rational men with whom they have no substantive disagreement. Addressing both sides: do not insist that the childish squabblings of the Great Schism constitute a substantive disagreement. Objectivists need to concentrate their attention on questions more fundamental than who insulted whom decades ago. Perhaps we should attend to the example of Galt who, involved in a literally life-and-death struggle, could live with, and even love, the woman who had sworn to kill him.

Life Support Systems

The most serious damage inflicted by the Great Schism and the destruction of the NBI organization was the abortion of the embryo of an Objectivist culture. The NBI lectures, and the clubs and discussion groups which grew out of them, brought isolated Objectivists together. The movement began to become not just an arena for learning and debate, but a social meeting ground. We started to learn how to interact with other people in a new way. Then it was mostly destroyed.

Each of us who accepts Objectivism faces exactly the same problem that tormented Rand throughout her life: How can a rational person live in an irrational society? How can a sane man live in an insane culture? We too readily forget Rand's insight that we cannot truly do so alone.

We have learned from Rand the first step only—how to live with ourselves. But we are on our own from there, for she left us only a few hints.

How do we live with the irrational? Rand taught us the need for independence, for consistency, for loyalty to our values in spite of all pressures. And she taught us the danger of emotional repression. Yet, as we find ourselves in an increasingly regulated, statist, and hazardous world, we encounter the need for new ways of coping. Nathaniel Branden has contributed much useful work on this problem both before and after NBI; more is needed.

How do we live with the rational? Rand gives us only a hint, with her brief vision of Galt's Gulch. Yet, in the long run, this is the most crucial question for the future of Objectivism. A society of rational persons will of necessity develop an entirely new set of social institutions. The organization not just of government, but of the economy, of education, of the family, and every other aspect of social life will be changed. It is none too soon to be thinking about these issues.

And, if Objectivism is to begin moving again, we must re-establish a thriving, collaborative Objectivist subculture. The influence of Objectivists as isolated individuals is too limited. More important, to maintain Objectivist ideals as a lone and lonely individual is too stressful. We do need many more social institutions which allow us to meet with one another. Fortunately the Internet has connected Objectivists everywhere.

Perhaps most important of all, how do we live with our families? Rand told us much about rational behavior in romantic relationships, but not all we need to know. Science, in the last few decades, has discovered whole vistas of new facts about the distinctive nature and functions of men and women; about the development of children; and about the structure and value of families. We had better develop the ethical and cultural implications of this knowledge, and on a very practical basis—for if we cannot transmit our values to our children, Objectivism will not have a future.

The Tactics of Sanction

Ideas are powerful. Rand herself, in her essay 'For the New Intellectual', took the position that ideas, and specifically philo-

sophical ideas, determine historical trends. This is a theory calculated to be congenial to intellectuals, new or old; Keynes's famous
assertion that politicians are the slaves of dead economists comes to
mind. But Rand's theory of history seems incomplete. If the most
consistent ideas win out, how did Platonism defeat Aristotelian philosophy? If people accept the wrong ideas at times, what makes
them do so? Perhaps we will eventually come to understand the
dynamics of history better. But meanwhile, we must recognize that
an idea, no matter how rational, can at best influence society only
over the very long run. In view of the urgent need to reverse the
current trend toward statism, Objectivists need a more active strategy than 'education' or even leading by example.

The key is Rand's concept of the sanction of the victim. A strike
of the mind is, unfortunately, fictional: a tactic which ought to be
practical, but isn't. But withdrawing the sanction of the victim
offers a general strategy that could have powerful implications.

For, in practical politics, there are certain key pressure-points
that exert immense leverage. In politics, as in war, one cannot be
strong everywhere; one must concentrate one's forces on the
strategic locations. And applying the concept of the sanction of the
victim exposes these inconspicuous but crucial issues. As Rand
emphasized in *Atlas Shrugged,* a speech supporting a political
regime from Dagny Taggart is worth a thousand such speeches
from famous politicians; the signature of Hank Rearden on a Gift
Certificate has more political impact than a battalion of tanks
rolling over a protest demonstration.

Here is a lesson for us. The greatest danger to our cause
comes from deserters—allies who have become morally cowed.
When businesses give money to universities and foundations that
attack capitalism, for instance, the moral force of their example
far outweighs the financial assistance. Whenever and however we
may choose to fight, this kind of issue is the where. Indeed,
Rand's last public speech, read posthumously at the Ford Hall
Forum by Leonard Peikoff, was devoted to the sanction of the
victim.

The First of Their Return . . .

How will history evaluate Ayn Rand? In a sense, it already has.
Her books continue to sell; her ideas continue to excite. In every

generation a new crop of teenagers discover *Atlas Shrugged* and find the answers they have been looking for. In *The Fountainhead* Rand compared the public acceptance of Roark's architectural ideas to an underground river; the simile applies as well to her own experience. Though largely invisible, the acceptance is still there. Though the organized movement shows slow progress, millions of people have been influenced by her ideas.

A hundred years from now, if civilization survives its present crises. Rand will be seen as a giant among twentieth-century thinkers. Not only will Objectivism be recognized as a major contribution to philosophical thought; not only will Rand's ideas be accepted as correct; but very likely our whole way of thinking about philosophy will have changed. Philosophy will be to every thinking person what it was to Rand: not an abstruse subject roughly comparable to Latin grammar in interest and importance, but the fundamental source of right thinking and right action, of crucial, everyday importance.

Strictly as a writer, Rand will certainly be classed among the top ten of her century. Her novels are already classics by any sensible definition, and they will still be read—by high-school students and by college professors alike—when more famous writers of our century are no more than footnotes on yellowing pages. Our descendants will envy us that we were her contemporaries.

Bibliography

Adler, Mortimer. 1940. This Pre-War Generation. *Harper's Magazine* (October).

———. 1985. *Ten Philosophical Mistakes*. New York: Collier.

———. 1988. *Reforming Education*. New York: Macmillan.

Aristotle. 1999. *Nicomachean Ethics*. Indianapolis: Hackett.

Baker, James T. 1987. *Ayn Rand*. Boston: Twayne.

Barnett, Randy E., ed. 1989. *The Rights Retained by the People*. Fairfax: George Mason University Press.

Barry, Norman. 1987. *On Classical Liberalism and Libertarianism*. New York: Palgrave Macmillan.

Berti, Jim, and Durrell Bowman. 2011. *Rush and Philosophy: Heart and Mind United*. Chicago: Open Court.

Binswanger, Harry. 1987. Ayn Rand's HUAC Testimony. *The Objectivist Forum* 8:4 (August).

———. 1990. *The Biological Basis of Teleological Concepts*. Los Angeles: Ayn Rand Institute Press.

———. ed. 1986. *The Ayn Rand Lexicon*. New York: New American Library.

Blundell, John, and Todd Tennant. 2011. *Female Force: Ayn Rand*. Comicbook. Vancouver: Bluewater Productions.

Boaz, David. 1997. *Libertarianism: A Primer*. New York: Simon and Schuster.

Braitenberg, Valentine. 1984. *Vehicles*. Cambridge: MIT Press.

Branden, Barbara. 1986. *The Passion of Ayn Rand*. New York: Doubleday.

———. 1990. Barbara Branden Speaks Out. *Liberty* 3:3.

Branden, Nathaniel. 1969. *The Psychology of Self-Esteem*. Los Angeles: Nash.

———. 1970. Rational Egoism. *The Personalist* 51.

———. 1971. Break Free! An Interview with Nathaniel Branden. *Reason* (October).

———. 1980. *The Psychology of Romantic Love: Romantic Love in an Anti-Romantic Age*. New York: Tarcher.

———. 1982. The Benefits and Hazards of the Philosophy of Ayn Rand: A Personal Statement (taped lecture). New York: Laissez Faire Books.

———. 1983. Love and Sex in the Philosophy of Ayn Rand (taped lecture). New York: Laissez Faire Books.

———. 1984. *The Disowned Self.* New York: Bantam.

———. 1989. *Judgment Day: My Years with Ayn Rand.* Boston: Houghton Mifflin.

———. 1994. *The Six Pillars of Self-Esteem.* New York: Bantam.

Branden, Nathaniel, and Barbara Branden. 1962. *Who Is Ayn Rand?* New York: Paperback Library, 1962.

Britting, Jeffrey. 2004. *Ayn Rand.* New York: Overlook.

Brook, Yaron, and Don Watkins. 2012. *Free Market Revolution: How Ayn Rand's Ideas Can End Big Government.* New York: Palgrave Macmillan.

Brooks, Arthur C. 2010. *The Battle: How the Fight between Free Enterprise and Big Government Will Shape America's Future.* New York: Basic Books.

Burns, Jennifer. 2009. *Goddess of the Market: Ayn Rand and the American Right.* New York: Oxford University Press.

Cerf, Bennett. 1977. *At Random: Reminiscences of Bennett Cerf.* New York: Random House.

Chambers, Whittaker. 1957. Big Sister Is Watching You. *National Review* (December 28th).

Cox, Stephen. 2004. *The Woman and the Dynamo: Isabel Paterson and the Idea of America.* Piscataway: Transaction.

Dalrymple. Theodore. 2001. *Life at the Bottom: The Worldview that Makes the Underclass.* Chicago: Dee.

Den Uyl, Douglas J., and Rasmussen, Douglas B. 1978. Nozick on the Randian Argument. *The Personalist* 59.

———, eds. 1984. *The Philosophic Thought of Ayn Rand.* Chicago: University of Illinois Press.

Doherty, Brian. 2008. *Radicals for Capitalism: A Freewheeling History of the Modern American Libertarian Movement.* New York: Perseus.

Dwyer, William. 1974. The Argument Against an Objective Standard of Value. *Personalist* 55.

Economist. 2009. Atlas Felt a Sense of Déjà Vu. *Economist* (February 26th).

Ellis, Albert. 1968. *Is Objectivism a Religion?* New York: Lyle Stuart.

Enright, Marsha Familaro. 1995. *Con molto Sentimento*: On the Evolutionary Neuropsychology of Music. *Objectivity* 2:3.

Franck, Murray I. 1994. Taxation Is Moral. *Full Context* (June).

———. 1998. The State, The Market and the Morality of Taxation (Taxation Is Moral IV). *Full Context* (September–October).

Friedman, David. 1989a. *The Machinery of Freedom: Guide to a Radical Capitalism.* Second edition. La Salle: Open Court.

———. 1989b. Simple Principles vs. the Real World. *Liberty* 3:1.

Gladstein, Mimi Reisel. 1984. *The Ayn Rand Companion.* Westport: Greenwood.

Gotthelf, Allan. 1999. *On Ayn Rand.* Belmont: Wadsworth.

Gotthelf, Allan, and James Lennox, ed. 2010 *Metaethics, Egoism, and Virtue: Studies in Ayn Rand's Normative Theory.* Pittsburgh: University of Pittsburgh Press.

Gould, Lawrence I. 2007. Issues in Science and Religion: A Critical Evaluation. In Laderman and Eisen 2007.

Hamel, Virginia L.L. 1990. *In Defense of Ayn Rand.* Brookline: New Beacon.

Harriman, David. 2010. *The Logical Leap: Induction in Physics.* New York: New American Library.

Hawley, Cameron. 1952. *Executive Suite,* Boston: Houghton-Mifflin.

———. 1955. *Cash McCall.* Boston: Houghton-Mifflin.

———. 1960. *The Lincoln Lords.* Boston: Little, Brown.

Haydn, Hiram. 1954. *Words and Faces.* New York: Harcourt, Brace, Jovanovich.

Heller, Anne C. 2009. *Ayn Rand and the World She Made.* New York: Random House.

Hicks, Stephen R.C. 2004. *Explaining Postmodernism: Skepticism and Socialism from Rousseau to Foucault.* Tempe: Scholarly.

Hospers, John. 1967. *Introduction to Philosophical Analysis.* Second edition. Englewood Cliffs: Prentice-Hall.

———. 1990. Conversations with Ayn Rand. *Liberty* 4:1

Huebert, Jacob H. 2010. *Libertarianism Today.* Santa Barbara: Praeger.

Hume, David. 1978 [1739–1740]. *A Treatise of Human Nature: Being an Attempt to Introduce the Experimental Method of Reasoning into Moral Subjects.* Oxford: Oxford University Press.

Jones, W.T., Frederick Sontag, Morton O. Beckner, and Robert J. Fogelin, eds. 1969. *Approaches to Ethics.* New York: McGraw-Hill.

Kelley, David. 1986. *The Evidence of the Senses: A Realist Theory of Perception.* Baton Rouge: Louisiana State University Press.

———. 1996. *Unrugged Individualism: The Selfish Basis of Benevolence.* Poughkeepsie: The Objectivist Center.

———. 1998. *A Life of One's Own: Individual Rights and the Welfare State.* Washington: Cato.

———. 2000. *The Contested Legacy of Ayn Rand.* Formerly *Truth and Toleration* Piscataway: Transaction.

———. 2011. Rand Versus Hayek on Abstraction. *Reason Papers* 33 (Fall).

———. 2012. *The Art of Reasoning.* Fourth edition. New York: Norton.

King, J. Charles. 1984. Life and the Theory of Value: The Randian Argument Reconsidered. In Den Uyl and Rasmussen 1984.

Kinni, Donna, and Theodore Kinni. 2001. *Ayn Rand and Business.* New York: Texere.

Klemke, E.D., A. David Kline, and Robert Hollinger, eds. 1986. *Philosophy: The Basic Issues.* New York: St. Martin's Press.

Kuhn, Thomas S. 1970. *The Structure of Scientific Revolutions.* Second edition. Chicago: University of Chicago Press.

Laderman, Gary, and Arri Eisen, eds. 2007. *Science, Religion, and Society: History, Culture, and Controversy.* New York: Sharpe.

Laudan, Larry. 1990. *Science and Relativism.* Chicago: University of Chicago Press.

Lester, J.C. 2012. *Escape from Leviathan: Libertarianism without Justificationism.* Buckingham: University of Buckingham Press.

Lichtenberg, Jacqueline, Sondra Marshak, and Joan Winston. 1975. *Star Trek Lives!* New York: Corgi.

Locke, John. 1967. *Two Treatises of Government.* Cambridge: Cambridge University Press.

Lugenbehl, Dale E. 1974. The Argument for an Objective Standard of Value. *The Personalist* 55.

Luskin, Donald L., and Andrew Greta. 2011. *I Am John Galt: Today's Heroic Innovators Building the World and the Villainous Parasites Destroying It.* Hoboken: Wiley.

Machan, Tibor. 1971. A Rationale for Human Rights'. *The Personalist* 52.

———. 1975. *Human Rights and Human Liberties.* Chicago: Nelson Hall.

———. 1977. Nozick and Rand on Property Rights, *The Personalist* 58.

———. 1985. *Introduction to Philosophical Inquiries.* New York: University Press of America.

———. 1989a. *Individuals and Their Rights.* La Salle: Open Court.

———. 1989b. Ayn Rand and I. *Liberty* 3:2.

Mack, Eric. 1971. How to Derive Ethical Egoism. *The Personalist* 52.

———. 1984. The Fundamental Moral Elements of Rand's Theory of Rights. In Den Uyl and Rasmussen 1984.

Manthey-Zorn, Otto, ed. 1964. *Nietzsche: An Anthology of His Works.* New York: Washington Square Press.

Mayhew, Robert. 2004. *Ayn Rand and Song of Russia: Communism and Anti-Communism in 1940s Hollywood.* Lanham: Rowman and Littlefield.

McConnell, Scott. 2010. *100 Voices: An Oral History of Ayn Rand.* New York: New American Library.

Mencken, Henry L. 1982. *The Philosophy of Friedrich Nietzsche*. Torrance: Noontide.

Merrill, Ronald E. 1991. *The Ideas of Ayn Rand*. La Salle: Open Court.

Merwin, Samuel, and Henry Kitchell Webster. 1967. *Calumet 'K'*. New York: NBI Press.

Minsaas, Kirsti. 2005. Mimesis and Expression in Ayn Rand's Theory of Art. *Journal of Ayn Rand Studies* 7:1 (Fall).

Monbiot, George. 2012. How Ayn Rand Became the New Right's Version of Marx. *The Guardian* (5th March).

Monod, Jacques. 1971. *Chance and Necessity*. New York: Knopf.

Moore, Stephen. 2009. *Atlas Shrugged* from Fiction to Fact in 52 Years. *Wall Street Journal* (9th January).

Narveson, Jan. 1988. *The Libertarian Idea*. Philadelphia: Temple University Press.

Nash, George H. 1976. *The Conservative Intellectual Movement in America*. New York: Basic Books.

Nichols, Rosalie. 1977 [1972]. *Confessions of a Randian Cultist: An Open Letter to Ayn Rand Regarding the Branden Interview*. New York: Ms. Atlas Press.

Nozick, Robert. 1971. On the Randian Argument. *The Personalist* 52.

———. 1974. *Anarchy, State, and Utopia*. New York: Basic Books.

Palmer, Tom G., ed. 2011. *The Morality of Capitalism: What Your Professors Won't Tell You*. Ottawa: Jameson.

Paterson, Isabel. 1993 [1943]. *The God of the Machine*. Piscataway: Transaction.

Paul, Ron. 2008. *The Revolution: A Manifesto*. New York: Grand Central.

Peikoff, Leonard. 1981. Maybe You're Wrong. *The Objectivist Forum* 2:2.

———. 1982. *The Ominous Parallels*. New York: New American Library.

———. 1983. Assault from the Ivory Tower: The Professors' War against America. *The Objectivist Forum* 4:5.

——— ed. 1984. *The Early Ayn Rand*. New York: New American Library.

——— ed. 1988. *The Voice of Reason: Essays in Objectivist Thought*. New York: New American Library.

———. 1993. *Objectivism: The Philosophy of Ayn Rand*. New York: Meridian.

Perkins, Richard, and Ernestine Perkins. 1971. *Rational Anarchy*. St. Thomas: Phibbs.

Perry, Ralph Barton. 1926. *General Theory of Value*. Cambridge: Harvard University Press.

———. 1954. *Realms of Value*. Cambridge: Harvard University Press.

Plasil, Ellen. 1985. *Therapist*. New York: St. Martin's Press.

Podritske, Marlene, and Peter Schwartz, eds. 2009. *Objectively Speaking: Ayn Rand Interviewed*. Lanham: Rowman and Littlefield.

Poole, Robert, Jr. 1988. Things Are a Lot Groovier Now. *Reason* 20:1 (May).

Rand, Ayn. 1936a. *We the Living*. New York: Macmillan.

———. 1936b. *The Night of January Sixteenth*. New York: Longmans, Green.

———. No date. *The Night of January Sixteenth*. Amateur edition, Nathaniel Edward Reid, ed. New York: McKay.

———. 1943. *The Fountainhead*. New York: Bobbs-Merrill.

———. 1944. The Only Path to Tomorrow. *Reader's Digest* (January).

———. 1946. *Anthem*. New York: New American Library.

———. 1957. *Atlas Shrugged*. New York: Random House.

———. 1959. *We the Living*. Revised edition. New York: Random House.

———. 1961. *For the New Intellectual*. New York: Random House.

———. 1968a. *The Night of January Sixteenth*. Authorized edition. New York: World Publishing.

———. 1968b. To Whom It May Concern. *The Objectivist* (May).

———. 1968c. A Statement of Policy: Part I. *The Objectivist* (June).

———. 1971. *The Romantic Manifesto*. New York: New American Library.

———. 1974. *The Virtue of Selfishness*. New York: New American Library.

———. 1975. *The New Left: The Anti-Industrial Revolution*. New York: New American Library.

———. 1982. *Philosophy: Who Needs It*. New York: Bobbs-Merrill.

———. 1983a. From Ayn Rand's Unpublished Writings: Philosophic Journal (1934). *The Objectivist Forum* 4:4.

———. 1983b. From Ayn Rand's Unpublished Writings: Notes for *Atlas Shrugged*. *The Objectivist Forum* 4:6.

———. 1984. From Ayn Rand's Unpublished Writings: Philosophic Notes. *The Objectivist Forum* 5:4.

———. 1988. *We the Living*. Movie starring Alida Valli. Video. New York: Angelika Films.

———. 1990a. *Introduction to Objectivist Epistemology*. Second edition. New York: New American Library.

———. 1990b. *The Fountainhead*. Movie starring Gary Cooper. Videotape. Culver City: MGM/UA Home Video.

———. 1997. *Letters of Ayn Rand*. New York: Penguin.

———. 1998a. *The Ayn Rand Column: Written for the Los Angeles Times*. Second edition. New Milford: Second Renaissance.

———. 1998b. *Ayn Rand's Marginalia*. New Milford: Second Renaissance.

———. 1999a. *Journals of Ayn Rand*. New York: Penguin.

———. 1999b. *Russian Writings on Hollywood*. Los Angeles: Ayn Rand Institute.

————. 2000. *The Art of Fiction*. New York: Penguin.

————. 2001. *The Art of Non-Fiction*. New York: Penguin.

————. 2005. *Ayn Rand Answers: The Best of Her Q&A*. New York: New American Library.

Rand, Ayn, Nathaniel Branden, Alan Greenspan, and Robert Hessen. 1967. *Capitalism: The Unknown Ideal*. New York: Signet.

Rockwell, L.H., Jr. 1990. The Case for Paleolibertarianism. *Liberty* 3:3.

Rockwell, L.H., Jr., and Jeffrey A. Tucker. Ayn Rand Is Dead. *National Review* (28th May).

Rothbard, Murray N. 1962. *Man, Economy, and State*. Princeton: Van Nostrand.

————. 1973. *For a New Liberty*. New York: Macmillan.

————. 1987. *The Sociology of the Ayn Rand Cult*. Port Townsend: Liberty.

————. 1989. My Break with Branden and the Rand Cult. *Liberty* 3:1.

Rubin, Harriet. 2007. Ayn Rand and the Literature of Capitalism. *New York Times* (15th September).

Schulman, J. Neil. 1990. *The Robert Heinlein Interview and Other Heinleiniana*. ebook. Mill Valley: Pulpless.

Schwartz, Peter. 1990. Libertarianism: The Perversion of Liberty. In Peikoff 1988.

Sciabarra, Chris Matthew. 1995. *Ayn Rand: The Russian Radical*. University Park: Pennsylvania State University Press.

Searle, John R. 1964. How to Derive 'Ought' from 'Is'. *Philosophical Review* 73.

Skoble, Aeon J. 2008. *Deleting the State: An Argument about Government*. Chicago: Open Court.

Smith, Adam. 1976 [1776]. *An Inquiry into the Nature and Causes of the Wealth of Nations*. Oxford: Oxford University Press.

Smith, George H. 1991. *Atheism, Ayn Rand, and Other Heresies*. Amherst: Prometheus.

Smith, Tara. 2000. *Viable Values: A Study of Life as the Root and Reward of Morality*. Lanham: Rowman and Littlefield.

————. 2007. *Ayn Rand's Normative Ethics: The Virtuous Egoist*. New York: Cambridge University Press.

Soto, Hernando de. 2002 [1989]. *The Other Path: The Economic Answer to Terrorism*. New York: Basic Books.

————. 2003. *The Mystery of Capital: Why Capitalism Triumphs in the West and Fails Everywhere Else*. New York: Basic Books.

Tannehill, Morris, and Linda Tannehill. 1970. *The Market for Liberty*. Lansing: no publisher given.

Torres, Louis, and Michelle Marder Kamhi. 2000. *What Art Is: The Esthetic Theory of Ayn Rand*. Chicago: Open Court.

Tuccille, Jerome. 1972. *It Usually Begins with Ayn Rand*. New York: Stein and Day.

Valliant, James. 2005. *The Passion of Ayn Rand's Critics*. Dallas: Durban House.

Veatch, Henry. 1962. *Rational Man: A Modern Interpretation of Aristotelian Ethics*. Bloomington: Indiana University Press.

———. 1985. *Human Rights: Fact or Fancy?* Baton Rouge: Louisiana State University Press.

Walker, Jeff. 1999. *The Ayn Rand Cult*. Chicago: Open Court.

Weiss, Gary. 2012. *Ayn Rand Nation: The Hidden Struggle for America's Soul*. New York: St. Martin's.

Wheeler, Jack. 1984. Rand and Aristotle: A Comparison of Objectivist and Aristotelian Ethics. In Den Uyl and Rasmussen 1984,

Zablocki, Benjamin. 1997. A Sociological Theory of Cults. Conference paper. Philadelphia (31st May).

Zamyatin, Yevgeny. 1924. *We*. New York: Dutton.

Index

abortion, 34, 36, 41, 110
academia, 46, 128–29, 171, 172–73, 195–96
achievement, 15, 52, 82, 86, 93, 100, 144, 189–190, 199; as central, 14, 17, 18; as function of the individual, 3, 14–15, 18, 17, 18, 22, 26
Adams, John, 50
Adler, Mortimer J., 129–130
aesthetics; *see* esthetics
Aglialoro, John, 4, 7–8, 12
Akston, Hugh (character), 43, 103, 114, 195
Alger, Horatio, 164
Allen, Jeff (character), 116, 120–21
Alessandrini, Goffredo, 78
Allison, John, of BB&T Bank, 4, 33, 196
altruism, 125, 169, 173, 174; as morality based on death, 140; definition of, 14; Robert Heinlein on, 10; Nietzsche's rejection of, 62–65
American Enterprise Institute, 191
American Founders, 46, 177, 186, 189
American sense of life, 54, 59, 189
American sensibilities, 18
Americanism, 15
analytic-synthetic dichotomy, 136–37
anarcho-capitalism, 176–79; as

purest form of libertarianism, 176; free-rider problem and, 179; social contract theory attacked by, 181–82; *see also* libertarianism
'The Anatomy of Compromise' (Rand), 174
Andre, Karen (character), 72–73, 92, 111
Anthem, 1, 6, 20–21, 61, 100, 102, 109–110, 114; analysis of, 98–100; influence on Rush, 11; parallels to Zarathustra, 98; relation to *We*, 99
anti-concept, 170
Apollo and Dionysus, 68
Approaches to Ethics (Jones *et al.*), 129
Apple Computer, 4
Argounova, Kira, 54, 61, 70–71, 74–82
Armey, Dick, 5
Argument from Intimidation, 48
Aristotle, 4, 27, 20, 30, 63, 73, 90, 128–131, 146–48, 150, 184, 186, 196; esthetics, 165; great-souled man, 17; metaphysics and Objectivism, 130; *Nicomachean Ethics*, 146; "Man is a political animal," 185
art; *see* esthetics
ArtGrok.org, 50
At Random (Cerf), 51–52

213

ATHEISM EXPLAINED

FROM FOLLY TO PHILOSOPHY

DAVID RAMSAY STEELE

"A clear, concise, complete, and convincing presentation of the case for atheism."

—Victor J. Stenger